Introduction to Religious Studies is more like a conversation than a textbook—a conversation about approaches, methods, and discoveries in the study of religion that draws students in, invites them to pose their own questions, and involves them in wrestling with the realities of religious experience and commitments. *Introduction to Religious Studies* provides a framework for inquiry that is flexible—adaptable to varied classroom contexts and readily paired with other readings and resources of the instructor's choosing. A particular strength of this volume is its attentiveness to the range and variety of religious expression. Each chapter explores its subject from multiple cultural and faith perspectives, enabling students not only to recognize religious diversity but to ponder the meaning and purpose of particular beliefs and practices. *Introduction to Religious Studies* is a well-written volume that fits the goals of the introductory religion course, *engages* students intellectually and interpersonally, and *models* a rigorous, reflective, and respectful approach to religious study applicable far beyond the classroom.

—Elna K. Solvang, Ph.D., Department of Religion, Concordia College, Moorhead, MN

Introduction to Religious Studies is the long-awaited answer to the question of how to present the foundational and contemporary dimensions of religious studies in a dialogical framework to the college undergraduate student. With faculty and student learning goals in mind, the authors share a wealth of scholarship and teaching experience on a variety of topics that invite both critical inquiry and personal exploration. Keeping in mind a broad range of student religious commitments, the text breaks new ground in presenting the complexities of the interrelationship of religion and contemporary life. Educators will find here content that is central to the introductory study of religion as well as resources and references for further investigation.

—Dr. Lucinda A. Nolan, Assistant Professor of Religious Education,
The Catholic University of America

Throughout the year, students doing independent work in various disciplines come to me asking for guidance on ways that their topics relate to religion. I often find myself scrambling to help them locate resources that are both written at the introductory level and still engaging and rich in content. *Introduction to Religious Studies* will be an invaluable resource in helping me to help my students. Not only are the topics timely and illustrative, but the list of additional resources at the conclusion of each chapter will help guide students toward doing the kinds of work they want to do.

This book will also be an invaluable resource for professors, especially those struggling to navigate the tricky waters of the introductory course in religious studies or in need of the energy boost provided by new pedagogical strategies and frameworks. Reading this book has gotten me excited again — re-energized — about this fascinating and incredibly difficult thing we do: teach about religion.

—Trina Janiec Jones, Associate Professor of Religion, Wofford College

AUTHOR ACKNOWLEDGMENTS

Special thanks to Jerry Ruff, Leslie Ortiz, Jack McHugh, and members of Anselm Academic publishing involved with this project. Their editorial and managerial assistance throughout the publication process has contributed significantly to the polishing and refinement required with any book project.

Special thanks to my wife, Carol, and daughters, Rachel and Leah, for their tireless and sustaining encouragement throughout the task of envisioning this project and during the subsequent research, writing, revising, and editing. They have been and continue to be sources of strength and inspiration.

Special thanks to my parents, Odell and Karen, and sisters, Carol, Ruth, and Kristine, for their generous spirits and capacity to engage tough questions about religious inquiry and theological imagination during my formative years. The space they provided to explore terrains of inquiry about religion on my own terms has enabled me to encounter, experience, and witness panoplies of global religious thought and practice.

Special thanks to Nadine Pence, Lucinda Huffaker, Thomas Pearson, Patricia Overpeck, Rita Arthur, Sherry Wren, Beth Reffett, Karen Myers, Raymond Williams, and William C. Placher at the Wabash Center for their support and encouragement as I engaged in the work associated with this project during my fleeting moments of spare time.

Special thanks to the chapter authors for their willingness to contribute chapters that fit within the overall vision for the book. The authors were attentive to student learning goals and needs throughout. Their shared commitment to excellence in teaching and writing has made work on this project a joyful one.

PUBLISHER ACKNOWLEDGMENTS

Our thanks to the following individuals who advised the publishing team or reviewed this work in progress:

- Professor Mary Joan Leith, Stonehill College, Easton, Massachusetts
- Professor Priscilla Pope Levinson, Seattle Pacific University, Washington
- Professor Rich Penaskovic, Auburn University, Alabama
- Professor Michelle Tooley, Berea College, Berea, Kentucky

INTRODUCTION TO RELIGIOUS STUDIES

ANSELM ACADEMIC

Created by the publishing team of Anselm Academic.

Cover images royalty free from iStock

The scriptural quotations contained herein, with the exception of those in chapters 7 and 11, are from the New Revised Standard Version Bible, Catholic Edition. Copyright © 1993 and 1989 by the Division of Christian Education of the National Council of the Churches of Christ in the United States of America. All rights reserved.

The scriptural quotations contained in chapters 7 and 11 are from the New English Bible with the Apocrypha: Oxford Study Edition (New York: Oxford University Press, 1976) and the New Oxford Annotated Bible with the Apocryphal/Deuterocanonical Books: New Revised Standard Version (New York: Oxford University Press, 2007), respectively.

Printed in the United States of America

7023

ISBN 978-0-88489-976-1

Library of Congress Cataloging-in-Publication Data
  Introduction to religious studies / Paul O. Myhre, editor.
      p. cm.
Includes bibliographical references and index.
  ISBN 978-0-88489-976-1 (pbk.)
      1. Religion. I. Myhre, Paul O.
  BL41.I59 2009
  200—dc22
                                                    2009023082

Contents

Introduction

FOR TEACHERS
USING THIS BOOK

An introductory course in the study of religion can be daunting for undergraduates. It is often a required course for students before taking courses in areas of study that may hold greater interest. Although some students come to the study of religion eager to learn, many arrive with mixed motivation and languid enthusiasm. Resistance to the study of religion may be a byproduct of student fears—real and imagined—that personal faith might somehow be dismantled by the study of religion. Perhaps students resist because they are convinced that the course will be irrelevant for study and life in general. There exists an array of student perceptions about what religion is and how it might be studied. For a host of educators teaching first-year religion courses, then, the classroom can seem to be more a like salted field impeding growth than a fertile one destined to produce abundance.

As for students, perhaps the majority might compare the introductory study of religion to being swept away by a flood of new ideas and concepts—most of them foreign to the students' own experience of religion and religious life. Hence, course design can greatly influence the students' experience.

North American higher education does not currently subscribe to a universal standard for teaching an introductory course in religion. Even denominationally related schools—Protestant and Catholic—have no universal curriculum for foundational courses in religion. Furthermore, students and faculty who engage in the introductory course find that it is not a *tabula rasa* on which the course is written. The classroom represents an array of commitments—both scholarly and faith-oriented—that directly or indirectly influence how a course is taught and how students engage the texts, stories, and ideas. Barbara Walvoord recently completed a study of the best practices of effective teachers of introductory courses in religion, theology, and Bible studies. Her findings, published in *Teaching and Learning in College Introductory Religion Courses* (Malden, MA: Blackwell Publishing, 2008), shed light on recurrent issues for the study of religion. One key finding concerns what Walvoord calls "the great divide," the line in many college and university religion classrooms where student and faculty goals diverge. Faculty are largely interested in fostering critical reflection in the study of religion, while students are primarily interested in their own spiritual and religious development. This book will try to walk in the liminal space between these two goals. Each chapter author has written with the intent of making his or her topic accessible to the student reader through keeping both faculty and student goals in mind.

Over the past century, some religion professors have maintained that a certain objectivity is preferred in the religious studies classroom.

This may be a lofty ideal, as objectivity is a rare commodity, difficult to attain and commonly illusive. Given that students come with a range of religious commitments and passions, emotions, experience, and opinions, objectivity may be hard to come by in the religious studies classroom. However, recognizing the densely layered subjectivity of students and teachers alike can liberate the student to explore a range of ideas and practices. In fact, subjectivity tempered by disciplined study, openness to new ideas, and attention to research and pedagogical methods can create an environment where the study of religion is exhilarating rather than something one must suffer through. Such an environment could potentially catalyze a new growth of ideas about religion, religious experience, and contours of faith, and prepare minds for subsequent growth in related subjects.

This book endeavors to foster a dialogical environment. It is not meant to serve as the only source of classroom material, but rather as a framework or scaffold for conversation. It is assumed that both teacher and student will draw from personal knowledge and experience as they dialogue about ideas central to the study of religion: truth, faith, religious experience, sacred texts, rituals, and so on. In a global environment where religion has been variously understood, it is my hope that this text will provide room for every voice to be heard and no one voice to be privileged above the rest. It is also assumed that the conversation will not be finished with the completion of the course, but rather that this book might serve as a prelude for a sustained, lifelong conversation.

This book takes into consideration common questions students raise about religion, cultural notions about faith, and what the lived experience of religion might entail. Sets of questions are offered throughout the book to serve as discussion prompts. The book is also designed to aid students and teachers in exploring perceptions about how religion is understood, to expose matrices of relationships between ideas and practices, and to serve as initial steps toward discovery of how religion and religious life are interwoven with an array of commitments—economic, cultural, political, and so on—in an increasingly globalized (and Westernized) world. The book introduces students to nomenclature unique to the study of religion and to ideas and concepts that religions share; it serves as a means for interpersonal as well as personal reflection; and it invites for interrogation of perceptions and beliefs about what connotes religion, faith, and religious practice. Though each author wrote independently of the others, certain concepts, ideas, and methods thread throughout the book, and it is hoped that students and teachers will weave these together as they engage in the study of religion.

The book is written with the first-year college student in mind; hence it will not introduce all of the nuances that could be covered. Because the study of religion is massive, the book confines itself to basic topics and ideas that could be investigated more thoroughly in subsequent courses. In addition, the text will not cover religious methods, ideas, or practices comprehensively, but rather smorgasbord style. Not all topics will be covered, and some readers may leave longing for more. Description, analysis, and interpretation of ideas and practices are imbedded in most chapters. Sometimes topics will surface for careful examination and at other times remain submerged and awaiting subsequent study. For this reason each chapter includes a list of references for further study. As with a smorgasbord, no one will be able to ingest it all. I hope this book will serve as a means of whetting student appetites for return visits to ideas and topics in the study of theology and religion.

Paul O. Myhre, editor

WHAT IS RELIGION?

Rev. Dr. Paul O. Myhre
Wabash Center for Teaching and Learning in Theology and Religion

Preface

What is religion? Some argue that religion is best understood as a construction of Western European scholars who sought to categorize the beliefs and practices of the peoples they encountered during the colonization period of the sixteenth through nineteenth centuries. Others contend religion is a system of culturally conditioned lived practices. Still others say it is a human construct rooted in a longing to extend life beyond death. And some maintain religion is a gift from deities or spirits for the well-being of humans. Whatever the answer, no simple, single definition will suffice. It might be helpful to hold a group of definitions loosely so as to begin to sense this diversity.

It is part of our human experience to engage in religious ideas and practices that change in subtle and significant ways over time. This chapter aims to disturb the calm waters of settled opinions on religion and to explore basic ideas about what religion is and is not from different vantage points and to offer alternatives for the study of religion.

Chapter Goals

- To promote critical reflection on religion and religious practices
- To introduce alternate definitions for and ways of understanding religion
- To examine personal perceptions and assumptions about religion and religious practices

INTRODUCTION

Throughout history, people have performed actions and held beliefs that are considered religious. Although the term *religion* is relatively recent, it has been used to describe time-honored actions and beliefs that are aimed at connecting people with what could be identified as most true, real, sacred, or divine. Religion has also been identified with beliefs and behaviors that connect us with what is most worth knowing or that steer us toward self-negation and material detachment. It is difficult, if not impossible, to read a newspaper, watch a television program, or surf the Internet without finding some direct or indirect reference to religion. Whatever the reasons, religion has been and continues to be one of the most pervasive and influential forces in people's lives.

From ancient times, people have created monuments and artifacts testifying to the human propensity toward religious belief and practice. Often religion is rooted in rational aspirations, linked with emotional attachments, inspired by some external idea or force, and connected with what people believe represents their cultural, communal, and individual truth. Consider the following examples:

- Pyramids constructed in Cairo/Giza in Egypt more than three thousand years ago served to orient people toward the mystery of death and what follows it.

- Kiva pits, dug by the Anasazi in the southwestern United States more than one thousand years ago, were meant to connect Anasazi with their ancestors and their emergence stories.

- Remnants of a temple in Jerusalem built more than two thousand years ago recall a structure raised for the right worship of one God above all others.

- Burial and ceremonial mound-complexes in North America associated with Hopewell and Mississippian cultures, now more than ten centuries old, testify to a fabric of life connected with the spirits of the sun, moon, and other forces in nature.

- Small-, medium-, and megasized Christian churches in the United States revolve around the worship of a Triune God; these worship centers also serve as pedagogical posts for preaching the Christian gospel.

- Islamic mosques, scattered across the globe, serve as centers for Muslim communal prayer five times each day. Those who gather face toward Mecca—the focal place for worship of Allah—and recite the Qur'an, which serves as a

means of worship and a pedagogical tool to inscribe the words of Allah on hearts and minds.

Hindu temples, Nazca lines, European and North American rock circles, Kiribati manyaba, Fijian Bure, Mayan pyramids—all of these constructions suggest that their architects were concerned with more than day-to-day existence. Each place, each structure, each artifact associated with these larger architectural monuments proclaims the depth and breadth of religious practice and belief. Each suggests ideas considered so fundamental that people devoted enormous amounts of time, effort, and resources to their creation. Some would defend these locations as places not to be defiled; others would regard these architectural spaces as sacred or special, claiming that here alone people might find security, safety, solace, and peace.

In some cases, new worship spaces were built on or near prior sites of worship for local inhabitants. The reasons for supplanting an old worship space with a new one were many, yet there was something about the geographical location that inclined the newer inhabitants to regard it as important and therefore to use it for their own purposes. Time and again this has been documented. For example, many early Christian churches in Europe were erected over sites already regarded by the locals as bearing religious significance, such as the Novgorod church (dedicated to Saint Sophia) in Novgorod, Russia, which was erected over the site of a non-Christian temple in 989 CE.

It seems that a disposition toward religion is somehow infused or encoded in our genetic makeup. Consider the history of any people and you will find numerous examples of religious beliefs and practices playing a part in wars, leadership succession, human relationships, purity codes, legal documents, social and environmental ethics, and so on.

Art documents well this connection. Some art historians maintain that 75 to 85 percent of all art has some type of religious connection or connotation. The art of native North and South America, of African and South Pacific cultures, of Byzantine Christianity, and so on is infused with religious symbols and meaning. It would be impossible to separate religion from art. The structures, histories, and artifacts of human creation are testimonials to the practice of religion. If religious belief and practice has had such a pervasive influence, it strongly suggests the study of religion might better our understanding of human history and human existence itself.

The beginning student of religion can easily become overwhelmed. The plethora of sacred texts, the complexity and diversity of languages and religious practices, and the multifaceted religious nomenclatures are daunting. The history and current systems of religion cannot all be studied even in a lifetime. So how might one be able to say anything about any religious belief or practice given this diversity and complexity?

Religions emerge out of specific cultures, geographies, and historical periods and thus represent myriad thought-worlds. Our own religious, social, and cultural context directly and indirectly affects how we understand religious commitments, ideas, and practices. How people construct knowledge, beliefs, and worldviews is often so culturally rooted that it is difficult for those outside the culture to discern the main contours of a religious belief or practice, let alone its subtler dimensions associated with that culture.

Western European students with Christian backgrounds often have difficulty understanding Eastern Asian Buddhism or Native American religions. Christian students often attempt to grasp these other religions by comparing them with their own only to end up frustrated, as Christian ideas do not mesh easily with Buddhist or Native American religious beliefs. Each of these religions developed within a unique cultural context, and each traces its founders and practices to distinct stories, circumstances, and events.

For example, complex Navajo chantway rituals involve sandpainting, prayers, chants, songs, and a host of people bearing specific roles; each ritual is part of an elaborate matrix of prescribed ceremonies passed down to practitioners through time. Chantway rituals are oriented toward healing and restoring balance to individuals and the Navajo community. The interrelationship and proper performance of each part of the ritual at each level is crucial for the efficacy of each chantway. Improper treatment of any aspect of the ceremony would cause imbalance and create disharmony in the Navajo cultural fabric and is to be avoided. For students who regard religion as a compartmentalized part of life, the idea of an integrated religious reality involving personal and communal practices, visible and invisible forces, and environmental elements may be difficult to comprehend.

Given the complexity of religious belief and practice and its intimate connection with an immense cultural variety, students of religion might well be baffled as to how to proceed. Perhaps students would do well to become hyperattentive to any opportunity to learn about religion and to cultivate a degree of self-awareness about their own assumptions and biases regarding religion and its study. Creating a chart or diagram of a personal understanding of what religion is or is not could aid students as they approach the study of religious belief and practice.

The study of religion is deeply rooted in a curiosity that is bolstered by acute observation, critical reflection, analytical investigation, and a willingness to ask the who, what, where, when, and why of a particular religion. But this study is not about knowing all of the answers. Instead, it involves a willingness to live with the ambiguities generated by diligent investigation and considerate thought. It is about closely observing the religious practices of others and trying to discern their importance and meaning. It is about reserving judgment of religious beliefs and practices that may seem strange, different, or odd because they are so different from our own. Those who reflect on the subject of religion will find themselves asking challenging questions that may require settling on tentative answers rather than quick solutions or resolutions. The study of religion also may cause students to rethink their own cherished practices and beliefs.

For example, I am currently working with an undergraduate student on a research project mapping geographical arrangements of Native American Mississippian mound-complexes in relation to movements of the sun, moon, and stars. After researching the ancient culture and religious beliefs and practices suggested by the archaeological record, early historical accounts, and stories from remnant tribes, we have developed a set of challenging questions. We wonder if we can discern something about this people even though the Native Americans left no written records. Their religious ideas and beliefs were probably passed down to contemporary Osage and Natchez tribes through oral stories and need to be more closely examined. So far we have discovered a correlation between the movements of the sun (summer and winter solstice, spring and fall equinox) and the location of mound structures. It may be that the mounds are directly aligned with the movements of the moon and constellations. And there may be a connection between Mississippian ritual practices and the Skiri Pawnee morning star sacrificial practice. The relationship of astrological and mound geographical alignments to particular religious practices is an open question.

Some students may want to throw this book against the wall at this point because it is not oriented toward correct answers about what religion is and how it ought to be studied. Others may think the study of religion should be largely catechetical, focused on learning what is True and what is False. Some may think they have already reflected on and studied religion enough and see its academic study as a waste of time. Instead, this text is oriented toward encouraging students to tour historic and current religious beliefs, practices, and thought; to explore a range of methods and disciplines for the study of religion; and to reflect on their own assumptions, opinions, and beliefs and the impact they may have on the world.

It may help to reflect that since religious practice is so common and takes on such varied expressions, studying it might serve people in everyday living. Nearly every job in North America intersects some facet of religious belief and practice. Every sporting event, concert, or political occasion contains elements of religious thought and practice. Student athletes pray before games, spectators pray during games, concertgoers give religious interpretations to songs and stage performances, politicians claim or deny that religious connections inform their decision-making, and religious beliefs and practices are interwoven with economic, social, and environmental issues.

The U.S. legal system is riddled with laws protecting religious beliefs and practices and preventing their proscription. The U.S. Senate and House of Representatives open their sessions with prayer and yet rule against compulsory prayer in public schools. U.S. currency proclaims, "IN GOD WE TRUST," while monuments that cite the Judeo-Christian Ten Commandments are barred from courthouse property. While forbidding imposition of one religious viewpoint on their constituents, lawmakers often model and enforce others. Laws pertaining to what is or is not permissible for the American public are often rooted in Judeo-Christian perspectives of right and wrong. For example, marriage laws are often bound up in the New Testament notion that only one man and one woman may be joined together as husband and wife. Hence, same-sex marriage is barred in most states and other practices such as polygamy—observed in many places throughout the world—are not permitted. With such a variety of thinking about what religion is and how it should be interpreted, it is striking that there isn't more civil unrest about how religion ought to be practiced—if at all.

In nearly every age, there are those who claim that religion and its study are dead or near death. People such as Friedrich Nietzsche, Sigmund Freud, and others regarded the very idea of religion as dangerous for humans and human relationships. To the skeptic or cynic, religion might be considered a means to enslave or corrupt minds, or simply a false hope and empty promise to those desiring a better life. For many, all one can count on is death; life after death is an illusion and the idea of a personal or impersonal God is false. The only religion worth having is none at all or one founded solely in oneself.

Likewise, there are those in every age for whom religion is alive and well; those who are adamant that religion should be more pervasive, at least in their part of the world—Mahatma Gandhi, Sathya Sai Baba, Billy Graham, Gautama the Buddha, the Apostle Paul, Benny Hinn, Mother Teresa, Pope Benedict, Emperor Hirohito, Osama bin Laden, and others. Each has made or is making claims about what religion is and ought to be and how it should be practiced.

Anyone reading this book carries a host of assumptions about what religion means and how it ought to be practiced. Some will identify with Roman Catholic Christian backgrounds, where the sacraments figure prominently in devotional and religious life. Others will identify with Protestant Christian backgrounds, where baptism and the Lord's Supper may be cornerstones for a life of faith. Or possibly, faith, justice, peacemaking, and personal ethics may be regarded as most relevant. For those from a Muslim, Jewish, Hindu, Sikh, Native American, Wiccan, or other religious perspective, assumptions about religious beliefs and how people encounter what is most true, sacred, holy, or divine will vary greatly. This chapter and book take seriously the different assumptions, perspectives, beliefs, and cultural worldviews the reader brings to the subject of religion, with the hope that active engagement with one's own assumptions will enable the reader to reflect on their merits, to critique and analyze them, and perhaps to build on them.

Questions for Reflection and Discussion

- What is your religion or religious tradition? If you have none, then what are your core values?

- From your experience, is the practice of religion dead or dying? Explain.

- What contemporary ideas are currently touted as the most religiously valid or invalid?

- What laws do you think are religiously motivated and why?

- Describe your own experience of religion.

- In what ways have you observed religious beliefs or practices conveyed through video, print, radio, Internet, or other media?

- Who are the major religious people in your life and what makes them religious?

DEFINING RELIGION

As we stated in the preface, no simple, single definition of religion holds for all. There is such diversity it seems part of being human is to engage in religious ideas and practices. These ideas and practices do not remain absolutely constant over time; they change in subtle and significant ways. And there is no seamless whole or commonality that binds together this complexity. Religious ideas and practices are ephemeral, defy simple explanation, and yet are held by most people in the world.

Given the propensity of humans to hold something called "religion," an introductory book on the subject can serve to enumerate approaches to religion, unmask hidden assumptions about what religion is or is not, engage one's imagination about historical and contemporary religious ideas and practices, and so on.

Definitions for religion abound. Huston Smith, an eminent twentieth-century scholar of religion, claims,

> Religion . . . confronts the individual with the most momentous option life can present. It calls the soul to the highest adventure it can undertake, a proposed journey across the jungles, peaks, and deserts of the human spirit. The call is to confront reality, to master the self. Those who dare to hear and follow that secret call will soon learn the dangers and difficulties of its lonely journey . . . [and] we shall never quite understand the religions that are not our own.[1]

Influenced by the writings of William James, Alfred North Whitehead, and others, Smith in part defines religion as the means by which human beings come to terms with what is most real in themselves and their world. Smith further argues for two things: first, a "need to see their [other religions'] adherents as men and women [and children] who faced problems much like our own. And second, . . . [a need to] rid our minds of all preconceptions that could dull our sensitivity or alertness to fresh insights [that might be gained through the study of other religions]."[2]

Friedrich Schleiermacher, the late-eighteenth-century theologian and founder of liberal Protestantism, argued that religion is largely a matter of emotion or feeling. In *Religion: Speeches to Its Cultured Despisers*, he contends that religion is basically a "feeling of ultimate dependence" on something that is immediately present and at the same time infinite and beyond apprehension.[3] The affective human experience is one that makes religion universally desired and intuitively understood; it is rooted in a self-conscious relationship to God. For Schleiermacher, religion is best understood through an experiential knowing, not simply through rational means.

People who study religion disagree over what it is and how it should be studied. Even the terms used lack universal definitions. The word *religion* is sometimes regarded as synonymous with *spirituality*. But are we talking about the same thing? Some regard spirituality as the lived experience of religion rather than the belief system itself. Others contend that spirituality is about connection with spirit entities or powers. Yet not all religions hold that spirits exist or that spirituality is a proper term for their religious beliefs and practices. Some try to distinguish between the two terms by using *religion* as a more general term for activities and beliefs that give meaning to life and connect people with truth, and *spirituality* for specific practices aimed at improving one's spiritual awareness. Others contend that religion concerns the eternal while

---

1. Huston Smith, *The World's Religions* (New York: HarperSanFrancisco, 1991), 9, 11.
2. Ibid., 11.
3. John Lyden, *Enduring Issues in Religion* (San Diego, CA: Greenhaven Press, 1995), 19.

spirituality concerns the inner life of individuals in relation to that permanent truth. Again, no single answer will suffice.

John (Fire) Lame Deer, a Lakota Sioux holy man, offers a Native American definition for religion that does not fit easily into European constructs. For him, religion is not something to be defined apart from other things, but rather an infusion of *wakan* or sacredness in everything.

For Lame Deer religion is found in multi-layered spiritual environments where people and creation intertwine. Religion can involve "numbers, names, stones, plants, animals, people, etc."[4]

Religion for him is bound up in relationships with all that can be observed and experienced in the natural world. It is breath, wind, movement, affective experience, intellectual assent, and as simple as grains of sand, buds on flowers, ravens calling, dew on grass, a rattle's sound, or an ant's movement.

Lame Deer claims, "We Sioux spend a lot of time thinking about everyday things, which in our mind are mixed up with the spiritual. We see in the world around us many symbols that teach us the meaning of life. . . . We Indians live in a world of symbols and images where the spiritual and commonplace are one."[5]

The Lakota (Sioux) people have a long history of religious practice that is intimately tied with the movement of seasons, the stages of life, notions of wakan, sacred directions, and a Great Spirit figure, "Wakan Tanka."[6]

In *Imagining Religion*, theologian Jonathan Z. Smith argues persuasively for a new approach to defining religion.

While there is a staggering amount of data, phenomena, of human experiences and expressions that might be characterized in one culture or another, by one criterion or another, as religious, there is no data for religion. Religion is solely the creation of the scholar's study. It is created for the scholar's analytic purposes by his [or her] imaginative acts of comparison and generalization. Religion has no existence apart from the academy. For this reason, the student of religion . . . must be relentlessly self-conscious. Indeed, this self-consciousness constitutes his [or her] primary expertise, his [or her] foremost object of study.[7]

Smith seems not so much concerned with finding some universal definition for religion as with the scholars' and students' personal quests to understand established categories for the study of religion. According to Russell McCutcheon, Smith is saying that the study of religion is about increasing our understanding of the diverse human practices that are lumped under the category of religion.[8]

Definitions of religion will vary depending on your starting point. If you start with an anthropological perspective, it is likely your definition will be science-based. If you begin with a christocentric perspective, your definition will likely be filtered through that lens. Likewise, whether your orientation is psychological, social, or political, it follows that how religion is defined and therefore studied will be determined by your starting point and assumptions.

---

4. John (Fire) Lame Deer and Richard Erdoes, *Lame Deer: Seeker of Visions* (New York: Simon & Schuster, 1972), cited in John Lyden, *Enduring Issues in Religion* (San Diego, CA: Greenhaven Press, 1995), 154.

5. Ibid.

6. For a fuller description of Lakota culture and religion, see: Stephen E. Feraca, *Wakinyan: Lakota Religion in the Twentieth Century* (Lincoln: University of Nebraska Press, 2008), and Joseph E. Brown, *The Sacred Pipe* (Norman: University of Oklahoma Press, 1953).

7. Cited in Russell T. McCutcheon, *Studying Religion: An Introduction* (London: Equinox, 2007), 68–69.

8. Ibid.

Questions for Reflection and Discussion

- What does the word *religion* mean to you?
- How does your definition of religion compare to the definitions of your peers?
- What are your particular questions about religion?
- If you had been raised without any religious belief or practice, do you think you would begin to practice some form of religion? Why or why not?

- Would you ever consider changing your religion? Why or why not?
- How do you define spirituality? How does your definition compare with various definitions for religion?
- What might be encouraging or rewarding about the practice or study of religion?
- How would you design an introductory course on the study of religion?

CORE VALUES

One way to approach the study of religion is to consider your core values. What are they? Why do you hold them? Where did they come from? How might they change depending on circumstance? What would happen if they disappeared? While religion and core values are not the same (an atheist would profess no religion but would still have core values), core values are often linked to foundational truths that stem from religious convictions. For example, the core value of not killing is for Christians a basic truth derived from God's commandment to Moses ("You shall not kill," Ex 20:13). Yet Christians do not always interpret this command the same way. Some would maintain there are circumstances in which it is permissible to kill.

Trying to clarify what religion is can be difficult. A personal definition might be a good start. However, a clarification of your own perspective will necessarily be limited and will resonate only within your sphere of like-minded acquaintances and others who are similarly disposed. Cultural background, economic stratification, gender, age, and so on affect how you identify your core values. And core values can change. A core value I held at age 18 might not be a core value I hold today. And while I might still hold particular core values since I remain a Christian, for example, I am now also an ordained minister in the Presbyterian Church (USA) and have studied and practiced religion in locations around the world. I have continued to reflect on what religion means and how a person might most effectively practice it. My beliefs and perspectives concerning religion continue to evolve, to change.

Questions for Reflection and Discussion

- Create a list of everything you value and why you value each item mentioned.
- What values do you hold that you think others do not? Why do you hold these values?
- Which values are you willing to compromise and which will you retain no matter what the cost?

- Are there values that others hold that you find offensive? Explain.
- Where did your values come from?
- Are there values that are held by a religious community with which you affiliate that you do not hold? Explain.

THE STUDY OF RELIGION IS DANGEROUS

Those who choose to study religion be fore-warned: it is dangerous work. When you begin to unravel the fabric of another's religious belief system and look more deeply at its practices, you risk doing likewise with your own. Some students claim the study of religion has eroded their faith or caused them to cease believing in what they once cherished as unassailable truths. Others say the study of religion has convinced them that all religions are really the same: if you study one you know them all. Regardless of how you approach the study of religion, the risks are real.

So how do people maintain their religious practices and beliefs when the study of religion causes them to question their faith? What if my religion discourages or even forbids the study of other beliefs? Is my salvation

RELIGIONS OF THE WORLD				
Religion	Date of Origin (Roughly)	Place of Origin	Sacred Texts	Founder(s)
Buddhism	520 BCE	India	Tripitaka, Mahayana sutras, and so on	Siddhartha Gautama, the Buddha
Christianity	30 CE	Israel, Middle East, Western Asia, and the shores of the Mediterranean Sea	Bible: Old and New Testaments	Triune God via Jesus the Christ and the Apostles
Hinduism	1500 BCE	India	Rig Veda, Upanishads, Bhagavad-Gita, Puranas, Tantras, and so on	Brahman via priests and people of India
Islam	622 CE	Saudi Arabia	Qur'an	Allah via Muhammad the prophet
Judaism	1500 BCE	Israel	Torah, Talmud	Yahweh (The name of God is considered too sacred to speak. Hence, when reading Hebrew the people refer to God as Adonai.)

in jeopardy if I study or attend religious rituals other than my own?

Could the study of a religion by an outsider even harm that religion or religious practice? Although it has been widely used to good effect, comparative theology is laced with dangers and may lead students to oversimplify what religion is and how it ought to be practiced. Learning the Four Noble Truths of Buddhism, the Five Pillars of Islam, the Christology of Christianity, the laws of Judaism, and so on doesn't qualify as solid knowledge of those religions. Compiling an essential-characteristics list for a religion may provide an instructive outline, but the risks are manifold. Religion, religious teaching, and religious practice are complex and not readily reduced to simple facts, formulas, and categories. Knowing the name of a founder or a core creation story tells us little about a religion and its practice. Crafting a simple chart does not permit me to conclude that I have plumbed the essence of every religion ever practiced.

Which leads me to the chart page 11 that provides an overview of several major religions—"major" because of the number of their adherents. The chart notes each religion's founders, dates of origin, and other relevant details usually covered in a comparative world religions textbook. This comparative method also carries with it the risk of missing or distorting much of each religion by virtue of what is included or left out. For example, when discussing the Christian Sacrament or Ordinance or Observance of the Lord's Supper, some authors prefer to focus on what members of different denominations believe as they partake of the bread and wine. They may discuss Roman Catholic transubstantiation, Lutheran consubstantiation, Presbyterian communion, Baptist commemoration, and so on. Even though this may highlight some of the salient differences among Christian doctrines, it does not begin to tell the whole story of the Christian practice of the Lord's Supper. In addition to the risk of oversimplifying a religion or religious practice, the comparative method is also prone to exoticizing religions and practices that are unfamiliar to the student. Although memorizing essential facts may introduce students to a religion, it cannot do much more than that. In addition, the chart on page 11 represents a Western European method for understanding world religions that counts such things as founders, sacred texts, places and dates of origin as pivotal and telling details.

For a good overview of world religions, students may wish to consult Robert S. Ellwood's *Many People, Many Faiths*; Huston Smith's *The Illustrated World's Religions: A Guide to Our Wisdom Traditions*; or a similar text. A summary chart of facts about world religions can also be found on the Web at *http://www.religionfacts.com/big_religion_chart.htm*.

Questions for Reflection and Discussion

- Other than the comparative method, how might religion be studied?

- What is your greatest fear regarding the study of religion?

- Is the practice of religion ever dangerous? Explain.

- Is the study of religion ever dangerous? Explain.

- What is your greatest hope regarding the study of religion?

CONCLUSION

One of the main arguments in this chapter is the notion that how you define religion will directly influence how you study it. For this reason, a single definition of religion is neither offered nor encouraged in this book. Instead, the variety of definitions of and approaches to studying religion presented by our contributing authors represent individual responses to religion, rooted in their respective disciplines. Questions to prompt reflection and discussion are offered throughout. We hope these will fuel your imagination and prompt a degree of excitement in your study of religion.

Any study of religion should raise questions about how culture, social and economic location, gender, lifestyle, ethics, and so on affect definitions for religion, as well as the beliefs and concepts within particular religious traditions. The practices of those following a particular religion will vary widely depending on the age, gender, location, and so on of the practitioner. Hence, the practices of children engaging in prayer within Judaism or Islam will vary widely from region to region and between male and female children. Some religions provide specific rules for how males and females should engage in religious activity. For example,

Coptic Christians separate males from females during worship services. In addition, only males may perform certain portions of the rituals and only men may serve as priests.

Hence, the study of religion requires maintaining an open mind toward the many alternatives that exist. Native American, South Pacific, and South Asian religions as well as the monotheistic traditions—Muslim, Jewish, and a variety of Christian denominations—will be examined to provide students with a more textured range of responses to questions such as "What is religion?" and "How might religion be studied?" As an ideological framework that merges directly with lived experience, religion is a complicated subject. Faith, belief, and lived practices are nurtured and expressed through particular texts, works of art, music, dance, physical adornments, artifacts (cups, furniture, masks, etc.), foods, ethical and moral codes, laws that govern human behavior, and more.

The aim of this first chapter has been to disturb the calm waters of settled opinion about religion and its study. In the ensuing chapters, we will navigate new waters in exploring some of the myriad faces and facets of religious practice and belief.

Questions for Reflection and Discussion

- What were the most difficult sections of this chapter for you to understand?
- What would you like to learn more about?
- Was it disturbing not to receive one simple definition for religion or one simple method for its study? If not why not? If it was

disturbing, what did you want the definition and method of study to be?
- What do you think will be the most difficult task in the study of religion?
- How do you think religion might best be studied?

Additional Resources

Berling, Judith A. 2004. *Understanding Other Religious Worlds: A Guide for Interreligious Education.* Maryknoll, NY: Orbis Books.

Fitzgerald, Michael L., and John Borelli. 2006. *Interfaith Dialogue: A Catholic View.* Maryknoll, NY: Orbis Books.

Haught, John F. 1990. *What Is Religion? An Introduction.* New York: Paulist Press.

Herling, Bradley L. 2007. *A Beginner's Guide to the Study of Religion.* New York: Continuum International Publishing Group.

Jakelic, Slavica, and Lori Pearson, eds. 2004. *The Future of the Study of Religion: Proceedings of Congress 2000.* Leiden/Boston: Brill.

Lyden, John. 1995. *Enduring Issues in Religion.* San Diego, CA: Greenhaven Press.

McCutcheon, Russell T. 2007. *Studying Religion: An Introduction.* London: Equinox.

Orsi, Robert A. 2005. *Between Heaven and Earth: The Religious Worlds People Make and the Scholars Who Study Them.* Princeton, NJ: Princeton University Press.

Pals, Daniel L. 2006. *Eight Theories of Religion.* New York: Oxford University Press.

Rodrigues, Hillary, and John S. Harding. 2009. *Introduction to the Study of Religion.* London: Routledge.

Roman Catholic Committee for Other Faiths. 2002. *Interfaith Dialogue: The Teaching of the Catholic Church.* London: Catholic Communications Service.

Segal, Robert A. 2006. *The Blackwell Companion to the Study of Religion.* Malden, MA: Blackwell Publishing.

Smith, Huston. 1991. *The World's Religions.* San Francisco: HarperSanFrancisco.

Strenski, Ivan. 2006. *Thinking about Religion: An Historical Introduction to Theories of Religion.* Malden, MA: Blackwell Publishing.

Web Resources

Internet Guide to Resources: *http://www.wabashcenter.wabash.edu/resources/guide_headings.aspx*

A selective, annotated guide to a variety of electronic resources of interest to those who are involved in the study and practice of religion: syllabi, electronic texts, electronic journals, Web sites, bibliographies, liturgies, reference resources, software, and so on.

Intute Arts and Humanities: *http://www.intute.ac.uk/artsandhumanities/*

A free online resource with access to more than 21,000 Web resources representing some of the best Web resources for education and research.

HOW IS RELIGION STUDIED?[1]

Dr. Debra Majeed
Beloit College

Preface

The question of how religion is studied—or perhaps, how to study religion—is answered differently depending on one's culture, gender, age, economic status, location, history, and so on. Methods for studying religion are as varied as the people practicing religion. To help readers discover some of the shapes, contours, and confluences in the landscape of the study of religion, in this chapter Debra Majeed introduces seven approaches to this study. Specifically, readers will examine anthropological, ecological, sociological, psychological, phenomenological, feminist, and womanist approaches to the study of religion.

Chapter Goals

- To help readers learn *how* to think about religion, rather than *what* to think about religion
- To show how the academic study of religion differs from the practice of religion
- To introduce seven methods for the academic study of religion

INTRODUCTION

"You mean we actually have to *go* there?" inquired a first-year student upon learning about the assigned ritual observation in my foundational course, Understanding Religious Traditions in Multicultural America. "I thought we could just read a book." "I'm not interested in conversion," added another. "I'm taking this class because it's open, fits my schedule, and I get credit for it."

These typical responses convey numerous presumptions, several of which we will consider shortly. For now, rest assured that as the semester evolved, these students became explorers,

---

1. For more in-depth looks at the study of religion, see Julia Corbett Hemeyer, *Religion in America*, 5th ed. (Upper Saddle River, NJ: Pearson Prentice Hall, 2006); Michael Molloy, *Experiencing the World's Religions: Tradition, Challenge, and Change*, 2nd ed. (Mountain View, CA: Mayfield Publishing, 2002); Jacob Neusner, ed., *World Religions in America: An Introduction* (Louisville, KY: Westminster John Knox Press, 2000); and Diana L. Eck, *A New Religious America* (San Francisco: HarperSanFrancisco, 2001).

confronting the challenge of defining religion and considering its study. They came to understand our varied religions as attempts by people like themselves to consider life's big questions, to "highlight certain words like Meaning, Ultimate, Reality, and Truth with capital letters." They had begun an important journey.[2]

These explorers came to appreciate the ritual-observation assignment as an opportunity to visit local religious communities, observe activities, and return to class to share their findings—all part of an introduction to the nonevaluative method of studying religion. And they came to know that to undertake the academic study of religion is to question ourselves and others, to position ourselves to learn from those we study, and to appreciate that "the building blocks of religion are also the building blocks in our own lives."[3]

When I first started teaching undergraduates in 1997, I was surprised by student comments like the ones above. Today I am not.[4] As a beginning teacher, I thought my students understood that the study of religion was a valuable opportunity to consider questions of ultimate reality, to challenge their own assumptions by encountering different experiences, and to grapple with theories and methods for interpreting religious phenomena.

I assumed they recognized this as a chance to develop the basic knowledge and vocabulary needed for informed and insightful discussions of religious thought and practice. I thought these "global citizens in the making" would be eager to understand religion's role as "the most critical and threatening marker of difference."[5]

You may or may not be a person of faith, spiritual, searching, or someone who limits anything religious to the private, personal sphere. You may be considering an academic major in a field other than religion, religious studies, or the humanities. Perhaps you have encountered an advisor or professor who is a bit self-conscious when it comes to thinking about religion and the most appropriate space for such theorizing to take place.[6] You may also have crossed paths with someone who did not value religion "in its living forms, but found [it] terribly interesting . . . in its dead ones."[7] By deciding to take an introductory course on religion and by reading this text, you have chosen to enter a world of "passion and drama" as humanity "discovers the truth of what it is to be human."[8]

As one former student, now a professor of religious studies, wrote: "Religion is a key ingredient in many of the puzzles we must solve if we are to understand our contemporary world."[9]

---

2. Donna Freitas, "The Big Questions: A Professor Links Children's Literature to Religious Imagination," *School Library Journal* (May 2005): 34.

3. Ibid., 35.

4. In truth, my initial reaction was based upon my own college experience and personal passions, rather than those of contemporary young adults. I had assumed the "uneducated" position of all educators who are less than informed about the religious activities of their students. Craig Calhoun examines this issue in the preface to the *SSRC Guide: Religious Engagement among American Undergraduates, http://religion.ssrc.org/reguide/printable.html.*

5. Natalie Gummer, "A Profound Unknowing: The Challenge of Religion in the Liberal Education of World Citizens," *Liberal Education* 91, no. 2 (Spring 2005), *http://www.aacu.org/liberaleducation/le-sp05/le-sp05perspective.cfm.*

6. See Barbara Walvoord, *Teaching and Learning in College Introductory Religious Courses* (Malden, MA: Blackwell Publishing, 2008). Moreover, my experience is consistent with the conclusion offered by Craig Calhoun: "most faculty members move in networks in which religious questions are seldom raised." See also the preface to "Essays Forum on the Religious Engagement of American Undergraduates," *SSRC Guide: Religious Engagement among American Undergraduates, http://religion.ssrc.org/reguide/printable.html.*

7. Jacob Neusner as cited in Laurence J. O'Connell, "Religious Studies, Theology, and the Humanities Curriculum," *Journal of the American Academy of Religion* 51, no. 4 (December 1984), 736.

8. Jonathan Z. Smith, *Map Is Not Territory* (Chicago: University of Chicago Press, 1998), 290–291.

9. Gregory Allen Robbins, "Why Major in Religious Studies?" University of Denver Department of Religious Studies, *http://www.du.edu/rlgs/whymajor.htm.*

Explorers get better at puzzles as they work them.

Too much of the critical inquiry that occurs in the college classroom could be characterized as a disconnected monologue, with the professor as the "product manager" and the students as "consumer-learners." Here, however, I invite you into dialogue; join me in questioning personal biases and presuppositions; permit the subjects of your study to speak to you, to teach you.

This chapter concerns how the study of religion proceeds—that is, the study of religion as opposed to its practice—regardless of the motivation or assumptions the learner brings to this enterprise. We are colearners and explorers here, whose backgrounds and expertise influence our starting places and biases.

Questions for Reflection and Discussion

- What variables might affect our study of religion, especially as we begin?

- What views do people hold that might be considered religious?

DIVERSE READERS SHARE COMMONALITIES

Let's now turn to the question, *why* study religion? Our answer allows us to distinguish between religion and theology. Both our motives for studying religion (say, for academic credit) and the context in which our study takes place (the academic classroom as compared to a religious setting) can influence how religion is taught. In the United States, introductory courses in religion attract undergraduates with a range of motivations. Many enter the classroom wanting to learn more about their own religious tradition and the beliefs of their neighbors. Some are attracted by the chance to affirm the superiority of a secular, scientific perspective; others, to prepare for some form of ministry. Those whose sole experience with the study of religion has been devotional may seek to confirm what they know. At this point you may be thinking about your personal motives for studying religion and what you might have in common with other readers.

Realize this: those of you who are taking a course in religion solely for academic credit need not apologize, nor does your pragmatism indicate a disinterest in so-called religious questions. More likely, on some level you are also curious about how religious ideas and practices orient those you now know and love or will one day meet.[10]

A foundational course or text in religious studies acknowledges religion as a phenomenon that continues to play a decisive role in North American history and society.

As early as European immigrants' first encounters with Native Americans in the 1500s and following through the forms of Christianity practiced by the New England colonists on up through the arrival of peoples practicing the hundreds of different faiths we see today, the tapestry of American religion has been an ancient, rich, and multilayered one. Today, our diversity continues to be a source for contest and celebration. Interestingly, nearly 60 percent of Americans say they enjoy living in a diverse

---

10. S. A. Nigosian, *World Religions: A Historical Approach*, 4th ed. (Boston: Bedford/St. Martin's, 2008), 1.

religious landscape, according to a 2008 Pew Research survey.[11]

You and other readers of this text represent this diversity and likely share some characteristics in common as well. A 2006 self-study by the Department of Philosophy and Religious Studies at Beloit College suggests undergraduates like yourself routinely

- bring with them a vested personal interest, either through adherence to a particular tradition or through a related, but no less powerful, feeling that spirituality plays a deeply significant role in their lives;
- become captivated by the challenge of viewing life from perspectives radically different from their own; and

- find the ethical questions we highlight in our courses to be compelling and worthy of investigation for personal and political reasons.[12]

By the close of the nineteenth century, advances in science led scholars to design five disciplinary approaches to inquiry: anthropological, philosophical, sociological, psychological, and phenomenological. These scholarly methods are briefly described here along with two noteworthy postmodern approaches, namely, feminist and womanist. Let's begin with the overall approach in which we are engaged, the academic study of religion.

Questions for Reflection and Discussion

- What about religion or religious studies makes you curious?
- What are your own learning goals for the study of religion?

- Compare yourself with the student profile outlined above. How are you similar or different?

COMPARING THE ACADEMIC AND DEVOTIONAL STUDY OF RELIGION

Religious studies courses in the humanities are divided by function. The guiding question is "What do we hope to accomplish with our studies?" When, for example, our goal is to expand our knowledge of religion without assigning a value to a specific orientation, we call this the *academic* study of religion.

Alternatively, when our objective is to learn, apply, and possibly teach a specific religious system and set of practices, we call this the *devotional* study of religion (which some refer to as *theology*). Historically, the two disciplines share a common root, specifically an investment in "the religious dimension of ordinary human experience."[13]

This fundamental compatibility between theology and the study of religion yields the potential for one to serve as an ally for the other.[14] Indeed, the two subjects represent the "yin and yang" of

---

11. Paul Taylor and Richard Morin, "Americans Say They Like Diverse Communities: Election, Census Trends Suggest Otherwise," *http://pewsocialtrends.org/pubs/719/diverse-political-communities*.

12. "Department of Philosophy and Religious Studies, Beloit College, Self-Study for External Review," October 2006, 13–14.

13. O'Connell, "Religious Studies," 731.

14. Ibid.

religion. In fact, you may be among those students who have chosen to study religion in order to probe some aspect of theology. That said, important distinctions will determine whether religious studies or theology—the academic or devotional study of religion—is appropriate and under what circumstances. Where religion is concerned, each subject offers different theoretical options that "proceed in dramatically different ways, relying on different tools and methods, researching significantly different ends."[15] The theologian routinely encounters religion or faith as a phenomenon that is connected with salvation, human frailty, or communication with spirits.[16] Thus theology answers the question of how to study religion in terms of indoctrination, particularly with regard to belief in a god or the experience of religious faith.[17]

The devotional approach routinely focuses on a single religion, religious organization, or community of faith with the goal of sharpening the knowledge or commitment of the practitioners of that faith and in some cases empowering them to evangelize others. It may be that the junior quoted below, who was studying theology at a Catholic institution, was encountering a devotional approach in her classroom:

> The professor uses the pronoun "we" when discussing Christian viewpoints, because the majority of us come from a Christian background. Yes, perhaps this is true, but not all are Christian. I sit behind a Buddhist from Vietnam. I wouldn't label myself Christian, either.[18]

Intellectual environments that press for acceptance, or that expect or compel religious homogeneity (as some private and religiously affiliated institutions do) favor the devotional approach. Such environments may seek to conform students to a particular belief system or stipulate that "personal religious commitments carry an authority that renders those commitments immune to critical analysis."[19] Ultimately, the devotional approach to the study of religion represents an epistemological encounter with religion that identifies and advocates a single belief system.

We want to introduce you to the reality of religion locally and globally as "the classification some of us give to various collections of artful but all too human devices that help to portray any given world in which we happen to find ourselves as the 'world without end.'"[20] That is, we seek an independent approach that neither places a value on a certain belief system nor seeks the "safe distance [of] supposed objectivity and abstraction."[21] In other words, our goal is to explore the "passion and drama" of "how human beings have mapped out or understood what it means for [one's] existence to be meaningful at different times and places."[22] Our goal is the academic study of religion.

---

15. Russell T. McCutcheon, ed., *The Insider/Outsider Problem in the Study of Religion: A Reader* (London: Cassell Publishers, 1999), 2.

16. Ibid., 150.

17. Nigosian, *World Religions*, 2.

18. Grace Manning Wallace, e-mail to author, November 11, 2007.

19. John Leach, ed., "Teaching about Religion in a Public School Classroom: Questions and Answers," in *A Teacher's Guide to Religion in American Life* (Cary, NC: Oxford University Press, 2002), 12; Patricia O'Connell Killen, "Encountering Religious Commitments in the Classroom," *Washington Center News*, Spring 2000, *http://www.aarweb.com/Programs/Awards/Teaching_Awards/2006/EncounteringReligiousCommitments.pdf.*

20. L. Albinus, review of Russell T. McCutcheon's *The Discipline of Religion: Structure, Meaning, Rhetoric, Journal of the American Academy of Religion* 74, no. 2 (2006).

21. I appropriate language that Stacey Floyd-Thomas uses in a related discussion of pedagogy. See "Cultivating a Pedagogy of Possibility: A Womanist Christian Social Ethicist's Teaching Philosophy," *http://www.aarweb.org/Programs/Awards/Teaching_Awards/2007/SMFT_Teaching_Philosophy.pdf.*

22. Carl Olson, ed., "Religious Studies as an Academic Discipline," in *Theory and Method in the Study of Religion: A Selection of Critical Readings* (Belmont, Calif.: Wadsworth/Thomson Learning, 2003), 15; Zayn Kassam, "Reflection on Teaching Islam at a Liberal Arts College," 2 (presentation to Pomona College, February 19, 2000, Pomona, Calif.).

In the eighteenth century, when a liberal education was paramount to the training of future Christian leaders, the academic study of religion in North America emerged from beneath the intellectual heap created by the distinction between teaching religion itself and teaching about religion.[23] The academic study of religion is the approach fostered by the American Academy of Religion, the largest international organization of scholars of religion, with more than ten thousand members teaching in fifteen hundred colleges, universities, and seminaries.[24] This multidisciplinary approach recognizes, as does E. Thomas Lawson, that "a great deal of 'knowledge' about religion is in fact knowledge about something other than religion. It also is about knowledge of the nature of the human personality, knowledge about the structure of society and its various operations, knowledge of the features of cultural systems."[25] Indeed, the academic study of religion reveals just how extensively religion pervades all aspects of our complex and diverse human world. This is a strategy that promotes a lucid understanding of the wide-ranging religious landscape of the United States.

The academic approach is a systematic framework that also enables what Stacey Floyd-Thomas calls a "pedagogy of possibility."[26] It does not conflate belief with knowledge; instead, it attracts those who appreciate the opportunity to question as they explore without fear. Perhaps the best feature of the academic study of religion is what distinguishes this approach from its devotional counterpart: inclusivity. As Sam Gill aptly puts it:

> The academic study of religion must not depend upon or require its researchers, teachers, or students to maintain any specific religious belief or affiliation, race, culture, or gender. The academic study of religion must be sensitive to multiculturalism: the awareness that there are many peoples, cultures, and religions, none of which has any exclusive claims to be made with regard to religion as an academic subject.[27]

The possibilities of this level of inclusivity are most apparent in the variety of approaches we have to the academic study of religion.

Questions for Reflection and Discussion

- What do you know about the academic study of religion?
- How does the academic study of religion connect or disconnect with your previous studies of religion?
- What aspects of the academic approach to religion appeal to you? Why?
- What aspects of the academic approach to religion do you find problematic? Why?

---

23. Olson, "Religious Studies," 16.

24. Sam Gill, "The Academic Study of Religion," *Journal of the American Academy of Religion* LXII, no. 4 (Winter 1994), 966; "Mission Statement," American Academy of Religion, *http://www.aarweb.org/About_AAR/Mission_Statement/default.asp.*

25. E. Thomas Lawson, "Academic Study of Religion," *Journal of the American Academy of Religion* XLI, no. 2 (June 1994), 299.

26. Derived from the "Religion and the Humanities: Program of Study," University of Chicago, *http://collegecatalog.uchicago.edu/archives/catalog02-04/50-HCD-RELH-02.pdf;* "Cultivating a Pedagogy of Possibility: A Womanist Christian Social Ethicist's Teaching Philosophy," *http://www.aarweb.org/Programs/Awards/Teaching_Awards/2007/SMFT_Teaching_Philosophy.pdf.*

27. Gill, "Academic Study," 965.

APPROACHES FOR THE ACADEMIC STUDY OF RELIGION: UNDERSTANDING LIFE

We now turn briefly to seven methods for the academic study of religion. These approaches are varied, often complementary, sometimes in competition, and routinely "enforce distance through contradiction."[28] Indeed, no single approach, regardless of popularity, perceived value, or history, has garnered the consensus of scholars. Yet whether a religious ritual has piqued your interest, you see religion as "an integral part of human life" or the idea of exploring religion in relation to culture fascinates you, the academic study of religion will enhance your understanding of your own and other peoples' lives.[29]

Methods for the Academic Study of Religion

The anthropological approach. The key tools for anthropologists of religion are ethnography, participant observation, and the knowledge gained through such fieldwork. The key assumption is that religious rituals and institutions are observable. Rather than assigning a value to the truth-claims of a community, this method promotes an examination of a religious body by first exploring its beliefs, institutions, and the behavior of followers and then allowing those findings to guide interpretation. Guided by the contributions of Clifford Geertz and Victor Tuner, the anthropological approach is most concerned with how cultures create and transform religious symbols, myths, and the religious imaginations of particular groups.

An interesting and perhaps controversial example of this approach is Karen McCarthy Brown's ethnographic study of Moma Lola, a voodoo priestess in Brooklyn, New York.[30] Brown's study not only highlights how an imported religious culture navigates the complex and varied American landscape but also documents the struggles of an anthropologist who feels herself drawn to join the movement she studies.

The ecological approach. Advocates of this approach believe humans interact with their environment in intentional ways and therefore believe that religion can best be understood by analyzing the natural ecological factors that shape faiths. Central to this approach is how people adapt their religious practices to their environments. The use of the Nile River in the rituals of ancient Egypt is a historical example of the contribution of an ecological force to the culture and religious sensibilities of a people. For case studies, religious ecologists turn to tribal and other cultures that depend more on nonhuman life than technology to survive. As Carl Olson has observed, this approach involves an activist stance concerning "whether it is best to attempt to improve [the natural environment] by altering, shaping, and developing it with the long-term hope of perfecting it."[31] Ake Hultkranz, Walter Burkert, Rosemary Radford Reuther, and other proponents of this approach advocate an "awakening," a way of demonstrating that religion is a feature in all cultures and that cultures can inappropriately employ religion to dominate nature.

The phenomenological approach. Phenomenology attempts to distinguish between the essence of religion and its diverse forms. A "descriptive" method, phenomenology balks at the

---

28. Rubina Ramji, "The Centrality of Veiling and Invisibility: The Construction of the Muslim Woman Identity in Contemporary Discourses and Media" (PhD diss., University of Ottawa, 2003), 15.

29. Nigosian, *World Religions*, 7.

30. Karen McCarthy Brown, *Moma Lola: A Voodoo Priestess in Brooklyn* (Berkeley: University of California, 1991).

31. Olson, "Religious Studies," 440.

notion that to observe one religious experience is to have witnessed them all. Rather, phenomenology claims that the essence of religion is the experience of the sacred or holy—an experience unlike any other. Still, this method assumes the existence of a "general" pattern to religion, with definable elements, and seeks to analyze features such as prayer, giving, or revelation.[32] For example, a phenomenological approach would draw attention to the centrality of the Eucharist in the Catholic Mass (in contrast to the "Lord's Supper" in most Protestant congregations), the function of prostrations in the congregational prayers of Muslims, and the significance of spiritual healing in a Pentecostal worship service. As religious rituals and practices, these activities offer us insight into the particularities of religion within specific contexts. The work of Chantepie de la Saussaye, Rudolf Otto, Mircea Eliade, and Edmund Husserl confirms the utility of this approach, especially when the goal is identifying the human need filled or the meaning provided by a specific religion or religious practice.

The psychological approach. For the discerning psychologist, religion is a treasure trove of material with which to study human emotions and behaviors.[33] This approach deals with conflicts between belief and unbelief as it explores religious consciousness. It also attempts to separate the "sacred" from the "profane," to better understand reality beyond appearance. Pioneers like William James, Carl Jung, and Sigmund Freud have called attention to the ways in which religion is used to control human behavior. James points to significant features that distinguish institutional religion (groups, organizations) from personal religion (involving individual mystical experiences). Freud, for one, views religion as a tool for enslavement, rather than as something

that helps people work through their problems. He argues that religious behavior can be a symptom of mental illness—a contention sometimes used to explain aberrant religious behavior, such as the suicidal actions of charismatic leader Jim Jones, leader of the People's Temple.[34]

The sociological approach. Based on the theory that social conditioning shapes human reality, this method examines how religion affects the formation of worldviews. The chief focus of this approach is the network of relationships that can transform an individual into a member of a group, which then can serve as a basis for that individual's identity. This approach demonstrates a willingness to understand a tradition from the believer's perspective. It also considers the lived realities of practitioners as vital information in advancing our understanding of religion's function in society and throughout history. The sociological approach tends to focus on the role of religion in the public arena (political, economic, and media); in intimate interpersonal relationships; and in issues related to race, gender, and sexuality.

To illustrate, sociologists would be interested in the government responses to differing religions. For example, the Circle Sanctuary, a Wisconsin-based community that affirms and supports neopagan beliefs, has actively campaigned for the right of Wiccans to display a pentacle on gravesites in public cemeteries, while Summum, a group that practices mummification rites in Utah, has sought permission to display its "aphorisms" in a local park alongside the Ten Commandments. Groups like Circle Sanctuary and Summum advocate for an active and visible religious presence that extends beyond the boundaries of their membership into the public arena where battles for social justice are

32. Nigosian, *World Religions*, 8.

33. Molloy, *Experiencing the World's Religions*, 16.

34. Olson, "Religious Studies," 343; see "Jim Jones and the People's Temple Suicide" (1978), *http://www.ronaldbrucemeyer.com/rants/1118a-almanac.htm*. Before allegedly killing himself, Rev. Jim Jones, ordered more than nine hundred of his followers to commit suicide.

commonly waged, especially in regard to equal access and free speech. The actions of these organizations confirm their perception of religion as an apt foundation for the preservation of fundamental rights for all citizens, including those whose worldview or lifestyle differ from the norm. They also raise public awareness of the communal identity of individual members. Circle Sanctuary has been successful in providing alternatives to displays of Christian crosses and Jewish menorahs, symbols of mainstream traditions. Conversely, Summum's appeal was denied by the U.S. Supreme Court, which in 2009 ruled that local governments have sole discretion over public park displays without "running afoul" of the First Amendment. Regardless of the outcome, some religious and nonreligious organizations maintain that such activities challenge the church-state separation. Peter L. Berger and other social scientists challenge us to closely examine the implications of religious language and practice within cultures and global societies.

The tools of sociology include quantitative methods (surveys, polls, census, demographics, focus groups) and qualitative methods (participant observation, interviewing, and archival, historical, and documentary materials). Building upon the legacy of William Robertson Smith, Émile Durkheim, and Max Weber, the sociological method views religions as emerging from conflicting social forces, rather than being independent of them.

Women-Centered Frameworks

Our final two methodologies are women-centered frameworks that evolved in response to perceptions among female *and* male scholars that the vocabulary and "terrain of religious scholarship must be 'recast' to expand the voices engaged in the process of describing, interpreting, explaining, and evaluating religion and the religious."[35] By promoting the marginalized voices and experiences of women and attempting to ensure that "racist and misogynistic 'subjectivities'" no longer influence what we learn and how we learn it,[36] these methods (like the ecological method) advocate change and social justice. Theory as well as praxis ground these methodologies because both feminist and womanist approaches highlight "the relationship between social processes and religion and how [it] can perpetuate oppression."[37] Moreover, each method requires "an explicit commitment" to the struggle of an oppressed group, often regarding the interrelationship between gender, race, or sexual orientation and religion.[38] Both approaches assume that "objective inquiry and universal truth" are realized only to the extent that we "answer the questions posed" by the diverse and multilayered experiences of women.[39]

The feminist approach. While scholars have yet to agree about precisely who is or can be a feminist, there is no doubt that gender influences the assumptions we bring to the study of religion. Feminists study and reinterpret the role of women in religious traditions, as well as their encounters with God or other forces considered sacred. Feminists work, as Ruether has long argued, to draw attention to "what has been lost to humanity through the subjugation of women and what new humanity might emerge through the affirmation of the full personhood of women."[40] Feminist concerns move beyond patriarchy to include the objectification of women

---

35. Katie Cannon, as cited in Stacey M. Floyd-Thomas, ed., "Writing for Our Lives: Womanism as an Epistemological Revolution," in *Deeper Shades of Purple: Womanism in Religion and Society* (New York: New University Press, 2006), 1.

36. Ibid., 2.

37. Marcia Y. Riggs, *Awake, Arise and Act: A Womanist Call for Black Liberation* (Cleveland, OH: Pilgrim Press, 1994), x.

38. Ibid., xi.

39. Floyd-Thomas, "Writing for Our Lives," 2.

40. Rosemary Radford Ruether, *Sexism and God-Talk: Toward a Feminist Theology* (Boston: Beacon Press, 1983), 45.

in religious texts and religious institutions. Feminists prompt us to consider how religious ideology could be interpreted and applied differently depending upon one's sex and help us examine complementary patterns that may exist between the sexes. Feminists challenge us to consider how male and female identity roles are performed and to notice the continued stereotyping of gender roles. Feminists challenge us also to reject the assumption that misogyny is necessarily on the minds of women when they talk about gender oppression within religions. Among the attractive characteristics of this method for today's college women is its consideration of how archaeological and feminist goddess discourses interact.

A key factor in launching the feminist revolution in religion more than thirty years ago was the appreciation that gender is important in understanding how religion and belief is codified, how men regard women, and how women understand themselves. Since then, feminists have successfully argued for female representations of the divine, published woman-centered readings of sacred texts, and organized religious movements that promote female leadership. Rather than encountering female agency, piety, and presence through the "matrix of patriarchy and male sexism," the feminist approach to the study of religion challenges conventional views of women and power in religious institutions, belief, and practice. Many scholars have acknowledged the discriminatory power of the masculine matrix, among them: Riffat Hassan, Rosemary Skinner Keller, Rita Gross, Judith Plaskow, Gerda Lerner, Delores Williams, miriam cooke and Rosemary Radford Ruether.

The womanist approach. This method is the youngest of the approaches to the study of religion we have considered here. First articulated in 1985, the womanist approach emerged when a group of Union Theological Seminary graduate students began to search for a "new" epistemology, or way of knowing, that drew upon and took as normative the experience of black women from their first arrival in the so-called New World.[41] These first-generation womanists—namely Delores Williams, Katie G. Cannon, Emilie Townes, and Jacqueline Grant—were Christian scholars who gave currency to the term womanist, which writer Alice Walker introduced in her text, *In Search of Our Mothers' Gardens*.[42] They conceived a womanist to be "a Black woman committed to defying the compound forces of oppression (namely, racism, classism, sexism, and heterosexism) that threaten her self-actualization as well as the survival of her community."[43]

In bringing this new category of intellectual discourse into the academic study of religion, these first-generation womanists sought to redefine the prevailing discourse on African American women, and at the same time question "their suppressed role in the African American church, the community, the family, and the larger society."[44] They "introduced a means of addressing Black women's concerns from their own intellectual, physical, and spiritual perspectives" and thereby tied theory to activism.[45]

One legacy these trailblazers left to third-generation womanist scholars of religion like myself is a womanist approach that "celebrates

41. Ibid., 3; Linda E. Thomas, "Womanist Theology, Epistemology, and a New Anthropological Paradigm," *CrossCurrents* 48, no. 4 (Summer 1998), *http://www.crosscurrents.org/thomas.htm*.

42. Alice Walker, *In Search of Our Mothers' Gardens: Womanist Prose* (San Diego, CA: Harcourt Brace Jovanovich, 1993), xi–xii.

43. Floyd-Thomas, "Writing for Our Lives," 4.

44. Thomas, "Womanist Theology."

45. Floyd-Thomas, "Writing for Our Lives," 4.

multiple and diverse positions of belonging."[46] As a "touchstone for liberation studies in religion," this method extends intellectual space to a variety of discourses on African American women and draws scholars who intentionally challenge "the christological centrality" that at one time minimized African American religiosity.[47] Womanist ways of knowing encourage exploration of the diverse religious imaginations of Americans of African ancestry, such as those of African American Muslims.

Still in development, Muslim womanist thought brings African American women into the center of the intellectual enterprise as both subjects and actors, and examines what their religious "authorities" (husbands, imams, and mosques) say about and to them. This framework begins with what I call the experiential triad of Muslim life. We address questions of how to live with individual and communal interpretations that are sometimes oppositional but nevertheless routinely direct our worlds. This method can be described as womanist because it concerns the multidimensional oppression (race, gender, religion, and class) of African American women. Amina Wadud, Aminah McCloud, Gwendolyn Zoharah Simmons, and I are among a growing cadre of Muslim and other women who are beginning to recognize the instrumentality of the womanist method.

CONCLUSION

In this chapter, we have explored how religion is approached in the humanities curriculum of a liberal arts college. I also have sought to respond to two fundamental inquiries made by Jacob Neusner more than two decades ago, namely, "what do people not know, if they do not know about and understand religions? What can they not explain and of what can they not make sense?"[48] We have considered how the study of religion is the study of human practices and beliefs that inform how many people live, make meaning, and honor their realities.[49]

Each of the seven methods sketched above frames questions of religion differently; the audience, goals, and constraints each method faces and the contribution each one makes vary in subtle and significant ways. Nevertheless, each methodological tool helps students and scholars better understand the experience of those we study as well as our own lives.

Regardless of the tools you use to study religion, this is a collaborative and "dynamic process of mining" in which students and professors begin to better understand the nature and power of religion and ourselves.[50] It is when students like yourself realize that the world around you contains rich mysteries yet to be uncovered that our work as explorers begins.

How is religion studied? In my view, this question is best answered when approached with a curiosity allowing both transformation and discomfort on the road to wonder.

---

46. In an earlier work, I adopt miriam cooke's understanding of "multiple belongings" as a way to best understand Islamic feminism. See miriam cooke, "Multiple Critique: Islamic Feminist Rhetorical Strategies," in *Postcolonialism, Feminism, and Religious Discourse*, eds. Laura E. Donaldson and Kwok Pul-Lan (New York: Routledge, 2001), 142–160; cited in Debra Mubashshir Majeed, "Response to Roundtable Discussion: Must I Be Womanist?" *Journal of Feminist Studies in Religion* 22, no. 1 (2006), 115

47. Floyd-Thomas, "Writing for Our Lives," 5; Majeed, "Response to Roundtable Discussion," 116.

48. Jacob Neusner, "Why Religious Studies in America? Why Now?" *Journal of the American Academy of Religion* 51, no. 4 (December 1984): 738.

49. Talal Asad, *Genealogies of Religion: Discipline and Reasons of Power in Christianity and Islam* (Baltimore, MD: Johns Hopkins University Press, 1993), 27.

50. Stacey Floyd-Thomas, Laura Gillman, and Katherine Allen, "Interdisciplinarity as Self and Subject: Metaphor and Transformation," *Issues in Integrative Studies*, no. 20 (2002): 13.

Questions for Reflection and Discussion

- What methods for the study of religion appeal to you the most? Why?

- What methods for the study of religion appeal to you the least? Why?

- If you were to devise a method for the study of religion, what would it involve?

- If you were to frame questions for the study of religion, what would they be?

Additional Resources

Aleas, K. P. 2004. *Dialogical Theologies: Hartford Papers and Other Essays*. Kolkata: Punthi Pustak.

Antes, Peter, Armin W. Geertz, and Randi R. Warne, eds. 2004. *New Approaches to the Study of Religion, Volume 1: Regional, Critical, and Historical Approaches*. Berlin/New York: Walter de Gruyter.

Antes, Peter, Armin W. Geertz, Randi R. Warne, eds. 2004. *New Approaches to the Study of Religion. Volume 2: Textual, Comparative, Sociological, and Cognitive Approaches*. Berlin/New York: Walter de Gruyter.

Braun, Willi, and Russell T. McCutcheon, eds. 2000. *Guide to the Study of Religion*. London and New York: Cassell.

Capps, Walter H. 1995. *Religious Studies: The Making of a Discipline*. Minneapolis, MN: Fortress Press.

Connolly, Peter, ed. 1999. *Approaches to the Study of Religion*. London and New York: Cassell.

Cunningham, Lawrence S., and John Kelsay. 2002. *The Sacred Quest: An Invitation to the Study of Religion*. Upper Saddle River, NJ: Prentice Hall.

Gothoni, Rene. 2005. *How to Do Comparative Religion? Three Ways, Many Goals*. Berlin/New York: Walter de Gruyter.

Henking, Susan. 2004. "Religion, Religious Studies, and Higher Education: Into the 21st Century." *Religious Studies Review* 30, nos. 2, 3.

Henking, Susan. 2000. "Does (the History of) Religion and Psychological Studies Have a Subject?" In *Mapping Religion and Psychological Studies*, eds. Diane Jonte-Pace and William Parsons. New York: Routledge.

Henking, Susan. 2000. "Who Is the Public Intellectual? Identity, Marginality, and the Religious Studies Scholar." In *ARC: Journal of the Faculty of Religious Studies*, McGill University 28.

Henking, Susan. 1996. "The Open Secret: Dilemmas of Advocacy in the (Religious Studies) Classroom." In *Advocacy in the Classroom: Propaganda versus Engagement*, ed. Patricia Meyers Spacks. New York: St. Martin's Press.

Klostermaier, Klaus K., and Larry W. Hurtado, eds. 1991. *Religious Studies: Issues, Prospects and Proposals*. Atlanta, GA: Scholars Press.

Olson, Carl. 2003. *Theory and Method in the Study of Religion: A Selection of Critical Readings*. Belmont, CA: Thomson Wadsworth.

Stone, Jon R., ed. 1998. *The Craft of Religious Studies*. New York: St. Martin's Press.

Strenski, Ivan. 2006. Thinking about Religion: *An Historical Introduction to Theories of Religion*. Oxford: Blackwell Publishing.

Sutcliffe, Steven J., ed. 2004. *Religion: Empirical Studies, A Collection to Mark the 50th Anniversary of the British Association for the Study of Religion*. Burlington, VT: Ashgate.

Taylor, Mark C., ed. *Critical Terms for Religious Studies*. Chicago: The University of Chicago, 1998.

ORIGIN STORIES AND RELIGION: HOW ARE RELIGIONS FORMED?

David C. Ratke
Lenoir-Rhyne University

Preface

How do we explain the human inclination toward religious belief? How are religions formed? There are as many answers to these questions as there are religious systems. And each answer helps to illumine the nature of these universal and inherently mysterious phenomena.

Some believe origin stories may hold crucial clues to the formation of religions. Nearly every religion has an origin story around which revolve its values, rituals, and belief system. This story is central to understanding the religion's practices and structures and the ideas and beliefs that inform them. Origin stories embody the foundational truths on which religions are built.

In this chapter, David Ratke explores different perspectives on the source of religion before examining origin stories from within their cultural and historical frameworks. Ratke explores the example of the Navajo sweat-lodge ceremony, which centers on the emergence story of that people. Entry into the sweat lodge prompts practitioners to move back to a spiritual and cultural center, thus reorienting adherents to ways of living in the world that connect with their cultural and religious origins.

Chapter Goals

- To introduce different perspectives on the formation of religion, including scientific, Hindu, and Christian
- To consider origin stories and the formation of religions and religious practices
- To introduce myth in relation to the study of religion
- To better understand mythic belief systems by introducing religious ideas such as "sacred" and "profane"

INTRODUCTION

What is the source of religion? How do we explain the human inclination and desire for religious belief? In this chapter, I propose that religions are formed at least in part to explain and understand our human origin and the origin of the universe and to thereby locate ourselves in the world. Our explanations are often overtly religious in character and give rise to religious practices and beliefs that satisfy our human need for meaning and belonging.

But exploring why religions are formed necessarily involves grappling with what religion is. Indeed, asking why religions are formed suggests that religion might somehow be merely a human fabrication. Some people of faith would counter that religion is a divine gift given to humans more or less complete and fully developed. They might add that human understanding of a religion may develop over time, but that the core of the religion itself would remain unchanged.

Asking why religions are formed also assumes the existence of something called "religion" that occupies a distinct realm in human life. While for those in Western societies this implied distinction between "religious" and "secular" or "sacred" and "profane" is self-evident, this distinction is not always made elsewhere. Yet most would agree that there *is* something that can be called "religion" and there are certain behaviors and practices that people the world over recognize as religious. Most cultures, for example, have one or more distinct communities that identify themselves as religious. In the United States, churches, synagogues, mosques, and other places of worship are locations where certain religious practices commonly happen. Prayer and meditation are widely recognized as religious activities. Certain holidays (literally "holy days") such as Christmas and Easter or Yom Kippur and Passover or Ramadan are seen as religious. Participation in and observance of certain ceremonies and rites such as baptism or the hajj (pilgrimage to Mecca) or the various Hindu life-cycle rites are seen as religious activities.

Nonetheless, it is often difficult to distinguish the sacred (the supernatural, metaphysical realm) from the profane or mundane (the everyday, material realm). In other words, it is often difficult to separate religion from culture. In fact, the practices of a particular religion are often strongly influenced by its cultural location.

As noted, in many ways "religion" is a Western concept. In fact, in other parts of the world, there is no word that readily translates to "religion." The sacred writings of Islam and Judaism, for example, speak of *din*, meaning "judgment," rather than religion. And the New Testament of the Christian Bible doesn't mention religion.

Rudolf Otto, a German scholar of religion (1869–1937), argues in *The Idea of the Holy* that there is something identifiable as beyond the human person (the *numinous*). He names this "something" the *mysterium tremendum* (literally: "awe-full" or "overpowering mystery") and says it points to the divine that is "wholly other." Otto's concept of religion (as well as others like it) probably overemphasizes a divide between the divine and the material, the sacred and the profane. This conception works well enough with the Abrahamic religions (Judaism, Christianity, and Islam), but not so well with Buddhism and Hinduism. After all, these latter religions tend to emphasize the oneness or unity of the sacred and the profane. Hindus and Buddhists say there is not only a harmony but also an essential unity between the ultimate and the penultimate, between the sacred and the profane.

Some thinkers conceive of religion as a sense of something beyond the material, the physical, while others conceive of religion in terms of doctrines and beliefs. Some religious scholars think about religion in ways that encompass behaviors and practices, and point to values and ethics. This latter view makes sense when we consider that the mystical strain of many religions tends to reject creeds and other statements of belief in favor of emotional (ecstatic) experiences of the divine that sometimes result in a lifestyle characterized by specific behaviors and values. Consider the great Hindu leader Mahatma Gandhi. In reading the Christian scriptures, he came upon the passage that states, "Seek ye first the Kingdom of God, and his righteousness; and all these things shall be added unto you." Gandhi said that this passage had a profound impact on him. He commented: "If you will understand, appreciate and act up to the spirit of this passage, you would not even need to know what place Jesus or any other teacher occupies in your heart." Gandhi clearly does not see religion as having primarily creedal (having to do with statements of belief) boundaries. He understood himself to be a devout Hindu, but that did not dissuade him from reading the scriptures of other religions. Gandhi read the religious writings stripped of any doctrinal or creedal content and focused on their ethical value. His concern had to do with how we act, not with how we believe. Or, at the very least, action is not divorced from belief, and in fact action trumps belief.

All these perspectives on religion notwithstanding, still there is something that we can call *religion*, even if it is difficult to precisely distinguish it from culture (*culture* is also tricky to define).

Questions for Reflection and Discussion

- Why do you think the formation of religion is a nearly universal human phenomenon?
- Do you prefer the Western notion of separation between the sacred and the profane or the Eastern idea of harmony and essential oneness? Explain.
- How would you define religion?

A SCIENTIFIC ACCOUNT OF THE FORMATION OF RELIGION

Some studying the origins of religion ask: "Can the formation of religion be scientifically accounted for? Are humans genetically wired to be religious? If so, are some more inclined to be religious?"

Some scientists, such as Stephen Jay Gould and Richard Dawkins, dismiss religion as merely a human fabrication, while others, like anthropologist Barbara J. King, are genuinely interested in exploring the formation and development of religion.[1] These latter are curious about how science might help us better understand religion—both its faith and practice.

In *Evolving God: A Provocative View of the Origins of Religion*, King notes that religion is common to all human cultures. Acknowledging the difficulty of defining religion, she settles on the idea of "belongingness" as a "necessary element" of religion. "[B]elongingness," King writes, "was transformed from a basic emotional relating between individuals to a deeper relating,

---

1. See Barbara J. King, *Evolving God: A Provocative View of the Origins of Religion* (New York: Doubleday, 2007), 235. It is important to note that King does not argue that science can "explain" religion. She is interested in how religion is formed. For a discussion of the neuroscientific study of the formation of religion, see Michael Brooks, "Born Believers: How Your Brain Creates God," *New Scientist*, February 4, 2009, 30–33.

one that had the potential to become *transcendent*, between people and supernatural beings or forces."[2] King studies the evolutionary basis for religion and its formation. This is why "belongingness" is crucial to her. "We humans crave emotional connection with others. This deep desire to connect can be explained by the long evolutionary history we share with other primates, the monkeys and apes. At the same time, it explains why humans evolved to become the spiritual ape—the ape that grew a large brain, the ape that stood up, the ape that first created art, but above all, the ape that evolved God."[3]

King is interested in the commonality of the religious experience or the religious imagination. When people talk about their religious experiences, there appears to be a fundamental similarity, King says: "People enter into a deeply felt relationship with beings whom they cannot see, but who are present daily in their lives and who transform these lives . . . [A]n intimate social relationship between living people and supernatural beings of some sort is characteristic of human societies everywhere."[4] We may not be able to satisfactorily define religion, but we can generally agree that *something* called religion can be found in cultures and societies everywhere, although not all people in these cultures and societies are necessarily religious.

Because religion is about belonging, it is also emotional. "Religion *is* emotion," King asserts, "because it is so grounded in belongingness; it is about feeling deeply for another creature, caring enough for someone to act compassionately, being in awe of the ineffable. To turn away from

the emotional life of hominids while trying to explain the development of their religion renders any explanation sterile right from the start."[5] Having made these assertions, King then examines apes, early hominid cultures, and human culture to make her case.

Apes are not religious. They do however exhibit behavior that is associated with religion: meaning-making, imagination, empathy, and obedience (following the rules). Apes make meaning when they interact with each other and change their behavior based on the messages they receive from each other. Apes are empathetic. They suffer with and for each other. Apes are imaginative. They will create tools and imaginary playmates. Finally they follow rules as established by the community. None of this by itself really proves anything, but it helps King explore what life might have been like for prehistoric humans.

Having examined the emotional lives of apes, King explores what the emotional (and social) life of early hominids might have been like. Neanderthals, for example, took care to position the bodies of the dead in one room and the bones of a bear in another room. Why? King is not certain, but is convinced that such positioning is a signpost "pointing to symbolic behavior."[6]

The cave paintings at Lascaux, France, were early hominid attempts to understand the cosmos, King believes. For hunting and gathering societies, the sacred is closely intertwined with daily activity. Animals are as closely connected to the supernatural and the divine as humans. There are no clear-cut divisions between the animal world, the human world, and the supernatural.

---

2. Ibid., 8. The scientist in King is apparent in her focus on the phenomenon of communicating with the transcendent rather than the efficacy of it. These attempts, she says, may or may not be successful: "A bedrock is the belief that one may be seen, heard, protected, harmed, loved, frightened, or soothed by interaction with God, gods, or spirits," 51.

3. Ibid., 1. King emphatically argues that humans did not evolve from apes.

4. Ibid., 13.

5. Ibid., 94.

6. Ibid., 100.

Animals are active beings in this worldview. The cave paintings at Lascaux therefore were likely a sophisticated attempt to show the place of animals and humans in the cosmos.[7] The paintings themselves demonstrate relationality or belongingness at many levels: (1) the images suggest the interconnectedness of animal and human life (the paintings almost exclusively depict animal life, suggesting that animals were a central concern of the artists); (2) the size and quantity of the paintings are such that the production of the images must have been a communal project (there are hundreds of paintings, the largest of which is more than 15 feet long); and (3) because art is symbolic, art is social (the function of a symbol requires another person to recognize and share in its meaning).[8] The Lascaux paintings provide a clear example of how the sacred and the earthly come together.

The bottom line, for King, is that religion evolved to serve our human need for belonging, for relationship. She notes that "the full [sense of inclusion] of a social network . . . is the single strongest factor in why people convert to a new religion or join an established religious group.

People become attached to those who already belong, and are drawn in."[9] This makes considerable sense. Children tend to have the same values (including religious values) as their parents. Pastors, preachers, and priests will encourage people to talk to their neighbors and coworkers about their place of worship. These religious leaders know that the top reason people join a church is because of an invitation from someone they know. For people who are active in a religious organization it's likely that they are active in that organization because they know somebody in that organization.

People seek belonging. They join groups because they know other people in that group. They also seek belonging or connections to powers or forces beyond the human. As humans evolved, they began to seek connections with the supernatural world.[10] It did not happen suddenly. It evolved slowly. Humans began by connecting with others immediately around them, then by connecting with others in ever larger circles. They connected with family members, then clans, tribes, nations, and so forth until finally they connected with a divine being who created the cosmos.

Questions for Reflection and Discussion

- Do you think religion is purely a human construction? If so, why? If not, why not?

- How is belongingness or social community related to the formation of religion and religious practices?

- What holy or special days in your experience would you count as religious? Why?

- Do apes or other nonhuman species practice religion? If not, why not?

- What is it about humans that make them inclined toward religious practices?

- How are religious perceptions related to human emotions? Are there specific religious issues that trigger an emotional response in you? If so, what are they?

---

7. Images may be viewed at *http://www.culture.gouv.fr/culture/arcnat/lascaux/en/*.

8. King, *Evolving God*, 136.

9. Ibid., 174.

10. Not all religions identify the "other" that people connect to with a divine being. Buddhism is a notable example.

RELIGION AND THE NEED FOR MEANING, BELONGING

In this chapter, I propose that people have sought to explain and understand their origin and the origin of the universe in order to locate themselves in the world. These explanations are often overtly religious in character and give rise to religious practices and beliefs that satisfy the human need for meaning and belonging.

Many religions, especially so-called primitive religions, seek to reenact the first moment of creation with rites and ceremonies. The Navajo sweat-lodge ceremony is one example. Traditionally constructed of soft saplings that are bent into an igloo-shape, the dome-like frame of the lodge is covered with animal skins, making it completely dark inside. A fire is built nearby and used to heat rocks until they are red hot and glowing. The Navajo place these rocks in the sweat lodge, where they pour water over them. The participants, who are now sitting in the darkness listening to prayers and invocations, experience nearly suffocating heat, steam, and darkness.

A participant explained to me that if you understood the earth to be a female that gave birth to creation, then you could easily see how the sweat lodge itself looks something like the distended, swollen belly of a pregnant woman. When you enter this "belly," you return to the place where creation began. A baby before it is born is cramped in the mother's belly. The womb is warm, moist, and dark. Sweat lodges are all of these things as well: cramped, moist, warm (hot!—temperatures can reach 150° F), and dark. As my friend said, "You want to get out just as a baby wants to get out of its mother's belly." The womb—and the belly—is a place of disorientation and discomfort. Indeed when you do get out of the sweat lodge you feel relieved, exhilarated. You're glad to be out even while you're deeply appreciative for the experience. Birth and creation are seen as similar experiences. The sweat lodge is an attempt to re-create

that experience and that time when primordial chaos became ordered.

Christian baptism has similar themes. Saint Paul writes that in baptism you die with Christ and then rise again in the "newness of life" (Rom 6:4). The water used in baptism reminds the believer of the primordial water described in Genesis 1 (or even Genesis 6 in the account of Noah and the Flood), which seeks to overwhelm with its power to destroy and disorient. In baptism, the believer enters into this place of disorder and death in order to rise again—with Christ—into a new life and become a new person (Rom 6:3–5; Col 2:12; Jn 3:5).

That first moment of creation is a captivating and compelling theme to which adherents of nearly all faith traditions turn for inspiration and renewal. It's a moment when believers attempt to find meaning in the midst of meaninglessness, order in the midst of chaos, and life in the midst of death. "Creation" thus functions as a kind of symbol.

Symbols, Paul Tillich famously said, participate in the reality to which they point (*Systematic Theology* 1:239). More importantly perhaps, these rites and ceremonies have symbolic power. The sweat lodge both stands apart from creation and participates in it. Clearly, the sweat lodge does not "create" the world or even a new person. It does, however, allow people to participate in the reality of creation. Likewise, Christian baptism stands apart from creation. Christians do not literally go back in time to the point when something was made from nothing. Nonetheless, baptism participates in creation in that the believer participates in a symbolic death and re-creation.

Symbols of faith (e.g., sweat lodge, cross, Passover, hajj) are more lasting than doctrinal statements of faith. Doctrinal statements are rational in nature and though reason transcends time and space, it does seem limited. Symbols, on the other hand, appeal to the heart as well as the mind. They stand both within and outside of time. They appeal to the imagination and not just the intellect.

Questions for Reflection and Discussion

- In what ways and for what purposes is religion formed?
- How has your understanding of religion been broadened so far in this chapter?

- What holy or special days in your experience would you call religious? Why?

MYTHS

Myths are closely related to symbols. For most people, myth has a pejorative meaning. In Christianity, myths are looked upon a bit negatively as well. One thinks of New Testament passages such as "We did not follow cleverly devised myths" (2 Pet 1:16). Myths have been contrasted with truth and reason: "People . . . will turn away from listening to the truth and wander away to myths" (2 Tim 4:3–4).

This negative view of myths has persisted. Many religion scholars, however, have a neutral or even positive view of myths. Most scholars would define *myth* somewhat like Tillich does *symbol*, as a narrative or story that points to a larger truth and thereby helps us understand everyday life. Sometimes myths shape our values and our lives. They are narratives that point to truths or realities that transcend time and space.

Typically myths concern founding or originating events. As such, myths are not ordinarily

MYTH

The definition of *myth* has changed over the last two hundred years. In the nineteenth century, myth was understood to be a religious explanation of an event, such as the falling of rain or thunder. Myths in this worldview serve the same function as science: they seek to explain natural events. Myths, like science, also seek to explain human behavior (see the above discussion of Barbara King's ideas about how religion is formed). Understood in this way, myths and science inevitably conflict because science and myths share the same function. The difference, of course, is that science does not self-consciously provide *religious* explanations for events.

Scholars seek to get past this impasse. Mircea Eliade, a prominent religion scholar,

suggests that myths explain both physical and social phenomena. Myths, in Eliade's view, allow people to escape the natural world and enter into sacred, original time and space. For example, in the sweat lodge, participants try to re-create the creation of the world. At these moments, people try to rub shoulders with the gods. Another theory proposes that myths concern humans' understanding of their place in the world. From this view, the sweat lodge would provide a medium for participants to tell themselves about themselves. The sweat lodge would remind participants of the deep and profound connection between humans and the earth. In the sweat lodge, the participant would have an experience of creation and self-understanding.

conflated with factual history. They tend to be described historically (otherwise they would be entirely removed from the mundane) but take place before written history. Consequently, although myths cannot be known objectively, they are not beyond subjective knowing. They have a sacred dimension. In this way, myths intersect the sacred and the profane.

Mythical time is eternal—myths communicate in every time and place, and the world of a myth can be experienced or imagined anew just as if it were happening here and now. Remember the account of the sweat lodge? The myth of creation for that Navajo community is experienced and imagined just as if it were really happening right then in that sweat lodge. For this reason, myths are not merely intellectual or aesthetic experiences. They are not simply intellectual experiences in which the hearer or reader appreciates them only for the beauty or message of the narrative. They invite the hearer or reader into their world.

The account of creation in Genesis 1, for example, invites the reader into a world in which God is sovereign. The world before God's creative acts is chaotic, and death and destruction threaten at every turn unless and until the sovereign God imposes order and life through simply uttering a word ("Let there be light"). People who take this account of creation literally ought not to be simply dismissed. They are doing what people have done for thousands of years: entering the world—the time and space—of a myth that attempts to explain why things are the way they are. Myths, therefore, are vehicles by which a culture or community establishes its own beliefs, values, rituals, and principles as normative and authoritative.

The *Babylonian Epic of Creation* (*Enuma Elish*)

The *Enuma Elish* myth (sometimes called the *Babylonian Epic of Creation*) is not so much about the origin of humans and of creation as about divine order. It is concerned with gods and the hierarchy of gods. It explains how Marduk came to be the god of Babylon and asserts the primacy of Marduk. Marduk is said to be the most powerful of all gods because he conquered the forces of chaos by slaying Tiamat (who is closely connected to water: *tiamat* means sea). Marduk created the cosmos out of the chaos of Tiamat's body. In images that are evocative of Genesis 1, Marduk creates heaven to serve as a barrier to the waters above, he creates the stars in the heavens to mark the days, and he uses other parts of Tiamat's body to make clouds, rivers, and mountains. Marduk then forms humans from clay (cf. Gen 2:7) mixed with the blood of a competing god (Qingu or Kingu). At the end of the account, all of the gods acknowledge Marduk's power (and implicitly all humans should acknowledge the power of Babylon) by building him a palace. This marks the end of the threat of chaos and the establishment of order.

Like the creation story in Genesis 1, *Enuma Elish* describes a primordial state of chaos in which nothing is yet formed. The narrative centers on a battle between the female Tiamat and the male Marduk, who represent the forces of chaos and order. The narrative and the characters are a little ambiguous. Tiamat, at the outset, is described as patient with and indulgent of the other gods who

> would meet together and disturb Tiamat . . .
> They stirred up Tiamat's belly,
> They were annoying her by playing inside Andurana.
> Apsu could not quell the noise
> And Tiamat became mute before them;
> However grievous their behaviour to her,
> However bad their ways, she would indulge them.[11]

Tiamat herself is the wife of Apsu. Together they are the parents of the gods who created the

---

11. "The Epic of Creation," tablet 1 in Stephanie Dalley, ed. and trans., *Myths from Mesopotamia: Creation, the Flood, Gilgamesh, and Others* (New York: Oxford University Press, 1989), 233; all citations for *Enuma Elish* are from this translation unless otherwise indicated.

world (e.g., one of their children is Anu, who created the four winds). Apsu was slain by Ea, father of Marduk, who built a residence over Anu's body, which then became an underground body of water. As it happens, even in death, Apsu gives life: "Inside Apsu, Marduk was created; Inside pure Apsu, Marduk was born."[12] Among these gods is Marduk, who comes to represent wisdom, order, and justice. The accounts in Genesis 1–11 also concern divine order. The author of the creation account in Genesis 2–8 assumes an agricultural world (as opposed to the urban world assumed in Genesis 1) that needs to be organized to produce fruitful harvests.[13] The first humans were created from soil, according to Genesis 2:15, to take care of Yahweh's garden.

Cosmology, how the cosmos are ordered and understood, often determines how the world began. Generally, it is assumed that gods existed long before humans (both Genesis accounts as well as *Enuma Elish* assume this). Various representations are used to account for the origin of the universe. Sexual intercourse between gods is one example: A female deity and a male deity have intercourse and conceive. Their offspring may be plants or animals or humans or the seasons. Another image is that of creating from clay as does a potter or sculptor. An example of this is the Genesis 2 account: "The LORD God formed man from the dust of the ground . . . out of the ground the LORD God formed every animal of the field and every bird of the air" (Gen 2:7, 19). Yet another image is that of simply speaking the world into existence, as in Genesis 1: "Then God said, 'Let there be light'; and there was light" (Gen 1:3). Genesis 1 uses this formula repeatedly to establish the power and sovereignty of God.

Questions for Reflection and Discussion

- If a myth points to a larger truth, beyond its story, how do we recognize the truth to which a myth points?
- How do myths help us understand everyday life?

- Do *Enuma Elish* and other ancient stories help or hinder your understanding of religion?
- In what ways does a cosmological story provide insight into a religion?

RIG VEDA

Let's take a look at two creation myths: the Hindu Rig Veda and the Sandy Lake Cree creation account. In the Hindu sacred writing the Rig Veda, there is a short hymn on creation (hymn 129) that, like Genesis 1, suggests there was a time before time, a time of nonexistence, a time when there was nothing:

1. Then was not non-existent nor existent: there was no realm of air,

no sky beyond it. What covered in, and where? and what gave shelter? Was water there, unfathomed depth of water?

2. Death was not then, nor was there aught immortal: no sign was there, the day's and night's divider. That One Thing, breathless, breathed by its own nature: apart from it was nothing whatsoever.

3. Darkness there was: at first concealed in darkness this All was

---

12. Ibid., 235.

13. Bernard F. Batto, *Slaying the Dragon: Mythmaking in the Biblical Tradition* (Louisville, KY: Westminster John Knox Press, 1992), 50.

indiscriminated chaos. All that existed then was void and formless: by the great power of Warmth was born that Unit.

4. Thereafter rose Desire in the beginning, Desire, the primal seed and germ of Spirit. Sages who searched with their heart's thought discovered the existent's kinship in the non-existent.

5. Transversely was their severing line extended: what was above it then, and what below it? There were begetters, there were mighty forces, free action here and energy up yonder.

6. Who verily knows and who can here declare it, whence it was born and whence comes this creation? The Gods are later than this world's production. Who knows then whence it first came into being?

7. He, the first origin of this creation, whether he formed it all or did not form it, Whose eye controls this world in highest heaven, he verily knows it, or perhaps he knows not.[14]

Interestingly, this hymn speaks of an "unfathomed depth of water."[15] "There was neither death nor life. All that there was, was nothing. There was no order, only chaos."[16] One might say that the cosmos begins with a question mark, with possibility. Hymn 129 states that desire was the first to arise from this "place" of nothingness and chaos. Desire, the hymn suggests, gives rise to a series of questions: Where does this creation come from? Who even knows about this creation? Even the gods were not there; they came after creation. Whoever formed

creation formed it all. Or perhaps this god did not form it all. The questions are endless and cannot be answered; however, this does not mean that the questions should not be asked.

This hymnal account reveals the ambiguity at the heart of Hinduism, which fluctuates between polytheism and monotheism. This hymn suggests the divine character of humans, who can raise these questions and ponder answers without arriving at certain and sure answers. What is certain and sure is that desire is inherent in creation and is a central feature of Hindu anthropology. This hymn says two things about humans: (1) they desire to know the unknowable and comprehend the incomprehensible; and (2) they are like the gods and, in fact, may be divine in some way. And this hymn says two things about gods: (1) gods desire to know the unknowable and comprehend the incomprehensible; and (2) gods are not so very different from humans. In short, there is continuity between the human and the divine.

SANDY LAKE CREE

I once volunteered for a year with a Christian mission organization, living with the Anishnabi in Sandy Lake, Ontario. Outsiders variously called them Cree, Ojibwa, or sometimes Oji-Cree, names that derive from a Western, non-native way of understanding and classifying that assumes distinctions between the Anishnabi and their neighbors, distinctions that the Anishnabi do not necessarily make. (*Anishnabi* means, simply, "human.")

The following account of creation that the Sandy Lake Cree share is considerably different from any we have thus far discussed:

---

14. Rig Veda, trans. Ralph T. H. Griffith, x, 129, *http://sacred-texts.com/hin/rigveda/rv10129.htm*.

15. Ibid., x, 129, 1.

16. Ibid., x, 129, 3.

The earth mother, O-ma-ma-ma, gave birth to the spirits of the world. O-ma-ma-ma is a woman who remains perpetually or eternally beautiful. Among her children are Binay-sih, the thunderbird who protects the animals of the world from the sea serpent, Genay-big, who seeks to destroy them. Thunder is the result of Binay-sih battling Genay-big. Another child of O-ma-ma-ma is Oma-ka-ki who is a sorcerer frog who often aids other animals when they are in need. Her third child is Wee-sa-kay-jac, a supernatural Anishnabi. He has many powers (for example, he can change shape), but is also a trickster who likes to have fun (sometimes, perhaps even often) at the expense of people. Other children are Ma-heegun, the wolf, and Amik, the beaver.

The fish, rocks, grass, trees and all the animals were created from womb of O-ma-ma-ma. For a long time this was all there was; there were not any humans (Anishnabi).

During this time, Wee-sa-kay-jac battled Mishipizhiw the god of the water who tried to destroy Wee-sa-kay-jac in a whirlpool in a river. Wee-sa-kay-jac was victorious in this battle. Another time, the waters of the lakes and the rivers began to rise and eventually flooded all of the land but for a small island where Wee-sa-kay-jac and the surviving animals retreated. Some of the creatures thought that Mishipizhiw was digging deep into a lake and had opened O-ma-ma-ma to bleed to death. Others thought that they had angered O-ma-ma-ma. In any case, Wee-sa-kay-jac had to build a great canoe so that he and the animals might survive the deluge. For many years they endured the unending rain and stormy seas.

One day, the rain stopped. Wee-sa-kay-jac was dismayed when he realized that he had not brought any clay to re-create the world. He asked Amik, the beaver, to dive below the surface and get some dirt, but the noble creature died in the attempt. Then he asked the otter to dive, but he too drowned. Finally, Wee-sa-kay-jac sent the muskrat who also drowned but succeeded in getting some clay. It was with much gratitude that Wee-sa-kay-jac pulled the vine to which the limp muskrat's body was tied. Wee-sa-kay-jac's first order of business was to use the clay to bring the three animals back to life.

Then he boiled the clay so that it expanded and overflowed the pot thus forming the world.

Humans were created when Wee-sa-kay-jac had a dream in which he saw many creatures just like him dancing, singing, and making music. The first human Wee-sa-kay-jac was black, but Wee-sa-kay-jac decided that was not a Anishnabi (human) and discarded this one. The second human was pale and white, but this one too was not a Anishnabi. This human was also discarded. The third was olive-brown in color. A success! Thus the first human or Anishnabi came into being.[17]

This account clearly places humans second to animal spirits. It is also tribal in that a certain race of humans are preferred or ranked over others, in this case Anishnabi over other humans. This element of the myth is probably a later addition; nonetheless, it tells us something about how the Sandy Lake Cree see themselves and other humans. Anishnabi are at the center of the world at least in comparison to other humans. However, Anishnabi do not see themselves as the first creatures or, we can safely assume, the center of the world. At the center are the animal spirits that O-ma-ma-ma created. Second in rank is Wee-sa-kay-jac, who serves as a prototype for humans. The story itself has much to say about the activity of O-ma-ma-ma and the spirits. In fact, the story even hints at a rich collection of myths about these characters, which behave

17. Carl Ray and James R. Stevens, *Sacred Legends of the Sandy Lake Cree* (Toronto: McClelland and Stewart, 1971), 20–25.

disturbingly—or perhaps encouragingly—like humans. They are given to anger, frustration, competitiveness, jealousy, joy, gratitude, compassion, sympathy, and love. By placing humans far from the center of O-ma-ma-ma's activity and concern, the account puts humans in their place. Much more important are O-ma-ma-ma and the animal spirits, whose activity is central to creation and the ongoing sustenance of the earth. Humans can participate in this, but because they are far down the hierarchy, their contribution is of less importance. According to the Anishnabi, there is an entire world beyond the one we can know with our senses, a world that plays a much larger role. In short, what humans do in the here and now is not nearly as important as what is happening in that other world, beyond our ken.

Wee-sa-kay-jac's role as a human prototype is important and should not be overlooked. He is a noble character: well-intentioned, but a bit bumbling. He sounds a bit like us. Many of us are well intentioned, but our efforts are too often misplaced or misdirected. Wee-sa-kay-jac depends on the animal spirits to get things done. He needs the muskrat to dive for clay so that he can make humans. This account suggests that we are far from the crown of creation; we depend on animals and the rest of creation in order to survive, much less thrive. Even our best efforts are dependent on forces and powers far beyond our ken, much less our control.

GENESIS: TWO ACCOUNTS OF CREATION

Genesis 1 and 2 actually tell two creation myths, with similar but different interests. Genesis 1 is generally ascribed to the "priestly" writer (P), while Genesis 2 is credited to the "Yahwist" (J) writer.

"In the beginning when God created the heavens and the earth, the earth was a formless void and darkness covered the face of the deep, while a wind from God swept over the face of the waters. Then God said, 'Let there be light'; and there was light" (Gen 1:1–3). Thus begins the priestly account of creation. I often ask my students to imagine in their mind's eye what it might have been like to be there at the beginning in this formless void where darkness covered the seas. They often describe a cosmos that is dark, lonely, chaotic, even terrifying. I suspect this was the effect the priestly writer was aiming for: A dangerous and terrifying world without God. The chaotic and perilous seas will swallow you up. These death-threatening seas, of course, don't swallow us up. God says, "Let there be light." If there is any doubt about God's power in this account, it is now removed. When humans create, they create with preexisting materials. Carpenters use wood and nails. Students and professors use the ideas of those who came before them. Bakers use flour and sugar and water and eggs. Humans need stuff to create. They cannot create simply by speaking something into existence.

God can. The divine voice is enough to bring order to the turbulent and chaotic seas. The divine voice is enough to bring light into being. The divine voice orders the cosmos in a way that nurtures and sustains life. Water is separated from the heavens. Dry land appears. The earth brings forth vegetation that bears fruit. The entire account in Genesis 1 contributes to a sense that divine order is keeping deadly chaos at bay. God is great, and while humans have a special place in this account (they are given "dominion" over the rest of creation), they are clearly second in every way to this Creator.

Genesis 2, the Yahwist account, is a very different creation myth. "In the day that the LORD God made the earth and the heavens, . . . the LORD God formed man from the dust of the ground, and breathed into his nostrils the breath of life; and the man became a living being" (Gen 2:4b–7). In this account, earth already exists, a desolate earth without plants or other life, but earth nonetheless. In this account, Yahweh uses soil to form the first man, unlike the priestly account in which God simply speaks the first humans into existence. The aloof nature of God in Genesis 1 is not apparent here. Yahweh is hands-on and involved. Indeed Yahweh gets up close and personal with the first man, breathing life into his nostrils. There is a warmth or relationality to the Creator in Genesis 2 that is not nearly so apparent in Genesis 1.

The first man is different too. For example, unlike Genesis 1 where God created the first male and female humans (Gen 1:27), this first man is alone. This solitude in Genesis 2 is something that Yahweh soon resolves. The Creator creates the animals not as creatures for humans to have dominion over as in Genesis 1 (Gen 1:26) but as companions for the first man. "It is not good that the man should be alone; I will make him a helper as his partner," says the Lord God (Gen 2:18). Animals are created in a failed attempt to find a suitable companion for the first man, who apparently needs a companion. The first woman is then created and when she breaths life, it is an "aha" moment and it is clear that intimacy is expected of the two humans. "This at last is bone of my bones and flesh of my flesh . . . a man leaves his father and his mother and clings to his wife, and they become one flesh" (Gen 2:23–24). Can you imagine a more powerful way of expressing deep intimacy between two people?

The Genesis 2 account of creation suggests a number of different religious and social values. One overarching value is that of relationship. Yahweh is in close relationship with the man and the woman. This is expressed not only by Yahweh's breathing into the man's nostrils but also by the conversations in which Yahweh expresses concern for the man's solitude. Relationship and intimacy are apparent in that the man is expected to be in a relationship and the relationship will be deep. Even the relationship with animals is not finally about dominion, but about companionship, something a modern pet owner would understand.

CONCLUSION

Myths, especially those that describe the origin of the world, can be powerful means for shaping our ideas about the world, ourselves, and the transcendent. The Genesis accounts assume monotheism. Yet there is some diversity even in the first two chapters of Genesis, which point to one tradition that posits a sovereign God who keeps the powers of chaos and death at bay, and another that posits a Creator (Yahweh) who compassionately attends to the first man's emotional and social needs. Both of these traditions play powerful roles in Western culture. Most Westerners, regardless of whether they see themselves as people of faith, would recognize humans' "dominion" or rule over nature.

The Cree of Sandy Lake, on the other hand, do not see themselves as having authority over nature in any sense. In fact, they understand themselves to be at the mercy of nature and animals. The reality of global warming, they might say, is nature's revenge; and in the future, life on earth may or may not include humans. Wee-sa-kay-jac and O-ma-ma-ma will look after themselves first and only then look out for humans. And in the Rig Veda, the account of creation is deliberately ambiguous. Who can be certain about the origin of the world? About ourselves? About God? Even King's scientific account of creation is deeply influenced by her notion of belonging as fundamental to the human experience.

All of this tells us that origin accounts are intended to obscure as much as they reveal. How did the world begin? Where is humans' place in the world? Where are humans located in relation to divine being(s)? Creation stories and myths are intended to ask such questions as much as answer them.

Questions for Reflection and Discussion

- How are the *Enuma Elish*, Sandy Lake Cree, and Genesis accounts of creation similar to and different from each other?

- What role, if any, does a creation story play in the formation of a religion?

- Have your perceptions about the formation of religion changed as a result of reading this chapter? If so, how?

- How would you answer the question: "How is religion formed?"

Additional Resources

Barber, Elizabeth Wayland, and Paul T. Barber. 2006. *When They Severed Earth from Sky: How the Human Mind Shapes Myth*. Princeton, NJ: Princeton University Press.

Batto, Bernard F. 1992. *Slaying the Dragon: Mythmaking in the Biblical Tradition*. Louisville, KY: Westminster John Knox Press.

Boyer, Pascal. 2001. *Religion Explained: The Evolutionary Origins of Religious Thought*. New York: Basic Books.

Bultmann, Rudolf. 1984. "New Testament and Mythology: The Problem of Demythologizing the New Testament Proclamation." In *New Testament and Mythology and Other Basic Writings*. Edited and translated by Schubert M. Ogden. Philadelphia: Fortress Press.

Dalley, Stephanie, ed. and trans. 1989. *Myths from Mesopotamia: Creation, the Flood, Gilgamesh, and Others*. New York: Oxford University Press.

Eliade, Mircae. 1960. *Myths, Dreams, and Mysteries*. London: Harvill Press.

Eliade, Mircae. 1957. *The Sacred and the Profane*. New York: Harcourt, Brace and World.

Fieser, James, and John Powers, eds. 1998. *Scriptures of the World's Religions*. New York: McGraw Hill.

Hinnells, John R., ed. 2005. *The Routledge Companion to the Study of Religion*. New York: Routledge.

King, Barbara J. 2007. *Evolving God: A Provocative View of the Origins of Religion*. New York: Doubleday.

Long, Charles H. 1983. *Alpha: The Myths of Creation*. Chico, CA: Scholars Press.

Ray, Carl, and James R. Stevens. 1971. *Sacred Legends of the Sandy Lake Cree*. Toronto: McClelland and Stewart.

Segal, Robert A., ed. 2006. *The Blackwell Companion to the Study of Religion*. Malden, MA: Blackwell.

RELIGION AS "TRUTH-CLAIMS"

Dianne L. Oliver
University of Evansville

Preface

Many religions claim to grasp the truth, and many religious followers claim that their truth is greater and truer than any other. After all, why would anyone want to hold something as most worthy of devotion and allegiance if it were not true? Followers of religions expend huge resources to defend and export their version of truth. Some even resort to violence. One need not look far to find numerous examples of such violence. Newspapers, television, and the Internet are littered with stories about believers seeking to defend truth and oppose anything they consider false or capable of leading others into falsehood or apostasy.

In this chapter, Dianne Oliver considers the "truth-claims" of various religions and reflects on how these claims may impact the ideas, practices, and behaviors of believers. In addition, the author invites you to explore what you consider true or certain, including your own religious convictions regarding truth. You may also want to reflect on historical and contemporary ideas about what could be called truth or religious truth.

Chapter Goals

- To present diverse perspectives on the truth-claims of religions
- To facilitate reflection on fundamental questions of human living and what could be regarded as religious "truth"
- To suggest ways to handle conflicts about truth-claims
- To introduce the ideas of exclusivism, inclusivism, relativism, and pluralism

INTRODUCTION

Religions are essentially ways of viewing and living in the world, of understanding such fundamental questions as why humans exist, what our purpose in life is, what we can expect in the future, what lies beyond our material existence, why there is suffering, and how we ought to conduct our lives. It should be no surprise, then, that many people understand their religious views as fundamental truths about the nature of reality and therefore worth defending.

When a Muslim declares Muhammad the final prophet who received the complete revelation of Allah; this is a truth-claim. This is a claim about the truth offered by the prophets sent by Allah, if not a claim about the nature of the ultimate reflected in Allah. Similarly, when a Hindu claims there is one supreme reality, and it is called Brahman, this is a claim about the oneness and unity that constitute the nature of the universe.

At some level, religions make claims about what is true. In this chapter, we will explore the nature of religious truth and ways of managing conflicts among truth-claims in religion.

Questions for Reflection and Discussion

- Imagine you are in the middle of a large room. Around the room are representatives from religious traditions from around the world. Along with the major traditions (Hindus, Buddhists, Sikhs, Jews, Christians, and Muslims), some of the smaller, more recent traditions (Ba'hais, Mormons, and New Age advocates) are also represented. Each person is given half a day to present his or her tradition, and each does so beautifully. Your task is to decide which tradition is true. How do you decide?[1]
- If you follow a particular religion, what truth-claims does your religion make? Do you also hold these claims to be true?
- If someone's truth-claim conflicts with yours, how do you handle the conflict?

NATURE OF TRUTH

What does it mean to claim that a religion is "true"? And if a particular religious tradition is in fact true, does that preclude other traditions, with seemingly different basic belief systems and ways of viewing and living in the world, from being true? For example, Theravada Buddhism rejects a theistic worldview; that is, it denies the existence of a god separate from the world. This reflects a different understanding of the basic nature of reality than Judaism, which insists on one and only one God. Truth-claims are a vital part of religions, but what does it mean to make such claims? Are religious truths propositions that should be evaluated according to logic, consistency, agreement, and so on? Or should religious truth-claims be evaluated differently?

These are difficult questions. Many of us have been raised in a particular religious tradition and assume that our tradition is true—otherwise our parents or friends or religious community would not have insisted we share certain ideas or rituals or practices that bond us as a family or community. Those not raised with a particular religious perspective might believe that all religious traditions are false. But what might it mean to make such universal claims about religious belief, my own or those of others?

In general, we can think of responses to questions about the nature of truth as falling roughly into camps on either end of a spectrum. The first camp suggests that truth is unified in nature: scientific, religious, and historical truths share one nature, and all tell us something about the way things *really* are. These truths are not affected by who does or does not believe

1. Ian S. Markham, *Do Morals Matter? A Guide to Contemporary Religious Ethics* (Malden, MA: Blackwell Publishing, 2007), 80.

them—they objectively describe the real nature of the world or the ultimate reality beyond the world. In other words, truth means how things actually are. Therefore, anyone who makes a claim of truth makes a claim that is universal (that is, true for anyone and everyone, regardless of time, place, or culture) and objective (that is, able to be evaluated by criteria and reason that transcend a particular situation or individual).

A second camp suggests that truth, especially religious truth, is not at all like scientific truth, or what we would call "fact," but is closer to opinion. This truth is affected by the perspective of the one making a claim about the truth and is therefore largely individual in nature. Essentially, this camp argues that what I claim is a religious truth is in fact really only true for me, from my perspective. Thus, one cannot judge different religious "truths," because everyone's perspective is different. There are certainly other views between these two ends of a spectrum, but considering these extremes might help us better understand the issue.

Most beginning students of religion probably fall into one of these two camps: (1) there is only one "true" religion, or (2) religious truth is largely a matter of opinion and is therefore relative—you believe what you want, and I'll believe what I want, and as long as we don't fight over it everything will be fine. Which of these descriptions best fits your current view? Each view holds different implications, and while these are not the only possible views, they represent basic, commonly held orientations.

Neither of these "camps" adequately grasps the complexity presented by truth-claims. Paul Knitter, a noted religion scholar, uses the metaphor of a telescope to help us understand something of the issues surrounding religious "truth."

[W]e might compare "truth" or "the way things are" to the starry universe around us. There is so much of it, and it is so far away, that with our naked eyes, we really can't see what's there. We have to use a telescope. But by enabling us to see something of the universe, our telescope also prevents us from seeing everything. A telescope, even the mighty ones used by astronomers, can take in only so much. This describes our human situation. We're always looking at the truth through some kind of cultural telescope, the one provided us by our parents, teachers, and broader society. The good news about this situation is that our telescope enables us to see; the bad news is that it prevents us from seeing everything.[2]

So Knitter suggests that religious truth-claims express different perspectives on "how things are." Religious truth-claims therefore involve the assumptions, presuppositions, and interpretations of people necessarily using different "telescopes."

In the study of religion, truth-claims are usually associated with the beliefs of a religious tradition. For example, a Zen Buddhist might believe that what is sought, religiously speaking, is not to be found in scripture or tradition, but in the direct experience of the unity of all existence. A Christian in the Methodist tradition might insist that her beliefs about God being incarnate in Jesus who is the Christ are "grounded in Scripture, informed by Christian tradition, enlivened in experience, and tested by reason."[3] These claims reflect basic beliefs that followers of these two traditions typically hold to be "true"—for the Zen Buddhist, the source of truth is direct experience; for the Methodist Christian, the sources of truth are Scripture, tradition, experience, and reason.

But it is too easy to boil down an entire religious tradition to a particular set of beliefs or even to one key belief, and then to decide whether that tradition is true or not. We could study differences between religious traditions and

2. Knitter, *Introducing Theologies of Religions* (Maryknoll, NY: Orbis Books, 2002), 11.

3. *The Book of Discipline of the United Methodist Church* (Nashville, TN: United Methodist Publishing House, 2004).

insist that if some key beliefs are true, then the apparently contradictory beliefs of other religious traditions must be false. We could insist that if "there is one God, Allah, and Muhammad is his prophet," as Muslims claim, then Islam is true, and by implication, Hindus, who claim that there are 330 million different gods and goddesses that manifest the one supreme reality, Brahman, must have it wrong. We might want to say that if it is true that Jesus is the Christ, the anointed one of God, then Jews who do not affirm that view of Jesus of Nazareth must be confused.

But as the introduction to this chapter suggests, basic beliefs are but one aspect of a religious tradition. Ritual practices, moral structures, goals and means of personal development, communities, and a variety of other components all come together to shape a particular religious tradition. Charles Kimball suggests,

> A religion cannot be adequately comprehended as a self-contained, abstract collection of teachings and practices. Discovering the facts about a religion is a good place to start, but much more is needed. Understanding religion requires reflecting on how adherents of the religion understand and interpret its elements, for religion does not exist in a vacuum; it exists in the hearts, minds, and behavior of human beings. It is a very human enterprise, a lived reality.[4]

It is somewhat peculiar to the West to focus acutely on a set of beliefs as the defining characteristic of a religion. In contrast, someone from another part of the globe might say, "Show me how you act, how you live, and I'll tell you what you believe." It is important to acknowledge the limitations created by strictly focusing on beliefs. For most people, religion is a lived reality of rituals, practices, and ways of being in the world that informs every day of their lives. If one is Jewish, this means more than affirming a belief in the

one God who made a covenant with the people of Israel; it also concerns synagogue weddings, celebrating Rosh Hashanah (the Jewish New Year), and reciting *kaddish* (memorial prayers) when mourning a loved one. Religions are more than just tenets of belief.

Religious traditions are complex. It might seem natural to begin the study of a religious tradition by asking, "How do its beliefs compare with mine?" or "Is the supreme reality of Brahman in Hinduism similar to the monotheistic focus of Judaism, Christianity, or Islam?" In dialogue with persons from other religious traditions, it is often easiest to focus on what we have in common, to try to find a connection and say, "See? They're really a lot like us." While this may be a good first step toward understanding, it can also undermine a clear grasp of the complexity of real, lived religious traditions. Being a Muslim is not just about a pilgrimage to Mecca or about worshipping one God. Islam itself is complex and practiced in many different ways around the world. Most of us, as we begin to study religious traditions, barely scratch the surface of these traditions' basic beliefs, practices, histories, and worldviews. We might think we've captured Buddhism in the Four Noble Truths laid out by Siddhartha Gautama, but such an understanding would be deceptively simplistic. To say that Jesus is God in the flesh may signal something important and central to Christianity, but to focus exclusively or even primarily on this distinct position only distracts us from how complex actually are Christian beliefs and practices around the globe.

All of this is to say we may be tempted, as we begin to study religion, to boil down a tradition to a few basic ideas so as to allow comparisons with our own or other traditions. (This tendency is discussed in chapter 1.) But such easy comparisons do not help us understand the tradition as it is actually lived by people around the world,

---

4. Kimball, *When Religion Becomes Evil* (San Francisco: HarperSanFrancisco, 2002), 21.

whether it be Hindus living and worshipping in the temple in Banaras, India, or Hindus living and worshipping in the temple in Nashville, Tennessee. This statement is not intended to cause us to despair of ever fully understanding a religious tradition, but rather to help us recognize that the lived reality of each tradition is more complex than might be indicated by a mere look at its truth-claims.

Yet if religions are more than mere sets of beliefs to be intellectually debated, they nonetheless certainly do contain such beliefs. And followers of a particular tradition do indeed claim that their view of reality is in some way true. It is important to consider what is meant by *true*. The Enlightenment in the West highlighted the importance of reason for correctly determining what was right and true. One legacy of the post-Enlightenment era, the rise of scientific method, has meant that "truth" has often been narrowed to factual claims and empirically verifiable statements—what reason shows to be true. While there are some such "facts" in religious traditions (there really was a temple in Jerusalem, and there really was a leader named Muhammad), much of what constitutes the claims of a religious tradition are not historically, scientifically, or empirically provable.

The rise of postmodernity in the late nineteenth century brought the advent of the social sciences: psychology, anthropology, sociology, and so on. The social sciences led people to see their worldviews as relative to their specific culture, geographic area, and community. These shifts led many in the last half of the twentieth century to contend that all knowledge—not only religious or cultural worldviews but also scientific and historical knowledge—is the product of conditioned interpretations of reality and not necessarily an explanation of how things *really are*. In this view, neither scientific nor religious knowledge is completely objective. Rather, there is no completely neutral, objective standpoint from which we can judge claims to truth because we are always influenced by our own traditions and limited perspectives. What is accepted as knowledge is open to dispute. Thus, the nature of truth-claims has been questioned in ways that were not true for earlier eras. Our attempt to view religion as truth-claims therefore must allow for a more complex understanding of truth than as simply either scientific or religious.

We close this section with an analogy. Is Harper Lee's classic novel *To Kill a Mockingbird* true? If the question asks whether the book is factually accurate and the characters of Scout and Atticus really lived as reflected in the story, then the answer is clearly no, this is a work of fiction. But if the question is whether the story points to basic human understandings and issues in the racially divided American South of the mid-twentieth century, or whether the attitudes, issues, and views described in the novel reflect those of today, then *To Kill a Mockingbird* contains truth. Taking the more complicated view of truth illustrated in this analogy, what would it mean, then, to declare that Judaism is true?

Questions for Reflection and Discussion

- What are some ways that religious truth-claims could be evaluated?
- How do you view religious truth-claims— your own and those of others?

- In what ways might our own cultural, social, and gender perspectives affect how we understand religious truth-claims?

Continued . . . .

Continued . . .

Questions for Reflection and Discussion

- What do you think of Paul Knitter's telescope analogy? In what ways might it be helpful? In what ways might it be problematic?
- What is your "telescope" and what does it tell you about what truth is?

- Can a religion be "true" if it is not a "lived" religion?
- Is it possible for someone to judge religious truth-claims from a completely neutral, objective position? Why or why not?

RELIGIOUS TRUTH

Wilfred Cantwell Smith, a famous twentieth-century scholar of religion, suggested that we cannot talk about a *religion*, like Judaism or Confucianism, being "true," because each tradition is comprised of a complex history of ideas, events, and people and is much too intricate to be evaluated in terms of overall truth. Smith writes, "It is not statements that are true or false but the use of them by individuals."[5] This implies that, at the most basic level, one cannot say whether Theravada Buddhism is "true" or not—one can only say if a Theravada Buddhist is living with integrity and faithfulness. Thus, according to Smith, we cannot argue about whether Sikhism or Jainism is true. Religious traditions are not simply sets of propositions that can be verified or rejected using scientific methods.

Other scholars of religion hold different views on the nature of religious truth. John Hick suggests that each religious tradition is "mythologically true," meaning that it has the power to direct people toward what is Real. *Real* is Hick's term for the transcendent or sacred at the heart of reality and toward which all religious traditions seek to move. For some traditions, like Judaism,

Islam, and Christianity, this is encapsulated in the idea of God, whereas for others, the Real might be found in a state of existence, like nirvana in Buddhism. Yet, according to Hick, each religious tradition cannot *literally* be true because none ever completely describes the Real. We can never really know the Real—we can only know explanations of it or our understanding of paths leading toward it. Every religious tradition is a partial understanding of the Real and is mythologically true, if it leads adherents toward what is Real.

Hick's view is similar to that held by Mahatma Gandhi, a twentieth-century Hindu famous for using nonviolent means to achieve Indian independence from Great Britain. Gandhi suggests: "(1) all religions are true; (2) all religions have some error in them."[6] This implies that there is truth and error in each tradition, and each is therefore able to represent truth and also unable to represent truth adequately. Thich Nhat Hanh, a Zen Buddhist monk and advocate for peace and social justice through what he calls "Engaged Buddhism," offers a similar view: "All systems of thought are guiding means; they are not absolute truth."[7] Jainism suggests the nature of reality is multifaceted, thus all views are but partial expressions of the

5. Smith, "A Human View of Truth," in John W. Burbige, *Modern Culture from a Comparative Perspective* (New York: State University of New York Press, 1997), 99.

6. Gandhi, *All Men Are Brothers: Autobiographical Reflections*, ed. Krishna Kripalani (New York: Continuum, 1980).

7. Nhat Hanh, *Being Peace*, ed. Arnold Kotler (Berkeley, CA: Parallax Press, 1987), 89.

truth and should always be preceded by the term *maybe*. All of these views remind us of Knitter's telescope analogy for religious traditions: we can see truth from the perspective of each tradition, but a complete understanding of religious truth is, by its very nature, limited and incomplete.

In reflecting on the nature of religious truth-claims, one might conclude that religions are sets of propositions that are either true or false, somewhat like scientific or historical claims. Or one might agree with Wilfred Cantwell Smith, that religions do not make truth-claims because they are about the faith of individuals and thus cannot, as a whole, be either true or false. Or one might affirm the position shared by John Hick, Mahatma Gandhi, and Thich Nhat Hanh that each religious tradition contains some part of the truth, but none contains the full truth. Or one might deny the existence of religious truth altogether.

Questions for Reflection and Discussion

- Do you agree with Smith that religious traditions are not simply sets of propositions that can be accepted or rejected based on their truthfulness? Why or why not?

- Can human beings distinguish what is "Real" from what is not? Why or why not?

- Is there a difference between something that is mythologically true and something that is literally true? If so, what is the difference?

CONFLICTS ABOUT TRUTH-CLAIMS

Throughout history, cultures and empires have gone to war when one worldview, often religious, conflicted with another. Typically the spoils involve the control of a particular geographical area or population of people. These conflicts most often arise during empire-building or other attempts to conquer and possess land and resources. For example, the Crusades began in the Middle Ages as Christians united in a holy war against Muslims to free Jerusalem from Muslim control, among other things. Western Christians viewed the Crusades largely as a conflict between themselves, the bearers of religious truth, and Muslims, seen by the Christians as "infidels." Economic and political factors also fueled the conflict, but claims to religious "truth" were integral. Historically, apart from such conflicts and encounters, one's cultural background and religious tradition were largely defined by where one was raised.

In the twenty-first century, with our ability to communicate across miles and cultures at the click of a mouse or the touch of a button, contact among different worldviews is the norm rather than the exception. While at their best such encounters can be enlightening, they can also lead to conflict about truth-claims. For example, the Taliban in Afghanistan viewed the blowing up of ancient Buddhist statues as good because they believed they were destroying something that could lead others away from ultimate truth. Islamic law, as they interpreted it, did not permit such statues. Another example is the Ayodhya Temple (formerly the Babri Mosque) in northern India, a site of conflict because it is considered holy by both Muslims (the Babri Mosque existed on the site for centuries) and Hindus (who claimed the site as birthplace of the Hindu god Ram). Significant violence has occurred at the site in recent years, with the destruction of the ancient mosque and the subsequently built Hindu temple. These are negative examples of what can happen when religious truth-claims conflict. Since it is now common to encounter people whose worldviews and religious claims are fundamentally different than ours, we must figure out what these differences mean and how to handle them. In religion, we must question what happens when the truth-claims at the heart of one religious tradition meet the very different and conflicting truth-claims of another tradition. Are there more constructive ways forward than destroying the statues and temples of those whose views conflict with ours?

In the study of religion, we are particularly interested in how people with different religious views interact. *Interreligious dialogue* is the formal engagement between followers of different religious traditions about commonalities and differences among religious views. Sometimes such encounters occur intentionally, when groups are trying to find common ground in a particular geographic area. At other times, such dialogue reflects deliberate efforts to have religious traditions learn from one another or to seek common ground in responding to an ethical issue. So when the Parliament of the World's Religions meets with representatives from religious groups around the world to discuss pressing issues such as the environment or terrorism, interreligious dialogue occurs as all parties offer wisdom from their traditions.

Religions differ in how they view the truth-claims of other faiths, both independently and in comparison with their own truth-claims. Does a religion teach that it alone contains true claims about the nature of reality, or does it teach that other traditions might have claims to truth as well? In the discussion that follows, I provide examples to illustrate both views. Bear in mind that it is risky to categorize any religion as strictly and exclusively holding one of these views. There are individual believers within any religion who will fall into either of these categories.

EXCLUSIVISM AND INCLUSIVISM

The belief that full truth is found only in one religious tradition is held in some form by two different views: *exclusivism* or *inclusivism*. Exclusivism suggests that a single religious tradition has exclusive claim to that constitutes religious truth, and truth is not found in other religious traditions. An exclusivist might claim, for example, that the basic statement of belief in Islam, that there is no God but Allah and Muhammad is his prophet, contains the only true claim about the nature of ultimate reality. Other claims, that there are additional gods or goddesses or that there are no gods, are considered false. The claims of other religious traditions about the nature of reality or how one is saved or liberated from worldly problems are not true. Exclusivists are found in many religious traditions, but all hold that religious truth is found in only one religious tradition.

Inclusivism suggests that while the complete and definitive truth is exclusively found in a single religious tradition, other traditions are *included* in some way in that one "true" tradition. For example, in the Christian tradition, the official Roman Catholic perspective on religious truth suggests that while the full revelation of God's salvation is found exclusively in Jesus Christ and is brought about by his life, death, and Resurrection, others who earnestly seek God can also reach eternal salvation, even though their access to that salvation is severely limited. That is, all are *included* in the means to reach eternal salvation found fully in the Christian tradition, whether they accept or acknowledge that means or not. So for inclusivists, a single religious tradition contains the truth, but that truth allows others outside of that tradition to benefit from that truth as well. Thus, for a Christian inclusivist, the salvation provided by Jesus Christ is available to the Hindu in India who seeks God, even if that Hindu has never heard of Jesus. Another way of understanding inclusivism suggests that a single religious tradition is the fulfillment of other views. The Baha'i tradition reflects this perspective, because it views all religious traditions as coming to fulfillment in the universal religion of Baha'i, thus ultimately including all religious traditions in the Baha'i faith and the fulfillment it offers.

RELATIVISM AND PLURALISM

On the other end of the spectrum are those who suggest there is a plurality of appropriate claims to religious truth, or that religious truth is relative. One view that falls into this category is *relativism*. While understandings of relativism differ, one view suggests there are no universal claims to truth, all are relative to the time, place, situation, and so on of the person or group making the claim. No truth-claim can be considered better or worse than others, since all are relative. There can be no judgment of a particular religious view from outside that view because it is dependent upon its context. For the relativist, there is no such thing as universal truth. Rita Gross suggests that "religions are language systems, and no language is universal and absolute."[8] Gross and others with this view argue that religions are essentially cultures with their own languages, and our choice of religion is no different than our choice of English or French or Swahili as a language. Choosing a religion or speaking a language is simply that—a choice, a preference, or an accident of birth, but not a matter of truth. This view of religion as a language is a form of relativism.

Pluralism is often mistakenly associated with relativism, but is actually distinct. Pluralism describes the idea that there are a plurality of religious claims that are true. One does not need to reject the principle of the Tao, an impersonal power that orders the universe according to Taoism, to accept the Jewish monotheistic claim that there is one God, who created the world and made a covenant with the people of Israel. Thus pluralism suggests there are many viable truth-claims found within religious traditions, and a single religious tradition does not have an exclusive claim to what is true. Some pluralists, like John Hick, suggest that all religious paths lead to the same center, the "Real," and simply constitute different trails to the same goal. The Dalai Lama, the Tibetan Buddhist leader, makes a similar claim about the nature of the world's religions. He insists the only 'definitive truth' for Buddhism is the absolute negation of any one truth as the Definitive Truth."[9] The Dalai Lama suggests that some people like spicy foods and some do not. One would not say that either view is right or wrong, they are simply different relationships to food. Likewise, the Dalai Lama says that is also the nature of differences between religious traditions—there are many ways to be religious, and each way constitutes a certain "taste."[10] What the Dalai Lama claims that makes his position different than relativism is the idea that accepting multiple "tastes" does not result in nihilism or a form of relativism.

Pluralism is probably the most difficult view to understand well because there are so many variations of it. One of the most robust descriptions of a pluralist position comes from Diana Eck, director of the Pluralism Project at Harvard University. Eck insists that pluralism "is not diversity alone, but the *energetic engagement with diversity*." Pluralism is not mere tolerance, but "*the active seeking of understanding across lines of difference*" and involves "*an encounter of*

---

8. Gross, "Religious Identity and Openness in a Pluralistic World," *Buddhist-Christian Studies* 25 (2005): 15.

9. Robert Thurman, "The Dalai Lama: On China, Hatred, and Optimism," *Mother Jones*, November/December 1997.

10. Dalai Lama, interview by Jules and Gedeon Naudet, *In God's Name*, CBS[0], December 23, 2007.

commitments."[11] Thus pluralism for Eck is about dialogue between persons of differing religious traditions so that learning is always taking place and all religions are contributing to the discussion. So pluralism recognizes truth within many traditions, and what is important is to bring our commitments into conversation with the commitments of others to further our understanding of religious truth.

IMPLICATIONS

There are clearly consequences for each of these approaches to the diversity of religious truth-claims—each has benefits as well as problems. If one takes the exclusivist perspective, this implies that a single religious tradition holds the real truth about the nature of reality and tells us about how things really are. What is clearly compelling about this view is its strong sense that a religion's claims are actually telling us something about how the world is and how we ought to live in it. In societies where people tend toward relativism, the postmodern idea that all truths are equal, the exclusivist approach may seem especially compelling, offering the security of having "the" truth. At the same time, however, it seems a bit credulous to assume that only one tradition holds the truth, given that each religious tradition emerged largely from a single geographical area and that it is only in recent history that individuals made choices about the religious tradition in which they would participate.

Inclusivism initially seems like a good "middle way" between the stark claims of exclusivism and the less robust claims of pluralism or relativism. Inclusivism claims there is one true way of understanding ultimate reality but all adherents of any religious tradition are ultimately included in that one way. This holds at bay those who

would argue that two conflicting beliefs cannot both be true. One truth is accepted in this view, but no one is excluded from that truth. Yet inclusivism still claims that a single religious tradition holds the fullness of truth—thus we end up with some of the same dilemmas posed by exclusivism. Is it not a bit arrogant for a Christian inclusivist to tell Hindus, who in no way affirm Christianity, that Christianity has it right and that Hindus can only know ultimate reality through Christianity?

Relativism clearly opens the door widest to a diversity of truth-claims and thus affirms the multiplicity of ways of being religious in the world. Relativism may seem appealing to those of us who live in a country and a world that is becoming more and more religiously diverse. But relativism, at its starkest, provides no foothold for contending that some views are better than others—thus it is difficult to claim that Hitler's brand of Christianity and Osama bin Laden's version of Islam are not acceptable. Yet most Christians and Muslims oppose Hitler's and Bin Laden's interpretations of their religion and do consider them wrong.

The pluralist view of religious truth-claims is probably the most widely accepted by academic scholars of religion. This view affirms that there are multiple truths and there are criteria indicating what is truth and what is not. Many traditions contain truth, though none exclusively. There are also traditions that do not guide us toward the Real (Hick) nor create space for conversation and learning (Eck). Thus there is room for discernment among truth-claims. Yet pluralism varies widely both on what it considers to be true and how important truth-claims are. Pluralism can devolve into its own form of relativism, with no place for discernment between better and worse, and is subject to criticisms similar to those levied against relativism. There is also some

---

11 Eck, "What Is Pluralism?" *The Pluralism Project,* http://www.pluralism.org/pluralism/what_is_pluralism.php.

question as to whether all religious traditions, given their widely varied views of the sacred and how to live in the world, are really seeking the same ultimate reality, a position that is implied by some (though not all) views of pluralism.

CONCLUSION

It is evident that studying religion is about more than simply learning a few facts and concepts regarding assorted traditions. Studying religion requires us to engage our own views on the nature of truth and to consider ways to deal with diverse views of this truth.

In the twenty-first century, some of the most profound questions we face are whether there is such a thing as "truth," whether the world and human beings specifically have a meaning and purpose in the universe, and how we can have a just and peaceful world in which to live and raise future generations. The study of religion can push us to ask these questions of ourselves and the world. How do we live in a world where there are diverse claims of religious truth? How do we constructively deal with disagreements about what is good or better, about what has value and what does not? How we handle encounters between different versions of the truth—different views of the nature of ultimate reality and what is to be valued in our lives and how we find meaning—will profoundly affect our lives.

As you embark on the study of religion, your own answers to these questions will affect how you study religion. It might be helpful to ask yourself why you are studying religion in the first place. Is it to learn more about different understandings of ultimate reality so that you can learn and possibly embrace new views? Or do you want to know about various religious traditions so you can determine where they are different than your own and where you think they might be wrong? Do you seek understanding because you want to know more about other people or is there something deeper in your quest? It is difficult to study religion seriously without asking profound questions. These may help you better understand religious traditions and their followers and may help you make better sense of your own basic convictions and ways of living in the world.

Questions for Reflection and Discussion

- What is the difference between exclusivism and inclusivism? Do you hold either view? If so, why do you hold that viewpoint?

- What is the difference between relativism and pluralism? Do you hold either view? If so, why do you hold that viewpoint?

- Does someone who doesn't share your religious convictions have the same access to what might be called "truth" as you do? Why or why not?

- In a world with so many different religious perspectives, it may seem easier to hold a "live-and-let-live" philosophy so that everyone can get along with one another. Yet such a philosophy might suggest that differences among truth-claims do not matter. What problems or concerns might arise with this philosophy?

- Has your perception of your own religious truth-claims changed as a result of reading this chapter? If so, how? If not, why not?

Additional Resources

References

Berling, Judith A. 2004. *Understanding Other Religious Worlds: A Guide for Interreligious Education.* Faith Meets Faith Series. Maryknoll, NY: Orbis Books.

The Book of Discipline of the United Methodist Church. 2004. Nashville, TN: The United Methodist Publishing House.

Dalai Lama. 2007. Interview by Jules and Gedeon Naudet. *In God's Name.* CBS, December 23.

Eck, Diana. "What Is Pluralism?" *The Pluralism Project.* http://www.pluralism.org/pluralism/what_is_pluralism.php.

Gandhi, Mohandas K. 1980. *All Men Are Brothers: Autobiographical Reflections.* Edited by Krishna Kripalani. New York: Continuum.

Gross, Rita. "Religious Identity and Openness in a Pluralistic World." *Buddhist-Christian Studies* 25 (2005): 15-20.

Hick, John. 1985. *Problems of Religious Pluralism.* London: Macmillan.

Kimball, Charles. 2002. *When Religion Becomes Evil.* San Francisco: HarperSanFrancisco.

Knitter, Paul. 2002. *Introducing Theologies of Religions.* Maryknoll, NY: Orbis Books.

Markham, Ian S. 2007. *Do Morals Matter? A Guide to Contemporary Religious Ethics.* Malden, MA: Blackwell Publishing.

Nhat Hanh, Thich. 1987. *Being Peace.* Edited by Arnold Kotler. Berkeley, CA: Parallax Press.

Pals, Daniel. 2006. *Eight Theories of Religion.* 2nd ed. New York: Oxford University Press.

Smith, Wilfred Cantwell. 1997. "A Human View of Truth." In John W. Burbige. *Modern Culture from a Comparative Perspective.* New York: State University of New York Press.

Smith, Wilfred Cantwell. 1979. *Faith and Belief.* Princeton, NJ: Princeton University Press.

Smith, Wilfred Cantwell. 1967. *Questions of Religious Truth.* New York: Scribner.

Strenski, Ivan. 2006. *Thinking about Religion: An Historical Introduction to Theories of Religion.* Malden, MA: Blackwell Publishing.

Thurman, Robert. 1997. "The Dalai Lama: On China, Hatred, and Optimism." *Mother Jones,* November/December.

Web Resources

Council for a Parliament of the World's Religions. *http://www.parliamentofreligions.org.*

Pluralism Project at Harvard University. *http://www.pluralism.org.*

CHAPTER 5

SACRED WORDS, STORIES, WRITINGS, AND BOOKS

Karl N. Jacobson
Augsburg College

Rolf A. Jacobson
Luther Seminary

Preface

Every religious group has sacred words, stories, writings, and books that are unique to it. Some groups believe that certain words are the actual words of a sacred being or beings and therefore hold a greater measure of truth than do ordinary utterances. Some aver their stories are embedded within layers of cultural memory and experience. Others suggest their stories and writings have power in their mere utterance and that indeed the breath alone contains a generative power derived from holy entities. Few scholars dispute the power of words, stories, writings, and books to evoke our human imagination, hope, longing, desire, and a range of other emotions.

In this chapter, Karl N. Jacobson and Rolf A. Jacobson consider how sacred words and texts are intimately connected to religious communities, histories, and traditions. We invite you to examine the nature and function of sacred or religious texts from different vantage points: What do the texts say about what is most and least valued? What do they offer as explanation for particular religious practices? Why do they so often evoke intense passion in adherents?

Chapter Goals

- To consider broadly the role that sacred words and texts play in the life of religious communities and traditions
- To invite readers to examine their assumptions about the nature and function of religious texts

INTRODUCTION

Because language is fundamental to human life and community, every faith tradition has sacred words that play key roles in their history and daily practice. These words come in about as many shapes and shades as do faith traditions themselves: consider, for example, a tradition's books, prayers, stories, histories, creeds, and rituals. These special words express the norms by which communal teachings and morals are judged; they provide the symbols that form the reality in which adherents live; they guide believers in mourning and in celebration and comprise the texts to be studied, prayed, or sung.

This chapter considers the vital role that special words, stories, writings, and books play in the world's religions. We also invite you to examine your assumptions about the nature and function of religious texts. We do not attempt to apply a single, overarching theory or unifying framework to the study of sacred words and texts. Rather, the diversity and individuality of these words and texts are respected. Although the sacred words of many traditions are mentioned, those of Judaism, Christianity, and Islam serve as the primary exemplars of our subject so that we might attempt to give it greater focus and depth.

SACRED WRITINGS AND BOOKS

Every sacred writing or book embodies the assumptions of its religious group and therefore raises certain questions for students of religion. These questions concern issues of style and derivation, dissemination and authority, and translation and role within the religion.

SELECTED RELIGIONS AND THEIR SACRED TEXTS		
Religion	Main Writing or Book	Other Important Writings and Books
Judaism	The Jewish Bible—also called the Tanak.	The Talmud (the Mishnah and the Gemara)
Christianity	The Christian Bible—comprised of the Old and New Testaments	The Nicene, Apostles', and Athanasian Creeds; various Christian denominations revere other secondary writings
Islam	The Qur'an	The Hadith
Hinduism	The Sruti (including the Vedas, the Brahmanas, the Aranyakas, and the Upanishads)	The Smriti
Buddhism	Various Buddhist groups recognize different writings, such as the Tripitaka (the Pali Canon), the Mahayana Sutras, or the Tibetan Book of the Dead	

Definition, Composition, Canon. What position does the text occupy within its religious tradition? By what names is it called? What words characterize it? What smaller texts comprise the writing? May the tradition add to, edit, or otherwise change the text?

Authorship. Who wrote the text—one person or many? Under what circumstances?

Transmission. How was the text preserved for future readers? How was it copied, translated, and disseminated?

Authority. Why is the text authoritative? How is the authority of the text understood and appreciated within the tradition? If there are other authoritative texts in the religion, is one more authoritative than others? How do the various texts within a religion relate to each other? How are the texts of other religions viewed?

Genre. What literary genre does the text comprise? Is it an anthology of different types of literature?

Interpretation. Who in the religion interprets and explains the sacred writing? How is the text studied?

Role. How does the text function in the daily life of the religion? How is it used in worship, in family life, or in personal life?

This list of issues and questions provides a helpful structure with which to consider the special words, stories, and writings of the world's religions. But the first thing to know about these writings and scriptures is that one size does not fit all.

DEFINITION, COMPOSITION, CANON

The concept *sacred text* varies from religion to religion. And within a given religion, groups may define the religion's sacred texts differently. For example, in Islam the Qur'an (which means "the recitation") is understood to record the literal words of God, revealed to Muhammad over a period of more than two decades. The Theravada school of Buddhism considers its scripture, the Tripitaka (or Pali Canon), to be the teachings of the Buddha and other early Buddhist disciples. The difference in how these two religions understand their scriptures is directly related to the core identity of each faith. In Islam, supreme value is placed on the oneness of God and submission to God's will. The understanding of the Qur'an as the direct recitation of God thus fits hand in glove with the identity of the religion. Buddhism, on the other hand, does not teach the existence of a personal god, but rather the Noble Eightfold Path to enlightenment. Thus, the understanding of the Tripitaka as the teachings of early wise figures who achieved enlightenment fits Buddhism's self-understanding.

As noted above, even within religions, different understandings of a faith's scripture can exist. Within Christianity, the Bible is widely considered to be the Word of God. Some Christian groups believe in the "plenary (full) inspiration of Scripture"—that every word of the Scripture was inspired by God, which is similar to Islam's understanding of the Qur'an. Perhaps the best illustration of this view is Michelangelo Caravaggio's famous painting of the angel dictating to the evangelist Mathew. Other Christian groups have a less fixed understanding of the Bible, believing that it is the word of God not because every word came from God, but because it testifies to God's activity, or because God continues to speak through the Bible. Still other Christian groups consider the Bible more as a source of wisdom than as direct divine revelation, which is similar to how Buddhists understand the Tripitaka.

A related set of questions addresses the issue of canon. A canon is an official list of those writings that are considered genuine and authoritative by a religion. This issue can become quite complex. Within Christianity, for example, while all Christian groups revere the same twenty-seven

Greek-language books of the New Testament, the number of Old Testament books is disputed. Protestant groups acknowledge only the thirty-nine books written in Hebrew that Rabbinic Judaism acknowledges as its Bible. The Roman Catholic Church acknowledges an additional seven books or parts of books that were either written in Greek or translated from Hebrew and for which the Hebrew original was lost: Tobit, Judith, Wisdom of Solomon, 1 and 2 Maccabees, Sirach, Baruch, and some additions to Esther, Daniel, and Jeremiah. Various Orthodox Churches accept all of these plus the Prayer of Manasseh; Psalm 151; 1, 2, and 3 Esdras; and 3 and 4 Maccabees. The question of translation is also an issue. The Roman Catholic Church officially acknowledges as inspired the Latin translation of the Bible known as the Vulgate, while some American Protestant groups make a similar claim about the English translation known as the King James Version. Other Christian groups do not have an official translation.

Perhaps because of canonical and translation differences among Christian groups, in Islam an effort was made to ensure that the text of the Qur'an did not change. Within twenty years of Muhammad's death, an official authoritative text of the Qur'an was established. It contains 114 suras (chapters) and is still used today. While the Qur'an has been translated from Arabic into many languages, Muslims do not recognize such translations as valid—they are not *qur'an*.

A related issue is the question of whether a canon is open or closed. In Islam, the canon is closed—the Qur'an cannot be edited or added to. In Christianity, similarly, the canon is basically closed, if not officially closed by all Christian groups; that is, while some Christian groups have not formally closed the canon, it is hard to imagine that any books could be added to the Bible. A different view exists in Mormonism, where the canon is explicitly open. One result of the Mormon belief that God still speaks today is that the Mormon canon is always growing. In addition, since the original version of the Book of Mormon in 1830, between three thousand and four thousand changes have been documented, most of which have been discussed in official Mormon publications.

In most religious traditions, books and writings of secondary authority also have been developed. One can understand these second-tier authoritative books as interpretations of the primary sacred writings of the tradition. Often these secondary texts were written or developed in response to crises or changes in context that occurred after the main text of the tradition was finished. In Christianity, for example, Lutherans developed the Book of Concord (1580) as a statement of official Lutheran interpretations of Scripture. The book is not considered to be inspired as is the Bible, but it is viewed as a faithful interpretation of the Bible. In Rabbinic Judaism, different interpretations and applications of the Jewish Bible developed. These views were collected and published in the Talmud. Unlike the Lutheran Book of Concord, the Talmud does not offer official interpretations, but offers various opinions.

Questions for Reflection and Discussion

- What writings do you regard as religious? What makes them so and why do you regard them as such?

- What do you know about the origin of the writings that are part of your faith tradition?

Continued . . .

Questions for Reflection and Discussion
Continued . . .

- If you do not ascribe to a particular religion, what do you know about the authorship, transmission, authority, and so on of any given religion's special writings and books?

- Do you think additional books and writings ought to be added to a religion's collection of sacred writings and books? Why or why not?

- Interview a member of a religious tradition other than your own. Ask the person some of the questions listed as we began this chapter. Ask the person for his or her personal beliefs, as well as the beliefs of others within the religion, regarding that religion's texts.

AUTHORSHIP

Some of the more complex and difficult questions about sacred texts concern authorship. Who composed the stories, instructions, and discourses that make up the numerous sacred texts? Were they written by an individual, by a group, or—like the tablets of the Hebrew Law—by God? Each religious tradition answers these questions differently. Again, while we caution against drawing conclusions that are too broad, some generalizations are helpful.

The Christian and Jewish Bibles contain clear evidence that they were written by many authors over a substantial period of time. The Old Testament/Jewish Bible is explicitly a collection of the work of numerous authors. Sometimes these authors are identified, as with the books of Amos, Hosea, Nehemiah, or Micah—books that were either written by these individuals or are collections of their sayings. Sometimes the authors are anonymous, as with the many psalms or books 1 and 2 Samuel or 1 and 2 Kings. The Old Testament/Jewish Bible is unified not by one writer or even a shared theological view but by a shared subject matter: the relationship of God to Israel and creation. In the New Testament, there are the letters of Paul and the letters written in Paul's name ("disputed" Pauline letters), various writings attributed to John, and four anonymous Gospels (the names Matthew, Mark, Luke, and John were later attached to these anonymously written books). The New Testament, similar to the Old Testament, is unified not by common authorship but by its witness to Jesus of Nazareth as the Christ of God. The question of authorship is often a source of dispute, with some arguing for an inspired, God-empowered authorship that instills the text with meaning and authority, and some recognizing an inspired authorship through which God may speak. These positions tend to cross denominational lines and are not limited to any one group or era. Regardless of the presuppositions that are brought to the Bible, the work itself has little to say about authorship. And what one finds in the biblical testaments is a cloud of witnesses (not a monolithic witness from the clouds) and a chorus of voices, not the stylings of a soloist.

As noted, the Arabic word *qur'an* literally means "recitation." The Qur'an is understood to have a single author: Allah. Allah dictated the words of the Qur'an directly to the prophet Muhammad over some twenty-three years. Understanding this view of the authorship of the Qur'an sheds light on issues ranging from the purity of the Islamic canon to the insistence on only the Arabic version of the text, because the words of the Qur'an are held to be quite literally the words of God given completely and perfectly to the Prophet. Similarly, the Book of Mormon is said to have one author/compiler, the prophet-historian Mormon, and one translator, Joseph Smith, who is believed to have translated the book from a set of golden plates with the aid of the spiritual *urim* and *thummim*.[1]

The Hindi Sruti takes the concept of authorship in a slightly different direction. There is no recognized "author" of the Sruti's hymns, spells, stories, and so on. Instead, numerous holy figures (called *rishis*) have heard the sounds of the universe and tapped into what may be called the divine "words" or emanations of the cosmos. The word *sruti* literally means "that which is heard," so for the Hindi the sacred texts are directly received from the cosmos—heard by the worthy and recorded for the faithful. In this sense, the Sruti is not the literal word of god spoken to an individual but rather divine utterances available to the saints.

Finally, the Pali Canon is widely held to be largely traceable to words spoken by Siddhartha Gautama himself that were recorded by his disciples, probably generations later. So Gautama Buddha is the source of the Tripitaka, but the authors came after him, and the writings of Buddhism are significantly later. The earliest surviving reference to the recording of the Pali Canon dates to the first century BCE and the oldest manuscript fragments are from the fifteenth century CE.

In short, attributions of authorship for sacred works vary widely among the religions of the world. Thus, assumptions that a person may have about the writings of his or her own religion may not be accurate when it comes to the writings of other faiths. There is no universal view of authorship that defines "scriptures" or sacred texts. What does seem clear is that there is almost always a connection between the importance placed on authorship and the authority that is attributed to the text in question, a point we will return to.

Questions for Reflection and Discussion

- Does not knowing the authorship of a sacred writing pose problems for a religious tradition? If so, in what ways? If not, why not?
- What do you know about the authorship of works that are part of your religious tradition or the tradition with which you are most familiar?
- Is the fact that many religious texts were written by many authors a concern? Why or why not?

TRANSMISSION

There are myriad ways that sacred writings are handed down and preserved. Here again we caution against overstating a simple and direct flow of textual traditions from one point to another, but it is helpful to think in broad terms of a continuum of starting and ending points:

Continuum of Transmission

oral tradition ⟶ precipitation to writing ⟶ redaction/editing ⟶ canonization

---

1. *Urim* and *thummim* are terms borrowed from the Old Testament. In the Old Testament *urim* and *thummim* are facets of the high priest's breastplate and may have been used for the purpose of *divination*, or consultation with the Divine. In Mormonism, *urim* and *thummim* are "seer stones" that Smith is said to have worn as glasses to help in his translation of the heavenly message, written down in an otherwise unreadable script.

At each point of change—from oral to early written drafts, from early written drafts to edited later drafts, from edited later drafts to official canonized texts—disputes, differences, and divergences can arise.

Generally, a religious text begins either as an oral tradition—stories, practices, regulations, and so on—that is handed down through the generations, or as the written record of those stories, practices, laws, and so on. Over time the stories are added to, edited, distributed, and finally established as the accepted, authoritative texts of the group. As noted above, there is no single pattern of transmission that characterizes all sacred texts. Even within a given group's texts there can be many modes of transmission. For example, the Pali Canon was passed down almost exclusively by word of mouth for the first five hundred years of its history. This is likely due to issues of climate and the durability of written materials and to the predominantly oral pattern of teaching and learning in Pali cultures. Only later, in the first century BCE, were these oral traditions committed to writing. On the other end of the spectrum stands the Qur'an, which achieved canonical status within a single generation after Muhammad's

death—largely due to claims about the nature of the text made in the text itself. Somewhere in the middle stands the Christian canon, with oral stories about the life of Jesus that spread abroad and were then written down thirty-five to sixty years after Jesus' earthly life (and not in one version but in several). Arising at the same time as the oral tradition—and predating the written forms of the Gospels—were the letters of Paul. So too with the Jewish Bible: the Jewish tradition probably began with oral stories of the matriarchs and patriarchs of Israel's earliest days, the stories of the Judges and the Exodus, and the earliest oracles of the prophets. Alongside these oral roots lie the Jewish liturgies, prayers, and hymns of the psalms written specifically for worship, and the missives of the so-called writing prophets (Amos, Hosea, and so on), whose words were set down at least in part as they were spoken.

Ultimately, written religious texts were codified to some extent, written down, and copied in "authorized" versions. But the transmission of these texts is neither fluid nor uniform, and in some cases the oral transmission and interpretation is still practiced.

Questions for Reflection and Discussion

- Since the oral transmission of stories and sayings often precedes the written transmission by dozens or even hundreds of years, does this make these stories and sayings somehow flawed? Why or why not?

- What reasons would you give for accepting or rejecting the above explanations for the transmission and development of texts?

- If you were to tell a sacred story to your closest friends, do you think they would faithfully tell it to others thirty years from now? Would their children's children be able to tell the same story?

AUTHORITY

In every religion there is a set of texts that achieves a level of influence that is authoritative for its adherents. In some cases this authority is absolute, a kind of etched-in-stone last word in terms of worldview and rules of conduct. In others these texts are more of a guide, a light to help the believer. One helpful way of understanding the authority attributed to a particular religious text is to consider its authorship or origins, and to follow the religious convictions around these issues to the point of claims for authority; another is to take the name given to the canonical material as a definitive characterization of the writing's authority.

We'll begin here with Buddhism. The word *pali* is sometimes translated as "norm," and *tripitaka* means "threefold basket." These two words describe well the authority of the sacred writings of Theravada Buddhism. The canon is the norm, the governing, constitutive material for discipline (*vinaya*), instruction (*sutta*), and reflection on "transcendent realities" (*abhidhamma*). In each case, the canon acts as the guide to one who is on the path to enlightenment. Other written materials, from mantras to histories to methods of interpretation (see, for example, the Nettipakarana), are recognized as helpful and to some extent authoritative. In general, Theravada Buddhism is open to the views expressed in the sacred writings of other religions; any path has its positives. For the Buddhist, the written material is simply a guide along the path that ultimately must itself be set aside if true enlightenment is to be realized.

The Christian Church has often used similar language to talk about the role and authority of the Bible; the key word is *normative*. A text that is normative sets the standard for matters of both faith (what is and is not central to religious belief) and life (how one is to live out faith both for oneself and with regard for one's neighbors). As early as the Council of Trent (mid-sixteenth century CE), the Roman Catholic Church described the Bible as normative, and many present-day Protestant denominations include in their constitutional documents language about the normative character of the Old and New Testaments.

One danger that has arisen, partly in response to Reformation-era biblical criticism, is what is often described as a "biblicist" view. At the Council of Trent, for example, the Roman Catholic Church decreed that the Bible was normative for life and faith, governing and guiding life, but that the Bible was above any "governance" or outside authority itself. A similar position is taken by many modern evangelical Christians who view any critical approach to the Bible as a threat to its authority. The goal of the biblicist view seems to be to maintain the purity and authority of the biblical text.

At the root of any discussion of biblical authority among Christians should be an awareness of the New Testament's understanding and use of the Old Testament. For the early church, the Old Testament was Scripture, but the New Testament's use of these Scriptures was anything but uniform. First, the most commonly quoted Old Testament books in the New Testament are Psalms, Isaiah, and Deuteronomy; not all of the Old Testament appears to have had such a strong impact. Second, the use of the Old Testament text varies: whereas some quotations are straightforward claims for authority, others reinterpret the meaning of the quoted text, and still others offer an intensification or expansion of the text's meaning. Take note that the authors of the New Testament took seriously the different character of the material it referenced from the Hebrew Bible; there is nothing "literal" or rigid about the New Testament view of Scripture.

Islam, naturally, has a simpler view of the authority of the Qur'an. As the literal words of God, the Qur'an is beyond question. For the Muslim there is no higher authority than the Qur'an. Muslims also find value in the *hadith*, the oral traditions surrounding the life of Muhammad, for the examples they provide of the right ways to live, be, think, and speak. One feature of the Qur'an that non-Muslim readers often find striking is its mention of many of the same people and stories that one finds in the Hebrew Bible and the New Testament (for example, Adam and Eve, Noah, Abraham, and more). These Bible stories are not repeated verbatim in the Qur'an but instead take on a different character. The versions of these stories in the Qur'an are understood by Muslims as corrective; that is, the Qur'anic versions are considered accurate and the biblical versions corrupted. In short, Muslims accept the Qur'an as the inspired, perfect word of God, and no other text compares.

The authority of sacred texts also differs at least minimally from religion to religion. Some, like Buddhism and Hinduism, emphasize the guidance of their texts while others, like Islam and in some cases Christianity and Judaism, emphasize the divine agency behind their texts and these texts' final authority over human life. Assumptions of authority clearly exercise a significant influence on the use and effect of a text in the daily lives of its readers.

Questions for Reflection and Discussion

- Is the authority of sacred texts important for you? Why or why not?
- How does one know if divine agency was involved in the development of sacred texts and stories?

- What are the risks associated with questioning the authority of a sacred text?

GENRE

We noted that religions have different concepts of what a "scripture" or sacred writing is. A related issue is that of the literary genres that a sacred text employs. *Genre* refers to the style, form, or content of literature, as for example, a letter, a story, or a law. Different genres fulfill specific functions. The function of a law, for instance, might be to sanction or prohibit particular behaviors; the function of a prayer, to interact and communicate with the divine; the function of a parable, to teach a lesson or illustrate a point; and the function of a chapter in an introductory textbook, to present basic information. The point here is that different genres serve different functions. Thus, the fact that various sacred writings employ different genres indicates that the writings were developed to serve different functions.

Speaking broadly, one may say that the Islamic Qur'an, which Muslims believe is the direct revelation of God to Muhammad, takes the form of speeches directed to the people of God. These speeches, in turn, take many different forms—stories, laws, directions, warnings. Here, by way of example, are two passages from the Qur'an. Both are the speech of God to the people; the first takes the form of instruction, while the second tells a story:

> Do not say of anything: "I will do that tomorrow," without adding: "God willing," and, whenever you forget, remember your Lord and say: "May my Lord guide me closer to what is right."[2]

---

2. The Qur'an, trans. M.A.S. Abdel Haleem (Oxford, UK: Oxford University Press, 2004), 184–185.

Tell them the story of Noah. He said to his people, "My people, if my presence among you and my reminding you of God's signs is too much for you, then I put my trust in God. Agree on your course of action, you and your partner-gods—do not be hesitant or secretive about it—then carry out your decision on me and give me no respite. But if you turn away, I have asked no reward from you; my reward is from God alone, and I am commanded to be one of those who devote themselves to Him." But they rejected him. We saved him and those with him on the Ark and let them survive; and We drowned those who denied Our revelations—see what was the end of those who were forewarned![3]

The Buddhist Tripitaka, on the other hand, can be described as the teachings of the Buddha and some early followers on the path to enlightenment, containing everything that a follower needs for the path to nirvana. These teachings often take the form of discourses between the Buddha and others, or poems, or rules for following the path.

The Christian and Jewish Scriptures, by contrast, are even more diverse in terms of genre than those of Buddhism or Islam—so diverse, in fact, that it is not possible to provide even an umbrella category under which these writings could be grouped. The genres include stories, laws, parables, fables, rituals, liturgies, prayers, histories, genealogies, letters, revelations, prophetic messages, proverbs, and many more.

When considering a scripture, it is important to note that the intended audience for that scripture may operate with an assumed genre that does not line up perfectly with the entirety of that scripture. For instance, many Christians believe that God directly inspired every word in the Bible. Yet the book of Psalms contains prayers directed to God expressing anguish and pleas for help. Thus, there is some disconnect between the genre the believer assigns to Psalms and the actual genre of the text itself.

A related issue is what a community of faith expects to learn or to occur when the sacred writing is studied. If a community understands a text as the words of God, then the community will expect to be confronted by and to learn God's will when the text is read. If, however, a community understands a text as offering wisdom about life's path, then the primary question will be, "What does this teach me about how to live?" Finally, if a community understands a sacred writing as telling the story of their faith, the community will expect to hear a part of their story and individuals will ask, "Where do I fit in this story? How is this my story?"

Questions for Reflection and Discussion

- How might knowing the genre of a text affect how one reads it?
- What genres are typically associated with sacred texts?
- What genre of text are you most exposed to in your daily life? Where do you encounter it? How do you go about making sense of it?

---

3. Ibid., 133.

INTERPRETATION

Every act of reading a text is an act of interpretation. To understand what a text says, what it implies, and what it means personally for a reader are acts of interpretation. Faith traditions have differing ideas about what kinds of interpretation should be encouraged (or even allowed) and thus what forms faithful interpretation should take.

Rabbinic Judaism, for example, has come close to canonizing debate as a faithful form of interpretation. The Talmud offers numerous views on the meaning of particular aspects of Scripture and Jewish life. Consider this excerpt from the *Pirke Avot*, one tractate of the Mishnah:

> 1.2 Simon the Righteous was one of the last of the Great Assembly. His motto was: "The world stands on three things — the Torah, the [Temple] service, and loving acts of kindness. . . ."
>
> *The world stands on three things.* Rashi and Maimonides differ on their understanding of the meaning of "the world stands." For Rashi, the world would not have come into being were it not for these three things. For Maimonides, proper human existence could not be maintained if it were not for these three things.[4]

This is not to suggest, of course, that this is the only form of interpretation one finds in Judaism. There are also academic-historical interpretations of the Torah, as well as mystical interpretations, artistic interpretations, and so on.

Different methods for interpreting a text can be illustrated by the fourfold exegetical method, popular in the Christian Church in the Middle Ages. This method emphasizes the difference between the letter and the spirit of a text. It focuses on four aspects of a text: literal (what the text says), allegorical (how the text relates to the doctrinal teaching of the Church), moral (how the text relates to matters of living), and anagogical (how the text relates to secret or hidden meanings).[5] In the modern era, Christian interpreters have focused mainly on the literal interpretation of the text, on what the text actually says. It should be noted that "literal" does not mean the reader interprets everything a text says in a rigidly historicist manner. Rather, this approach understands a text as the text wants to be understood — so a recipe for bread is understood as a recipe for bread, not as a metaphor for happiness; and a parable is understood as a parable, not as having actually happened; and a historical text is understood as reporting something that is believed to have actually happened.

Other modes for interpreting sacred writings include meditation, singing, art, and dance. In Islam, for instance, passages of the Qur'an are often memorized in childhood. Reciting these texts in a meditative fashion is considered to have a beneficial effect on the believer. The Qur'an is to be studied only in Arabic, the language of heaven. Translations of the holy writing are not considered scripture because a translation is always an interpretation, and hence prone to error. Translations of the Qur'an are therefore always referred to as expressions of the "meaning" of the Holy Qur'an, or as "interpretation." Furthermore, Muhammad forbade artistic representations of human beings, including himself. Thus, artistic representations, or interpretations, of the stories in the Qur'an are not allowed. Compare this with Christianity and Judaism, in which artistic interpretations of biblical stories form a major part of the

---

4. *Pirke Avot: A Modern Commentary on Jewish Ethics*, eds. and trans. L. Kravitz and K. Olitzky (New York: UAHC Press, 1993), 2–3.

5. In Jewish tradition, there is a similar, though not identical, system of interpretation represented by the acronym PaRDeS: *peshat* (literal), *remez* (allegorical), *derash* (moral), and *sod* (anagogical).

tradition, as the myriad paintings, carvings, and stained-glass windows in Christian and Jewish sanctuaries give witness.

CONCLUSION: ROLE OF TEXT

A final set of questions regarding the role of sacred texts concerns how the texts are used in the life of those who practice the faith. As we have noted throughout this chapter, it is unwise to generalize, other than to note the diversity of practices throughout the world. So it is with the use of sacred texts. Readings from sacred texts may be read and expounded upon in public worship, they may be read and meditated on devotionally by individuals, they may be studied in small groups, they may be sung, and so on. There is an almost infinite number of ways that special words function in the lives of religious people. Perhaps the only generalization one can safely make is that in every religion, certain teachings, prayers, or laws of the faith are more central than others. To illustrate this, we will consider key prayers and practices in various faith traditions.

In Buddhism, prayer, which frequently consists of the recitation of mantras, is an important discipline in achieving and maintaining the ideals of Buddhist living—tranquility, mindfulness, and concentration. Prayer is practiced to discipline the mind and focus one's attention away from the self and on the Four Noble Truths, which are central to Buddhist teaching. Prayer is also essential to walking the Noble Eightfold Path, enabling one to escape suffering and achieve enlightenment. C. S. Lewis said of prayer that it is not so much about changing God or God's mind as it is about changing us—those who pray. While this may be true of Christian prayer (which Lewis was talking about), it could also just as easily (and perhaps better) describe the intent of Buddhist prayer.

The same is true of prayer in Hinduism. The repetition of mantras makes up the core of Hindu spiritual life and is directly related to Hindu sacred writings—those that Hinduism hold highest and most dear are the mantras central to spirituality, worship, and daily living. Prayer and recitation express the innermost desire of the practitioner, that one's reality might be transformed from suffering and trial into peace. Consider a representative Hindu prayer taken from the Vedas:

> Lead Us from Untruth to Truth,
> Lead Us from Darkness to Light,
> Lead Us from Death to Immortality,
> Ohm. Peace, Peace, Peace.

In Islam, daily prayer is one of the five pillars of faith and forms the warp and weft of daily life. The required prayers (*salat*) are performed five times daily at specific times. In Muslim cultures, the call to prayer (*adhan*) is sounded at dawn, midday, midafternoon, just after sunset, and two hours after sunset. An example of *salat*:

> God is great.
> I bear witness that there is no divinity but God.
> I bear witness that Muhammad is
>   God's messenger.
> Hasten to prayer!
> Hasten to welfare!
> Prayer is better than sleep.
> God is great.
> There is no divinity but God.

The prayers are highly regularized, with motions and words that are prescribed with one opportunity to choose the recitation of a sura (the divisions of the Qur'an) of one's choice. After the prayer, composed of several *rak'as* (ritual movements and recitations performed two times in the morning; four at noon, afternoon, and evening; and three at sunset), a more free form or devotional prayer (*du'a*) may be said.

Daily prayer and sacred words also play an important part in Jewish life. Consider, for example, daily prayer for Jewish men. Men must pray three times daily and wear a *tefillin* (a small leather box containing the text of Deut 6:4–9, 11:13–21; and Ex 13:1–16) and a *tallit* (a prayer shawl with numerous knots and fringes, symbolizing the biblical commandments) during the morning prayer. The morning prayers include psalms, rabbinic prayers, and other elements. One of the most central elements of the Jewish daily prayer is the recitation of the *Shema* (meaning "Hear!") from Deuteronomy 6:

> Hear, O Israel! The LORD is our God, the LORD alone. You shall love the LORD your God with all your heart and with all your soul and with all your might. Take to heart these instructions with which I charge you this day. Impress them upon your children. Recite them when you stay at home and when you are away, when you lie down and when you get up. Bind them as a sign on your hand and let them serve as a symbol on your forehead; inscribe them on the doorposts of your house and on your gates. (Deut 6:4–9, Jewish Publication Society Tanak translation, 1985)

The centrality of this text, which emphasizes God's oneness, is evident in its recitation during morning and evening prayers and its inclusion in the *tefillin*.

By contrast, daily prayer is an important element in the life of many Christians, but Christianity as a whole does not prescribe any set rituals or patterns for daily prayer. The Lord's Prayer, which Jesus taught in response to his disciples' request that he teach them to pray (Lk 11:1–3), may be the most central prayer in Christianity:

> Our Father in heaven,
> Hallowed be your name.
> Your kingdom come,
> Your will be done,
> On earth as it is in heaven.
> Give us this day our daily bread,
> Forgive us our trespasses,
> As we forgive those who trespass against us.
> Save us from the time of trial,
> And deliver us from evil.
> For the kingdom, the power, and the glory
>   are yours.

The prayer is recited weekly in a majority of Christian worship services; it is prayed individually by followers of Jesus; it is used to open and close meetings and small groups; and it is often sung.

Compare the special words of the central prayer activities of these three faith traditions. What do they have in common? How do the practices shape the lives of members of the different faiths in different ways? How do the names for God shape the imaginations of members of these traditions? When one begins to ask questions such as these, the depths and subtleties that the special words and writings of the world's religions play in the lives of adherents emerge.

Questions for Reflection and Discussion

- In what ways might prayer be regarded as sacred text?
- How might the role of a text influence how it is understood?
- How do words shape the imagination and reflective capacity of religious practitioners?
- Are there risks associated with prayer? If so, what are they? If not, why not?

Additional Resources

Abdel Haleem, M. A., trans. 2004. *The Qur'an.* Oxford, UK: Oxford University Press.

Antes, Peter, Armin W. Geertz, and Randi R. Warne, eds. 2004. *New Approaches to the Study of Religion.* Vol. 2, *Textural, Comparative, Sociological and Cognitive Approaches.* Berlin and New York: Walter de Gruyter.

Assman, Jan, and Rodney Livingstone. 2006. *Religion and Cultural Memory: Ten Studies.* Stanford, CA: Stanford University Press.

Cohen, Abraham. 1949. *Everyman's Talmud: The Major Teachings of the Rabbinic Sages.* New York: Schocken Books.

Holtz, Barry W., ed. 2006. *Back to the Sources: Reading the Classic Jewish Texts.* New York: Simon and Schuster.

Rinpoche, Mipham, trans. 1997. *Gateway to Knowledge.* Hong Kong: Rangjung Yeshe Publications.

Smith, Wilfred Cantwell. 1993. *What Is Scripture? A Comparative Approach.* Minneapolis: Fortress Press.

AN AESTHETIC APPROACH TO RELIGION

S. Brent Plate
Hamilton College

Preface

The cultivation and appreciation of art and beauty—or aesthetics—is integral to religious traditions the world over. Nearly all religions reserve some form of art for devotional purposes. Individuals are often inspired to create works of art to express their faith or reverence for a sacred entity. Varied forms of music are employed by religions globally as expressions of belief. Even the beat of a drum can serve as a call to faith or a means to convey an affective desire. And many religions use certain carefully stylized physical postures or movements to support spiritual experience

Material culture pulses with themes that evoke and provoke religious observance and communicate much about belief. In North America, for example, religious symbols pervade nearly every dimension of lived experience. Everywhere, the faiths of the world are embedded in cultural customs that create or ascribe to human experience that which might be regarded as beautiful. Aesthetics is inseparable from our human sensory experience and our cultural, social, and religious history. In this chapter, S. Brent Plate explores the terrain of aesthetics in relation to religion and religious practices.

Chapter Goals

- To introduce and reflect on aesthetics as a category of religious sensory encounter
- To provide readers with the means to begin to consider aesthetics as an approach to religion
- To provide an opportunity for reflection on how the senses relate to religious practice and religion generally

INTRODUCTION

There are two popular, related understandings of the word *aesthetics* (sometimes spelled *esthetics*). The first is found in intellectual circles and tends to relate to theories of art, often in attempts to define *beauty*. The second is found in general cultural environments and refers to ways of altering the human body to make it more beautiful: stores specializing in aesthetics may offer pedicures, manicures, facials, and so on, while the more extreme "aesthetic surgery" beautifies the body through cosmetic nips and tucks.

This chapter will touch on the common understanding that aesthetics relates to beauty, with a critical emphasis on the body, but will expand the concept and apply it to religions. The modern *aesthetics* comes from the Greek *aesthesis*, which pertains to sensory perception. Aesthetics, as introduced here, is about the ways human bodies sense their religious worlds, particularly through sight, sound, taste, touch, and smell. While sometimes the sensual encounter enables people to be touched by beautiful art, more typically these aesthetic experiences occur on an immediate and everyday basis: in the candle lit before Sabbath prayer, in the incense smelled upon entering the temple, in the bitter herbs eaten at Passover, in the chanted call to prayer of the Muezzin, in the watercolor portrayal of the head of Jesus Christ, in the stroll through the gardens of Kyoto. An aesthetic approach to religion therefore pays attention to senses as they engage with the material objects and activities that comprise the religious experience.

By focusing on the vital role that materiality and the senses play in human experience, we are able to investigate religious traditions in ways that complement and expand traditional approaches to religion. The conventional study of religion continues to focus heavily on the interpretation of sacred texts and the intellectual exploration of philosophical doctrines. In contrast, experiencing religion through its material and artistic practices challenges the student of religion to reconsider the seemingly mundane dimensions of religion: what religious people taste and see in their sacred settings. It is not enough to say that wine and bread symbolize the sacrifice of Jesus Christ, as some Christian churches do; rather one must actually drink and eat the symbol, ingesting through the body, not merely comprehending with the brain.

Exploring each of the senses and some of their roles within religious environments, this chapter will outline ways that a multifaceted understanding of aesthetics is vital when approaching religion. Various objects mediate the experience of religion in connection with the senses, and the arts play an essential role in ongoing religious renewal. The examples that follow come from prominent global religions such as Islam and Christianity, and also from lesser-known traditions in Latin America and Africa. Drumbeats or chants do not register in the same way across all religious traditions, nor do images of gods and goddesses, since some traditions vehemently oppose representational imagery while others exalt it. Different religious traditions elevate the senses differently. But all religions are formed in part by sensual engagements with the material and artistically created world.

THE SENSES

In December 2005, the *New York Times* reported new scientific findings on a strange and often mythically imagined creature, the narwhal, a smallish whale with a long "tusk" on its head, looking something like a submarine unicorn. Long thought to possess magical powers, the tusk of this arctic dwelling mammal is now understood to contain more than ten million nerve endings that can "detect subtle changes of temperature, pressure, particle gradients and probably much else." Beyond its mythology, the tusk is, in strict terms, an extended tooth that functions as a sense organ. The lead scientist in the study suggests of the creature in its chilly, aquatic environment: "Of all the places you'd think you'd want to do the most to insulate yourself from that outside environment, this guy has gone out of his way to open himself up to it."[1]

The point here is to see how sense organs operate as "openings" that connect an individual creature and its surrounding world. Further, those openings have adapted to fit particular animals in particular places as a means of survival. They are not wide openings that allow all forms of information to pass through. Instead, they function in highly specialized ways, filtering what goes in and out.

Humans, like narwhals and all sentient beings, can only exist in the world in and through the senses, especially as the senses are finely attuned to the environment in which we live and move and have our being. The remaining senses of people who lack sight, hearing, or another sense faculty become vastly more powerful in order to compensate for the missing sense. The bottom line is we would die without the senses, for not only would we fail to sense danger using our sense-based survival instincts, we would also fail to give and receive love, a deep-rooted and vitally necessary emotional experience that we exercise through touching, hearing, and seeing.

Moreover, without the senses there would be no religion, for religion is founded on a relation between embodied beings and the world around them. We are creatures with bodies, and these bodies learn about their environment—whether social, familial, religious, or other—sensually as well as intellectually. Even intellectual learning, though the modern world has gone to great lengths to deny it, can only operate through sense perception. As William Paden, a scholar of religion, suggests, religions build "worlds" for their participants: "Religions do not inhabit the same world, but actually posit, structure, and dwell within a universe that is their own." Paden says that "all living things select and sense the

---

1. Quoted in William J. Broad, "It's Sensitive. Really," *New York Times*, December 13, 2005.

'way things are' through their own organs and modes of activity. . . . They see—or smell or feel—what they need to, and everything else may as well not exist."[2] Recall the narwhal's tooth-tusk: it senses what it needs to—temperature, pressure, particles—and connects with the environment through those data most critical to its survival in the icy northern waters. We humans, in creating specific religious worlds, do the same. In writing about the spaces that people inhabit, anthropologist Edward T. Hall suggests that "people from different cultures not only speak different languages but, what is possibly more important, inhabit different sensory worlds."[3] Some worlds lend credence to certain senses, while others offer a different version of reality.

The remainder of this chapter explores the various human senses, noting diverse examples of the ways the senses help construct and allow people to participate in religious worlds. There is a tendency in the modern world to think of seeing and hearing as the most important senses, yet in religious worlds, all the senses come into play, and a brief examination of various rituals and myths from around the world demonstrates the importance of each of the senses and the ways they come into contact with each other.

HEARING

Humans receive sonic vibrations through their ears. We quickly learn to tell the difference between a voice raised in anger and sweet whispers in the ear, between punk rock and J. S. Bach. Sometimes sounds are harmonic, sometimes melodic, sometimes spoken, sometimes screamed, sometimes sung. Words, chants, and music are all media of devotional expression, interhuman communication, and religious revelation: God speaks the cosmos into being at the beginning of Genesis, God speaks the Qur'anic revelation to Muhammad at Mount Hira and the revelation of the Torah to Moses on Mount Sinai. God and gods and goddesses are often understood to speak audibly to humans, just as humans speak, sing, and make music with each other. In traditions around the world, sounds and the objects that make them are living things through which divine revelation occurs.

For the South Asian religious traditions that find their early origins in the Vedas, it is sound that exists before anything else. The Vedas are literally books of "knowledge" (Sanskrit, *veda*) and are primarily regarded as oral texts, eternal in nature, without human or divine origin. In the beginning, and evermore existent, is the primordial sound of the universe, usually identified as the ultimate reality, *Brahman*. The early "seers" (*rishis*), of which there were seven, were able to take this sound and turn it into comprehensible verse. The Vedas are intended to be heard and not "read" in the modern, silent sense of the term. There is an ongoing sound that sustains the cosmos, and Brahmin priests are often called upon to connect with that sound, offering a chant as part of a Hindu ritual.

Similarly, though centuries later, the literal translation of Qur'an, Islam's central sacred text, is "recitation." Allah spoke this revelation to Muhammad who, legend has it, was illiterate, and the first word spoken was the command "recite!" (cf. Surah 96). All the early engagements with the Qur'an were oral. Although this text was ultimately written down, the beautiful styles of calligraphy that have emerged in Islam—after all, the Word of God must be made beautiful in its material manifestation—often represent a musical score, with diacritical marks telling the reciter how to orally chant the words on the

---

2. William Paden, *Religious Worlds* (Boston: Beacon Press, 1994), 51, 52.

3. Edward T. Hall, *The Hidden Dimension* (Garden City, NY: Doubleday, 1966), 2.

page. Muslim children in madrasas, or religious schools, learn the Qur'an "by heart," they do not simply memorize. The flowing, poetic Arabic language in which the Qur'an is spoken, written, and heard is pleasurable to recite and hear, far beyond the specifics of what is said.

Moving away from the oral-aural nature of sacred texts, we find divine drumbeats in the Afro-Cuban religion of Santería. Like Candomblé in Brazil and other localized practices across Latin America, Santería has its roots in West African rituals, especially from Yoruban religious cultures. The African traditions, including their rituals, deities, and sounds, traveled with enslaved people to the New World where they mixed and merged with other traditions, including Roman Catholicism, and were practiced by people in the Caribbean. One of the central rituals in Santería is a drumming ceremony (*toque de tambor*) that invokes the deities (*orishas*) to manifest themselves in the bodies of willing adherents. Importantly, the drums (*batá*) themselves are sometimes consecrated, as the deity *aña* is incarnated in these special percussion instruments, and there are distinctive ways of drumming that invoke various other *orishas*. These drums can be regarded as living beings, and their sounds comprise a central role in ritual, connecting humans with their deities.

SMELL

To understand local cultures and religious worlds more broadly, it is necessary to attend to the "aromascape." Smell is, admittedly, the most difficult of the senses to discuss in writing. Nonetheless, aroma's subtlety for comprehending the ways religions operate is all the more powerful because of its potential to be literally overlooked.

Ritual sacrifice is a sacred act, and holiness is often sensed through the nose. The God of the Hebrew Scriptures, like many humans, seems to enjoy the smell of cooking meat. Biblical passages such as Genesis 8:21, Exodus 29:18, and many places in the first few chapters of Leviticus, indicate how God is "pleased" by the smells of burnt animal sacrifices. The twelfth-century Christian mystic Hildegaard of Bingen comments on a curious passage in Isaiah 11 by suggesting: "By our *nose* God displays the wisdom that lies like a fragrant sense of order in all works of art, just as we ought to know through our ability to smell whatever wisdom has to arrange."[4] Throughout the Hebrew Bible, there are striking passages that suggest olfaction is associated with judgment, discernment, and knowledge.

In the Christian New Testament, we find Saint Paul suggesting of the followers of Jesus Christ: "Through us spreads in every place the fragrance that comes from knowing him. For we are the aroma of Christ to God" (2 Cor 2:14–15). Throughout Christianity until modern times, smell has often been linked with holiness, and there are accounts in which sweet smells wafted over an area upon the death of a saint. One of the most famous examples is Saint Teresa of Avila, who throughout her life was said to emit a pleasing fragrance. After her death in 1582, her body retained a particular scent for years to come and is connected with several healing miracles, especially as relics of her body were distributed across Europe, with some of these continuing to emit a sweet, healing odor.

The scent of sacrifice is a pungent odor that can be smelled across the worlds of religious people. The sacrifices are not always animal, however, and incense has become an almost universal ritual substance. It can be found as part of Christian,

---

4. Hildegard of Bingen, *Book of Divine Works with Letters and Songs*, ed. M. Fox (Santa Fe, NM: Bear and Company, 1987), 130; quoted in Constance Classen, *The Color of Angels: Cosmology, Gender, and the Aesthetic Imagination* (London: Routledge, 1998), 59. Many dimensions of this section are indebted to Classen's work.

Jewish, Buddhist, Muslim, and Hindu worship, and many smaller scale traditions as well. The burning of incense symbolically operates in two ways: it has a pleasing aroma, and as smoke rises upward (toward the gods in most cosmologies), it is clear that the burning is an offering "lifted up."

With a contemporary mixture of indigenous practices and Islam, the Tuareg of West Africa use incense extensively in wedding ceremonies and other rites of passage, especially as incense is believed to ward off evil spirits. Persons going through the rite, particularly in the liminal phase, must be protected since they are especially susceptible to harm at this time. The Tuareg also use aromas as part of healing ceremonies, and diviners utilize scents as well. All this leads anthropologist Susan Rasmussen to say that "aromas carry messages, open up boundaries, and suggest alternative ways of interpreting experience."[5]

TASTE

The crucial religious dimension of memory ultimately connects with all the senses, though it seems smell and taste have the strongest relations to the past. Strangely enough, those two senses are perhaps the most interlinked, even as they are the most overlooked in religious studies.

Every spring, Jews around the world celebrate one of the oldest ongoing rituals, the Passover Seder, which narratively and gustatorily celebrates the Exodus of the ancient Israelites from slavery in Egypt. The historian Yosef Hayim Yerushalmi explains this story and annual ritual of liberation:

[I]n the course of a meal around the family table, ritual, liturgy, and even culinary elements are orchestrated to transmit a vital past from one generation to the next. . . . Significantly, one of the first ritual acts to be performed is the lifting up of a piece of unleavened bread (*matzah*). . . . Memory here is no longer recollection, which still preserves a sense of distance, but reactualization.[6]

In eating the *matzah*, the bitter herbs (*marror*), and drinking the wine, the religious past is reactualized in the Passover meal. In reenacting the drama of slavery-to-liberation via eating and recitation of texts and prayers, the ritual participants become the slaves in Egypt and eventually the liberated captives who celebrate their freedom. The structure of this liturgy tells us both of the importance of ritual in reenacting ancient myths, and also of the central role that sensory perception plays in such activity.

Christianity takes its most fundamental ritual—Communion/the Eucharist—from the Jewish Passover. Indeed, according to the Gospels (cf. Matthew 26, Mark 14, Luke 22), the so-called Last Supper of Jesus with his disciples was a Passover meal at which Jesus memorably spoke, "Take, eat; this is my body." And as he lifted the bread and wine, according to Luke 22:19, he said, "Do this in remembrance of me." In other words, sometimes remembering requires physical activity, not merely intellectual thought. Memory can be enacted through the ritual use of the body. Sacred remembrances and therefore also traditions are created through the body and mind of the religious follower, who through bodily participation reenacts the past.

In Hindu devotional (*bhakti*) practices, the devotee makes offerings (*puja*) to the deities, who are often manifested with icons and statues. This sensual worship practice involves offerings of sweet-smelling flowers, chants and drumbeats,

---

5. Susan Rasmussen, "Making Better 'Scents' in Anthropology: Aroma in Tuareg Sociocultural Systems and the Shaping of Ethnography," *Anthropological Quarterly* 72, no. 2 (April 1999): 69.

6. Yosef Hayim Yerushalmi, *Zakhor: Jewish History and Jewish Memory* (Seattle: University of Washington Press, 1996), 44.

brightly colored dyes dabbed on the forehead of the deity, and foods. Hindu gods and goddesses have different tastes — Krishna likes dairy products, Ganesha likes sweets, some goddesses are vegetarian while others are carnivores. Devotees make offerings, which are consecrated through this ritual process, and then the blessed food (*prasad*, "grace, a gift") is offered back to the devotee as a sacramental substance. The consumption of the *prasad* by the devotee completes the rite. This is similar to the Christian rite of Communion: bread is just bread, a profane substance, until it is sanctified in the rite of Communion. The consumption of the host by the church member then completes the ritual.

TOUCH

Though the human skin is the largest organ of the body, touch is often the least valued sense in modern religious discourse. As with all the senses — and especially with the sense of touch — religious philosophers and others often contrast information received by the body to that received by the mind. Touch is, in a real sense, *proof* of what we know, and so it is contrasted with "true faith," which believes even if it does not see or feel. There are many indications that the need for touch to verify truth is a sign of weak faith, and so there ends up a paradoxical situation in which touch becomes confirmation, even as it shows that the person touching is not a true believer. The evidence needed by "doubting Thomas" (see Jn 20:24–29) speaks to the human need for "felt" evidence, evidence beyond that which is seen. Yet the supernatural *vision* of the Resurrection of Jesus is supposed to be enough for all his followers: both Mary and Thomas see the Resurrected Jesus, but each, in turn, are not supposed to touch. Seeing provides evidence enough, and to touch would be to diminish faith. Still, 1 John 1:1 makes it clear that sensual

evidence is important to understanding the "word of life."

Touch and the skin in general provide a natural mediating point between the natural and the supernatural. The skin is painted upon, cut into, used as parchment for sacred texts, just as sacred icons are felt and kissed by fingers and lips, wearing away surfaces. In many societies, rites of passage (ceremonies that mark a transformation from one phase of life to another, such as child to adult or single person to married person) use the skin to mark the difference between one stage of life and another. The transition is often made to be *felt* by the person experiencing it, and so we have many felt rite-of-passage ceremonies, including circumcision among some Jewish, Christian, and Muslim groups and coming-of-age scarification rituals in some African cultures. Thus, the ritual is embedded in the body and at the same time created as a visual display for others to see and witness. Religious individuals and communities are often identified by the external symbols they show to others, and this includes marks on the body. For the ancient patriarch Abraham, the sign of the covenant made with God was circumcision, a tradition that exists today, even as its original religious context has mostly died away.

For the Yoruba of Southwest Nigeria, there is a belief that malevolent spirits can enter the womb of a pregnant woman. The child who is so affected is called an *abiku* ("born-to-die-again child"), and in order to prevent an early death, a scarification ritual is sometimes conducted. During this time the image of a gecko is literally etched into the belly of the child. (This is in many ways a practice not unlike that of circumcision.) The process is understood as preventive medicine, warding off the evil spirits, and is performed by a priest/medicine man (*babalawo*). Geckos are seen as easygoing, nonmalevolent members of Yoruban households, almost like part of the household architecture, especially since they typically appear on the walls of houses. The etching of the gecko into the child's abdomen (a central, vital location) is an act of protection or preservation, intended to ensure the child's survival to older ages.[7]

Beyond its role in rites of passage, the skin serves as an envelope for the human body as it moves and feels its way through space and time. In Japan, a tradition of landscaped gardens grew alongside certain strains of Buddhism, most prominently the Pure Land (Jodo) and Zen sects, and mixed with the indigenous Shinto traditions as well as some Taoist ideas and practices. Japanese garden traditions have developed over the past millennium and pay special attention to the role of the human body as it moves through the garden. Japanese gardens are omnisensual, invoking engagement with each of the senses. Strolling along such a garden's irregular paths, moving up and down, the body of the visitor physically experiences the doctrines of Buddhism, including impermanence and meditative awareness.

VISION

Among modern Western religious believers, vision is considered the most prominent sense, and this arguably could be true for human consciousness in general. Religious language frequently reflects the deep-seated nature of vision. There are spiritual "seers" and "visionaries"; religious people hold "worldviews" and "perspectives" as they await "insight" and "clarity." Even *revelation* and *apocalypse* are terms of sight. Of course such language metaphorically points beyond the readily apparent material world, and yet these metaphors are based on the physical. Religious seeing is a vital part of traditions around the world, as visual activity serves to heighten the faith of communities, teach individuals, and guide those seeking deeper devotion.

In Hinduism, a prominent element of worship is *darshan*, or the interaction between the devotee and the deity. Significantly, *darshan* takes place through a mutual engagement of the eyes. The devotee goes to *see* the image of the deity, but she or he also goes to be seen by the deity in return and thereby receive a blessing. As Diana Eck, a scholar of Indian traditions, explains, "The central act of Hindu worship, from the point of view of the lay person, is to stand in the presence of the deity and to behold the image with one's own eye, to see and be seen by the deity. . . . The prominence of the eyes of Hindu divine images also reminds us that it is not only the worshiper who sees the deity, but the deity sees the worshiper as well. The contact between devotee and deity is exchanged through the eyes."[8] Although touch and taste and smell are also prominent in many Hindu ceremonies, sacred power often resides in the eyes.

A similar, though distinct, activity emerges in Eastern Orthodox Christian traditions. For more than a thousand years, icons have held a significant place in the ritual life of the Eastern Church. As with Hindu devotees, the Eastern Orthodox worshiper engages these icons through the eyes, and sometimes through touch, and the icons are carefully created to draw attention to the eyes. They tend to have slightly enlarged eyes set with a frontal presentation so that the eyes "look back" at the viewer, as the viewer receives blessings. The power of these icons is immense, and historically many authorities in the Christian church have worked to denigrate them because they seem to make the divine directly accessible, thus bypassing the church hierarchy. Indeed,

---

7. Information on this practice is indebted to the research of Tunde M. Akinwumi, in an unpublished paper on wall-gecko scarification motifs.

8. Diana Eck, *Darshan*, 3rd ed. (New York: Columbia University Press, 1998), 3.

disagreements over the place and power of such icons in Christian worship became one of several factors that instigated the first great split in the church between the Eastern Orthodox and Roman Catholic branches. Based in Constantinople, the Orthodox Church reaffirmed the power of icons as a direct means of connecting to God, while the Roman Catholic Church pointed toward their symbolic and teaching value only.

Vision plays an important role in the Qur'an, the sacred scripture of Islam, in comprehending the holiness of this text. Not long after Muhammad received revelations from God, he and his community realized the necessity of writing down God's words to preserve them. But since these were the very words of God, they needed to be treated specially, and so the artistic enterprise of Islamic calligraphy developed. Because most early Muslims, like early Christians, Buddhists, and other religious adherents, were illiterate, there was a need to find various ways for people to connect with the sacred. Thus, forms of calligraphy (literally "beautiful writing") and associated artistic schools emerged in order to make the Qur'an a beautiful text. Not only were particular Arabic scripts used, but entire pages of the Qur'an were decorated with ornamentation and richly colored dyes, making for a deeply visual experience that might enable worshipers to receive blessings just by looking at the pages. The Qur'an, in its visible, audible, tactile, and intellectual dimensions, necessitates a sensuous engagement.

THE SIXTH SENSE?

In the modern-day West, sense perception is typically understood as comprising five distinct senses. Yet, throughout history, philosophers have proposed numerous systems for categorizing our senses, and the number of human senses has ranged from as few as one to as many as six. The most prominent sense was often considered that of touch: all other categories could, in many ways, be relegated to aspects of touch. But there are ways of separating the proximate senses (that is, touching and tasting) from the distant senses (that is, seeing and hearing), as well as ways of grouping these sensual components together. What this tells us is that the senses themselves are subject to cultural and social arrangements, and that we are all trained to perceive the world in various ways.

Moreover, what is most important to recognize is that even the so-called five senses cannot be distinguished from each other. The functions of the human mind-body are organic, holistic, and interconnected. There is evidence to suggest that a person without a sense of smell cannot taste the difference between coffee and wine, thus smell and taste cannot ultimately be distinguished. Meanwhile, what we perceive through our eyes or ears is always dependent on all the other mutually informing senses. We do not hear, taste, touch, see, or smell in a material vacuum: we are always smelling as we are touching, seeing as we are hearing, tasting as we are smelling. The senses work in tandem with each other, sometimes affirming each other, sometimes offering conflicting views. Each sense informs the others, creating a general experience called *synesthesia*. Nonetheless, various religious cultures, myths, and ceremonies might each emphasize a different sense, and it is important to notice the consequences of this.

Further, these five senses are not the only ones to be conceived in religious communities. A number of recent studies have documented other ways of conceiving our senses. Anthropologist Kathryn Linn Geurts' study of the Ewe people in West Africa, for example, suggests the Ewe have a sense—something like "balance"—that informs their modes of being in the world. Geurts detects this in their mythical and everyday language and by the objects they use to construct their environments.

Similarly, C. M. Woolgar's in-depth study *The Senses in Late Medieval England* notes numerous ways the late medieval sensorium was different than the modern scientific one. In that time, some people understood speech to be a sense, while qualities like holiness were conveyed through a process similar to that of touch. And throughout the Christian tradition there have been "spiritual senses" such as understanding, desire, and delight. Different times and places, different cultural and environmental situations, different religious authorities and traditions can each affect how the senses are categorized and even experienced.

Questions for Reflection and Discussion

- Which of the senses do you favor most in your practice of religion?
- Which of the senses do you favor least in your practice of religion?
- What memories of religion, religious practices, and religious experience do you associate with assorted human senses?
- How are the human senses important for the study of religion?

CONCLUSION

To understand religions, it is important not only to study their sacred texts, rituals, doctrines, myths, and symbols but also to understand how religious worlds are constructed using the senses. Media theorist Marshall McLuhan posits that there are "ratios" of sense perceptions that differ from culture to culture. Some religious worlds strongly emphasize hearing in their rituals, for example, while others might emphasize touch in their mythology. Every religious world explicitly or implicitly has a sense ratio that suggests certain senses are more important than others in shaping their own particular worlds. Such insights make analyses of religions more complex and more complete.

As we have seen, material-sensual activities should not be seen as somehow opposing the supernatural realm; rather, it is through sensual activity that humans participate in and experience religion, including its "immaterial" elements: incense is a prayer, drums evoke gods, body scarification declares identity, drinking wine and eating bread invoke a shared past, and icons convey supernatural power. Myths, rituals, and symbols define the religious worlds that communities of people inhabit, even as they work in and through the senses to do so. Even sacred texts point to the emotional and evaluative function of the senses.

All traditions use material objects to elicit emotional, physical, and intellectual responses in their adherents. Candles and incense, wine and bread, beads and drums, tattoos and icons: in a real way, religions are lived through their *sensational forms*, as anthropologist of religion Birgit Meyer terms it. Media—whether drums, icons, or worship podcasts—are used to invoke our experience of the sacred, and within religious traditions there are authorized and unauthorized forms and contents of media. Incense and candles are often authorized. Representational images of holy figures are sometimes authorized, sometimes not: Hindus are quite free to display deities represented in human forms, while Jews are not. Likewise, particular musical styles are sometimes authorized, sometimes not, particularly for use in worship or other religious ceremonies. Images of holy figures are only sometimes authorized, and editorial or otherwise "politicized" use of such images can give tremendous offense. Many

Muslims protested the printing of cartoon caricatures of Muhammad in the Danish newspaper *Jyllands-Posten* in 2005. Likewise, many Christians protested Cosimo Cavallaro's sculpture of a crucifixion image of Jesus Christ made entirely out of chocolate and entitled *My Sweet Lord*, when it was displayed in a midtown Manhattan gallery in 2006. The point here is that religious authorities regulate the participation of adherents in sensational forms.[9]

To conclude, let us return to the arts. Artistic expressions are a conduit for innovation and change, in society, culture, and religion. Art sometimes offends religious adherents, but at least as often it spurs devotion and community, helping adherents adapt to new situations and environments. The history of religion reveals that tradition itself changes, adopting and adapting to newer cultural manifestations. These qualities of versatility and innovation allow traditions to remain both fundamentally consistent and adaptable. Through the senses and the sensational forms of the arts, religious practice is felt and experienced in ever-new ways.

Questions for Reflection and Discussion

- How does our language use metaphors that reflect a sensual perception of the world? For example, "Her worldview was influenced by modern philosophy." Or, "She swept me off my feet!" Think of similar examples from religion.

- What sense(s) did you use as you read this chapter? What sense(s) will you use as you demonstrate your knowledge in class? What does this say about how modern education functions?

- If you have attended a worship service unfamiliar to you, or if you were invited over to a new friend's house, how did you feel welcomed in the new place? What was said and done to welcome you?

- Recall the last religious service you attended. What senses were engaged? Was there singing? Flowers to see and smell? Were texts read? If so, what did they look like? Did you eat? Oftentimes, eating takes place just before or after the "official" services: why might this be so?

Additional Resources

Carp, Richard M. 2006. "Teaching Religion and Material Culture." *Teaching Theology and Religion* 10, no. 1: 2–12.

Chidester, David. 1992. *Word and Light: Seeing, Hearing, and Religious Discourse*. Urbana: University of Illinois Press.

Classen, Constance. 1998. *The Color of Angels: Cosmology, Gender, and the Aesthetic Imagination*. New York: Routledge.

Howes, David, ed. 2005. *Empire of the Senses: The Sensual Culture Reader*. New York: Berg Publishers.

Lamothe, Kimerer. 2004. *Between Dancing and Writing: The Practice of Religious Studies*. New York: Fordham University Press.

Meyer, Birgit, ed. 2008. "Media and the Senses." *Material Religion: The Journal of Objects, Art, and Belief*. Special Issue. Oxford, UK: Berg Publishers.

Continued . . .

---

9. See S. Brent Plate, *Blasphemy: Art That Offends* (London: Black Dog Publishing, 2006).

Additional Resources

Continued . . .

Morgan, David. 2005. *The Sacred Gaze: Religious Visual Culture in Theory and Practice.* Berkeley, CA: University of California Press.

Paine, Crispin, ed. 2000. *Godly Things: Museums, Objects, and Religion.* London: Leicester University Press.

Plate, S. Brent, ed. 2002. *Religion, Art, and Visual Culture: A Cross-Cultural Reader.* New York: Palgrave Macmillan.

Sells, Michael. 1999. *Approaching the* Qur'an. Ashland, OR: White Cloud Press.

Seremetakis, C. Nadia, ed. 1994. *The Senses Still: Perception and Memory as Material Culture in Modernity.* Chicago: University of Chicago Press.

Stoller, Paul. 1997. *Sensuous Scholarship.* Philadelphia: University of Pennsylvania Press.

Sullivan, Lawrence E. 1990. "Body Works: Knowledge of the Body in the Study of Religion." *History of Religions* 30 (1), 86–99.

Woogar, C. M. 2006. *The Senses in Late Medieval England.* New Haven, CT: Yale University Press.

CHAPTER 7

RELIGIOUS ETHICS, MORAL VALUES, AND STANDARDS FOR HUMAN CONDUCT

Jack A. Hill
Texas Christian University

Preface

Moral behavior and ethical decision-making are central to any discussion about the study of religion in today's world. Stem cell research, abortion, euthanasia, drug use, and so on, are hotly debated around the world. It is no surprise that religion plays a monumental role in framing conversations about morality with regard to hotly debated ethical issues. While many people are keenly aware of the dynamics associated with these issues, they may not be familiar with how discussions about them presuppose religious values and standards or how they are understood differently in different religious traditions. In this chapter, Jack Hill provides readers with an introductory exploration of religious ethics from a more globally encompassing religious context.

Chapter Goals

- To prompt critical reflection on religious ethics, moral values, and standards for human conduct
- To introduce moral teachings from Islam, Hinduism, and Christianity
- To present basic terms and ideas regarding the study of ethics
- To describe current trends in the international quest for a global religious ethics

INTRODUCTION

Religion and ethics are often mentioned in the same breath. But how *religious ethics* is understood depends on the respective definitions of *religion* and *ethics*. For example, religion is popularly understood to mean believing in and worshipping a god. But there are long-standing religious traditions, such as Theravada Buddhism, which do not espouse belief in a god. Scholars in religious studies generally define *religion* more broadly, for instance, as a means toward ultimate transformation[1] or as an appeal to the transcendent. In other words, religion has to do with reaching far and deep into the most significant wellsprings of our lives, however these are identified. And frequently, this reaching intersects with what we take to be good behavior or right decision-making. In short, religion and ethics seem to work together.

But what is ethics? *Ethics* can be defined as a rigorous reflection on moral experience. Moral experience, in turn, refers to all those times in our lives when we are aware of feeling obliged to be or to do something, or to refrain from being or doing something. It refers to an intuitive sense, learned from childhood, that we *ought* or *ought not* to do thus and so. Thus, *religious* ethics is thinking about this sense of "oughtness" in terms of the teachings of a particular religious tradition. For example, among the great world religious traditions, we have Islamic ethics, Christian ethics, Hindu ethics, and many others.

Religious ethics has spawned a broad, evolving field of study that employs an array of methods to approach its subject. For instance, scholars of religious ethics frequently use comparative, historical, phenomenological, anthropological, or philosophical methods—or various combinations of the above—to glean insights into our ethical behaviors and decisions. But central to all such inquiry is the need to approach religion and ethics in ways that are not simply sectarian or limited to the language and conventions of one faith tradition.

In this chapter, we use a primarily phenomenological approach and begin with a look at three elements of religious ethics that are crucial to making moral choices: facts, worldviews, and values and standards of conduct. Later, a fourth element is introduced—moral decision-making—and four modes of decision-making

A FEW KEY TERMS

Phenomenology is the attempt to understand (or interpret) the elements (or phenomena) of other people's lives as closely as possible to how *they* understand them. It presupposes that all of us to a certain extent construct our own versions of how things are and that our constructions affect how we view other persons' constructions of reality.

The **comparative** method compares similar phenomena and draws general observations. It assumes that it is possible to extract common denominators from varying traditions and sets of behaviors.

Moral values are principles that we cherish, such as compassion, justice, and integrity. We hold such values in high regard and believe we should strive to live by them.

Moral standards are rules of conduct that serve to guide behavior, such as, "Treat others as you would like to be treated" or "Forgive your enemies."

1. *Ways of Being Religious: Readings for a New Approach to Religion*, eds. Frederick J. Streng, Charles L. Lloyd Jr., and Jay T. Allen (Englewood Cliffs, NJ: Prentice-Hall, 1973), 7.

are summarized, with special attention paid to recent developments in liberation and contextual ethics. Following this discussion, the general contours of the religious ethics of three distinct traditions are sketched. We then utilize a comparative approach that suggests how each of these three religious traditions might address an ethical issue: economic justice. Finally we focus on some of the ways religious ethicists are working toward a shared global ethic.

Learning Exercise

Brainstorm about the terms *ethics* and *morality*. In two minutes, write down as many words as you can for each term. Compare and contrast the two lists and then discuss them with three other students. What might these lists suggest about your own sense of ethics? morality? religious ethics?

Questions for Reflection and Discussion

- Can someone who is not religious be ethical? Explain.
- Do you know someone who follows a different religion than your own?

What core moral values do you seem to share with that person?

RELIGION AND MORAL CHOICES: MAKING THE CONNECTION

Many of us associate religion with public worship (at church, temple, or mosque), private ritual (praying or meditating), or holding certain beliefs. Understood in this way, we might wonder how religion connects to making moral choices.

Suppose I'm a practicing Christian. I attend church regularly and read my Bible daily. And then my uncle, who is terminally ill, takes an overdose of sleeping pills and thereby brings about his own death. What am I to think about

this? If the action was intentional, did he do something wrong? The Bible says, "Thou shalt not kill!" but offers no example of someone who was really sick like my uncle. Does that commandment apply to cases like his? And, if not, how do I decide whether he did the right thing?

Such a case poses the kinds of difficult questions that arise in religious ethics. A full-fledged ethical analysis would involve consideration of three elements: facts, worldview, and moral values or standards of conduct.[2] First, we would need to know the *facts* of the situation. Who did what to whom? Was the action intentional or a mistake? And then there is the question of loyalties or commitments to others. Was the decision taken

---

2. In the following paragraph, I draw on the typology used by the Harvard ethicist Ralph Potter in *War and Moral Discourse* (Richmond, VA: Westminster John Knox Press, 1970).

unilaterally or were friends, family, and church members consulted? Was the uncle a member of a euthanasia support or advocacy group—that is, did he belong to a group that believes we have a right to decide how we will die? Did his suicide accord with accepted attitudes and practices in that community?

A second factor is the uncle's *worldview*. A worldview is an individual's perspective, which results from the combination of their attitudes, beliefs, skills, knowledge, education, experiences, and opinions; a person's worldview affects how that individual makes sense of his or her life. Perhaps the uncle believed the end of the world was imminent or perhaps he lived with a profound distrust in himself and others. Or maybe he felt that he had lived a meaningful life but that there was no point in prolonging it at this stage, especially because he wanted to leave his heirs part of his estate. Perhaps his savings were being

exhausted by long-term and what he considered invasive life-supporting medical procedures. And if he were religious, the uncle's worldview would include faith in a transcendent belief system.

To complicate matters further, let's suppose he was a convert to Buddhism. At one level, Buddhists do not believe there is an "I" or personal ego.[3] Thus, from a Buddhist perspective, it could be argued that in overdosing on pills, the uncle was not actually killing a determinate self. On the other hand, Buddhists believe we should have compassion for living beings. Can taking one's life be an act of love toward oneself? an act of un-love? This raises the third element, what are the relevant *moral values* or *standards of conduct*—the norms and principles that guide actions—in a religious tradition and how do I understand or interpret them? How do I apply a fairly abstract standard to a particular case like this one? And what if the religious tradition involved is different from mine?

Learning Exercise

Recall a tough moral decision you made in the last year. Write down three reasons you made that decision. Then ask yourself, "What moral values and standards are implied by each of these reasons?" Write these down. Finally, ask yourself if any of these values or standards come from your own religious faith tradition (whether in sacred scriptures, practices, traditional teachings, or experiences). Congrats! You have just experimented with religious ethics.

Questions for Reflection and Discussion

- What is your view of euthanasia? Give two reasons for your views that relate to the religious tradition with which you are most familiar.

- Think of a time when someone did something to you or someone you know

that you found morally despicable. Describe why you found it so by considering the three elements of ethics (facts, worldviews, and moral values or standards of conduct) discussed so far.

3. In the following gloss of Buddhist ethics, I draw on Hammalawa Saddhatissa, *Buddhist Ethics* (Boston: Wisdom Publications, 1977).

RELIGIOUS ETHICS

Traditionally, ethics is intertwined with reasoning and decision-making, and there are three classic modes for making moral decisions. The first was proposed by the Greek philosopher Aristotle (ca. 384–322 BCE) in *Nichomachean Ethics*.[4] In *Ethics*, Aristotle argues that moral reasoning is concerned with *telos*, the ultimate end of human living. *Telos* is found in the good to which we naturally aspire. For Aristotle, this good was *eudaemonia*, or a sublime happiness. According to Aristotle, we make decisions by judging which course of action will most likely produce the greatest amount of *eudaemonia*. Aristotle's method is known as *teleological ethics*, the ethics of the good.

A second method of ethical decision-making asks not, "What is the end to be achieved?" but rather "Who is the supreme authority?" or "What is the right standard or command to follow?" This mode of decision-making concerns duties or obligations, or *deontics*, and is called *deontological ethics*. A famous deontologist, the German philosopher Immanuel Kant (1724–1804),[5] argued that there are certain standards or principles that are universally valid. Religious adherents who justify a moral judgment by appealing to a law or command in a holy scripture are using a deontological method. And such an appeal can have a double force if it is both an appeal to a "right standard" and that standard is believed to be the command of a divine being. Kant believed that we could determine which standards or principles are universally valid by using reason alone. For example, he talked about a principle of universalization, which said if we can in good conscience will that everyone in a similar circumstance act in a particular way, then it is acceptable to act in that way.

Both teleological and deontological modes of decision-making have weaknesses, however. Teleological ethics presumes we can predict what will achieve the highest good; the consequence is that it can degenerate into a calculating rationality that runs roughshod over the rights of minorities. For example, the English teleologist philosopher Jeremy Bentham (1748–1832)[6] argued that we should always do what will be in the best interests of the greatest number of people for the longest period of time. But this could mean sacrificing the lives of a few for the well being of the many. Deontological ethics, on the other hand, does not consider the consequences of actions. If one must always tell the truth, but telling a lie might prevent someone from being murdered, we are still to tell the truth. In its rigid focus on rules and supreme authorities, deontological ethics may ignore other morally relevant factors.

The third classic mode of decision-making, relational ethics, combines aspects of the first two. In relational ethics, we ask not only what is the standard or authority and what will produce the greatest good, but also what is the most fitting action in this particular situation. It is thus sometimes referred to as situational ethics. In *The Responsible Self*,[7] American Christian theologian H. Richard Niebuhr (1894–1962) argued for a religious ethics that asks, "What is the most fitting response to the way God is acting here and now in this specific place?"

In such an "ethics of response," we need to respond to the broadest range of morally relevant relationships, including our relationship with ourselves, other human beings, communities, nature, and God. We need not only consider values and norms from the past but also anticipate responses to our actions in the future. Relational ethics thus allows for respecting authorities and

4. In *Introduction to Aristotle*, ed. Richard McKeon (New York: Random House, 1974).

5. Immanuel Kant, *Critique of Pure Reason*, trans. F. Max Müller (London: Macmillan, 1881).

6. *A Bentham Reader*, ed. Mary Peter Mack (New York: Pegasus, 1969).

7. *An Essay in Christian Moral Philosophy* (Louisville, KY: Westminster John Knox Press, 1999 [1963]).

time-tested rules as well as for thinking about the likely consequences of actions. But while relational ethics enables us to remain open to teleological and deontological approaches to decision-making, in practice it is often difficult to apply. The problem is not so much whether we appeal to rules or ends, authorities or the greatest good, but *which* rules are relevant, *which* authorities are to be invoked, *which* ends are worthy, and *which* consequences are desired?[8]

Individual scholars reasoning alone about moral experience in the abstract cannot find answers to these questions. Rather, answers are generated by dialoguing with communities of others who self-consciously identify with historically specific social contexts. This brings us to contextual ethics, a fourth mode of decision-making. Contextual ethics allows us to "begin where we are" with our basic experiences of social life and to clarify our values, rules, and notions of good by reflecting on key symbols and narrative themes that are part of the heritage of our people.

What role do symbols have in ethical decision-making? A symbol is any object, person, event, or context that stands for something else. A so-called key symbol is a root metaphor that evokes a set of categories summarizing many aspects of cultural experience. Key symbols might be woodcarvings of the Buddha, holiday gift exchanges, or sacred groves on mountaintops. The physical image of the Buddha, to follow that example, evokes many meanings that have ethical efficacy. The stillness of the statue and the alignment of the posture of the Buddha are invitations to self-control. The eyes of the Buddha evoke ethical teachings such as shunning all evil and purifying the mind. The very size of large statues suggests a greatness of moral stature.

Key symbols are often interwoven in narrative themes. Narrative themes are emotionally charged stories that move communities of people and provide meaning to their lives. The Exodus of the Israelites from captivity, pilgrimages to Mecca, the transformative power of the land, slave revolts on plantations, and women's struggles for equality are all examples of narrative themes in contextual ethics.

Because contextual ethics is rooted in the history of specific traditions, there are many different versions of such ethics. In the South Pacific, for example, contextual ethics is rooted in a strong sense of place—in what islanders call "the Pacific Way." For instance, in the Fiji Islands, there is an allegiance to what Fijians call the *vanua*. The *vanua* refers to the land with which a person or group is identified, together with its flora and fauna, and to the people—living and deceased—who are associated with that locale. The *vanua* is a key symbol for all the social protocols, myths, rituals, ancestors, and Fijians who are associated with the land. The *vanua* gives rise to narratives of interpersonal sharing or mutual aid, known as *kere kere* (responsible exchange), and hierarchical notions of good conduct, known as the *vakaturaga* (chiefly path).[9]

During the last forty years, contextual ethics has given rise to liberation ethics, especially in Latin America, Asia, and Africa, and among women and persons of color in North America. For these ethicists, "liberation" symbolizes freedom from social, economic, and political subjugation. A central narrative in Western religious liberation thought is that the God of the ancient Israelites is a God of liberation, working to free oppressed peoples everywhere. In Latin American countries under oppressive military dictatorships, Christian liberation theologians reimagine

---

8. See Charles L. Kammer III. *Ethics and Liberation: An Introduction* (Maryknoll, NY: Orbis Books, 1988).

9. See the detailed discussion of Fijian mores in Asesela D. Ravuvu, *The Fijian Ethos* (Suva, Fiji: Institute of Pacific Studies, University of the South Pacific, 1987).

faith and life as "one salvation history"—where people are simultaneously being liberated from legacies of imperialism, poverty, and religious hegemony.[10] Teaching in the North American context, the Hispanic ethicist Miguel De La Torre[11] emphasizes the theme of solidarity with the world's have-nots and critiques capitalism and classist biases—or attitudes reflective of social class advantages. The Hispanic ethicist Julio de Santa Ana argues that economic systems can cause ecological imbalance and poverty.[12] Using the Holocaust as an ethical lens, the Jewish liberation theologian Marc Ellis argues that a liberation ethic is embedded in the Exodus.[13] And in India, the Buddhist liberationist B. R. Ambedkar calls for an "emancipatory identity," arguing that one cannot pursue one's own enlightenment without struggling against social injustice and poverty in the wider community.[14]

African American theologians such as James Cone (in *God of the Oppressed*)[15] and J. Deotis Roberts (in *Black Theology in Dialogue*)[16] stress the need for liberation from racism (systems that produce race-based advantages) and economic oppression. Labeling all white ethics "satanic," Cone calls for the aggressive dismantling of white privilege, the affirmation of black history, and the realization of Martin Luther King's vision of the "beloved community." In this community, we stand in solidarity with the poor in the "two-thirds world," the developing countries at the periphery of the developed countries, or the much-advantaged "one-third world." (Pockets of poverty also exist within the latter.) Using humanist principles as an ethical framework, the African American liberationist Anthony Pinn calls for a nonsectarian, fuller sense of being.[17]

Feminist ethics represents a rethinking of ethics that critiques male bias, or the ideology of patriarchy—a system of ideas that excludes women and rationalizes their subordination. Drawing on women's experiences of oppression, Christian feminist ethicists question traditional interpretations of biblical passages, cite historical evidence showing that churches reflect cultural influences, and seek to recover unheard women's voices from church history. In *Feminist Theological Ethics*,[18] Lois Daly envisions a nonsexist world in which a more just community that nurtures reciprocity and friendly coalitions replaces a male ethos of domination and hierarchy.

African American women ethicists approach ethics from the standpoint of those who have not only experienced sexism but also racism. Affirming their roots in the black church, many African American women ethicists self-identify as "Womanists" rather than as feminists. They critique the white, middle-class presuppositions implicit in feminist ethics, along with the sexism

10. Gustavo Gutiérrez, *A Theology of Liberation: History, Politics, and Salvation* (Maryknoll, NY: Orbis Books, 1973).

11. *Doing Christian Ethics from the Margins* (Maryknoll, NY: Orbis Books, 2004).

12. In Leonardo Boff and Virgilio Elizondo, eds., *Ecology and Poverty: Cry of the Earth, Cry of the Poor* (Maryknoll, NY: Orbis Books, 1995).

13. *Toward a Jewish Theology of Liberation*, 3rd ed. (Waco, TX: Baylor University Press, 2004).

14. See Surendra Jondhale and Johannes Beltz, eds. *Reconstructing the World: B. R. Ambedkar and Buddhism in India* (New Delhi: Oxford University Press, 2004).

15. (New York: Seabury Press, 1975).

16. (Philadelphia: Westminster John Knox Press, 1987).

17. *African American Humanist Principles: Living and Thinking Like the Children of Nimrod* (New York: Palgrave/Macmillan, 2004).

18. Lois K. Daly, ed., *Feminist Theological Ethics: A Reader* (Louisville, KY: Westminster John Knox Press, 1994).

in male ethics generally. The Womanist Katie Cannon calls for a recognition of black women's contributions to the church and academia[19] and the Womanist Marcia Riggs champions a new nonracist, nonheterosexist vision of reconciliation and justice.[20]

Learning Exercise

Revisit the moral decision you wrote about in the previous learning exercise. In reasoning about that decision, were you more of a deontologist, teleologist, or relationalist? How so? Discuss how factors associated with your own racial, economic, and cultural context may have influenced your decision.

Questions for Reflection and Discussion

- How would you define "the highest good"? How could you reorder your life to more effectively and consistently realize that good?

- Were you familiar with any of the perspectives of contextual ethicists? If so, when and where did you learn about them? If not, why do you think you have never been exposed to those perspectives?

LAWS, PATHS, AND PRINCIPLES OF MORAL CONDUCT

Religious ethics is concerned with discovering, discerning, and clarifying basic sources of moral guidance for the faithful. As noted in the previous section, for some believers, these sources already exist in the form of laws or rules that are prescribed as binding by a supreme authority. For others, moral guidance is progressively discovered by following a way or path; that is, by conforming one's mode of conduct to a course or scenario of duty or discipleship. For still others, sources of guidance are created through processes of discernment that involve deriving principles or generalizations of fundamental truths from reflection on texts, long-standing traditions, reason, and personal experience.

Most religious ethical systems involve combinations of all three types of sources. Moreover, each system entails different ways of interpreting sources of moral guidance. Therefore, we need to be mindful of the complexity and variety of ethical stances, even within one tradition. It is possible, nonetheless, to generalize about the core features of moral conduct in quite different religions. Let us consider examples from Islamic, Christian, and Hindu traditions.

Islamic Moral Teachings: The Straight Path of Kindness

Since the events of 9/11, there has been a renewed focus on the religion of Islam in the international media. It is also probably safe to say that no religion has been subject to more negative

19. *Black Womanist Ethics* (Atlanta, GA: Scholars Press, 1988).
20. *A Womanist Call for Black Liberation* (Cleveland, OH: Pilgrim Press, 1994).

stereotyping in the United States than Islam. The Arabic word *Islam* is a verbal noun, the infinitive of a verb meaning "to submit," or even "to surrender"; but in modern religious language it might also be rendered as "to commit."[21] The word implies submission to the will of Allah, or God. A Muslim is one who makes or does *Islam*; that is, one who lives out a faith commitment to Allah. Muslims believe that Allah's intentions for humanity are revealed in the Qur'an, a sacred text disclosed to the prophet Muhammad (ca. 570–632 CE) and mediated in the *hadith*, teachings and accounts that reportedly convey what Muhammad said and did.[22]

As Islam spread to different parts of the world, four schools of Muslim *fiqh*, or jurisprudence, developed.[23] These schools each represent a different way to study *shari'ah* (Islamic Law). Although *shari'ah* is usually translated as "law" in English, it means "path" or "road" in the Qur'an (45:18).[24] While the Qur'an and *hadith* are the first and second sources of *shari'ah*, Muslims can also appeal to *ijma*, or the consensus of the community. Finally, if a question cannot be resolved by reference to the Qur'an, *hadith*, or *ijma*, then one can use *qiyas*, or reasonings by analogy through *Ijtihad* (exerting personal effort to form a legal opinion).

Islamic standards of moral conduct are thus specified in the *shari'ah* and issue from a personal commitment to Allah.[25] This commitment is acknowledged in the first three verses of the *al-Fatihah*, the opening to the Qur'an that is recited in everyday prayers: "Show us the straight way."[26] Since Allah is depicted as *al-Rahman*, or "the compassionate one,"[27] followers of Allah seek to walk the "straight way," and *shari'ah* originally meant "the path leading to water."[28]

Islamic ethics could be characterized as "the straight path of kindness that leads to the source of life." This path is lived out in five "pillars" or practices:[29]

- *Shahada*—profession of faith ("I testify that there is no God but Allah and Muhammad is Allah's messenger.")
- *Salat*—ritual prayer fives times daily
- *Zakat*—giving resources to help others
- *Sawm*—spiritual discipline of fasting
- *Hajj*—pilgrimage to Mecca

Each of the pillars provides a framework for moral values and standards. In affirming the absolute oneness of God, the *shahada* forbids *shirk*, or the association of Allah with anything from the created world.[30] An example would be worshipping an idol made by humans. The act of physically bowing down in s*alat* engenders a strong sense of unity with others as well as a

---

21. Charles J. Adams, ed., "Islam," in *A Reader's Guide to the Great Religions* (New York: Free Press, 1968), 287–288.

22. Toshihiko Izutsu, *Ethico-Religious Concepts in the Qur'an* (Montreal, QC: McGill University Press, 1966), 18.

23. For a highly readable discussion of the principle schools, see Neal Robinson, *Islam: A Concise Introduction* (Washington, DC: Georgetown University Press, 2007), 149–160.

24. John Kaltner, *Islam: What Non-Muslims Should Know* (Minneapolis: Fortress Press, 2003), 55.

25. As Esposito remarks, "It is here that we see the roots of Islamic ethics. God ordains; humankind is to implement His will"; *Islam: The Straight Path* (New York: Oxford University Press, 2005), 26.

26. Ali Ahmed, *Al-Qur'an: A Contemporary Translation by Ahmed Ali* (Princeton, NJ: Princeton University Press, 1988), 11.

27. Reuben Levy, *The Social Structure of Islam* (Cambridge, UK: Cambridge University Press, 1965), 194.

28. Frederick Streng, *Ways of Being Religious: Readings for a New Approach to Religion* (Englewood Cliffs, NJ: Prentice-Hall, 1973), 237.

29. See Theodore M. Ludwig, *The Sacred Paths: Understanding the Religions of the World* (Upper Saddle River, NJ: Prentice Hall, 2001), 465–468.

30. Kaltner, *Islam*, 54.

disposition of submission toward Allah. In practicing *zakat*, Muslims share a portion of their wealth to help the poor, those in debt, and those in need. During *sawm*, Muslims are to be particularly mindful of donating money and food to the needy. They should take care not to be wasteful. And during *hajj*, when everyone dresses alike in white garments, Muslims experience a powerful egalitarian spirit with others of different races, cultures, and social classes.[31]

These practices, in turn, entail moral predispositions, such as justice and fairness in financial dealings; showing compassion toward all human beings, including one's enemies; giving due regard to nonhuman creatures and nature—plants, animals, and the ecosystem; and comporting oneself in a lawful manner regarding dress, diet, the consumption of beverages, and cleanliness.[32] While some individuals, such as the 9/11 terrorists, have appealed to Islamic sources to justify violent acts of martyrdom, both the Qur'an and *hadith* forbid suicide. Indeed, Muslims adhere to a principle of "no-harm" to oneself and to others. Furthermore, the Arabic word *jihad* does not mean "holy war." Rather, it connotes both an internal spiritual "striving" (which the *hadith* call "the greater *jihad*") and the effort required to expand the Islamic community ("the lesser *jihad*").[33] While the latter may sometimes require military activity, many Qur'an passages stress that warfare is only justifiable when it is a defensive response to attack; and, in any case, most Muslims are primarily concerned with the greater *jihad*.

The Ten Commandments in Islam (Qur'an 17:23–39) prohibit certain acts such as adultery and exploitation of orphans, while extolling virtues such as forgiveness, peace, balance, kindness, and humility. Gambling, stealing, and fornication outside of marriage are strongly prohibited in Islam. Nevertheless, there are differing viewpoints on issues such as polygamy (a marriage in which a husband takes more than one wife), divorce, and women's dress.[34]

Christian Moral Teachings: The Sacrificial Way of Discipleship

Just as Islamic ethics cannot be separated from the Muslim's faith commitment to Allah, so Christian ethics is incomprehensible apart from the Christian's faith in God as revealed and modeled by Jesus Christ (ca. 4 BCE–27 CE). Jesus Christ is believed to be a unique incarnation of God, or at the least an extraordinary human being. He was born in Palestine as a carpenter's son nearly two thousand years ago, was crucified, buried and, according to the majority of Christians, rose from the dead. Christians are those who profess to follow Jesus' precepts and example, as disclosed in the New Testament, although most Christians also appeal to the entire Bible as the full narrative of God's working in history. Because the lynchpin of this narrative is God's sacrifice of Godself for the redemption of humankind in the person of Jesus, and those who follow Jesus commit themselves to walking in his footsteps, Christian ethics could be described as the sacrificial way of discipleship.

In addition to biblical sources, Christians draw moral insight from church traditions, individual conscience, guidance from the Holy Spirit, and reason. Given the wide range of sources for moral guidance in Christianity, it is especially

31. Ibid., 75.

32. I am indebted to Dr. Yushau Sodiq, my colleague at Texas Christian University (TCU), for these and other insights about Islamic mores noted in the subsequent paragraph.

33. Kaltner, *Islam*, 123.

34. Ibid., 89–92.

difficult to generalize about a single Christian ethic. As in Islam, there are different strands of adherents. But whether Roman Catholic, Protestant, or Orthodox, all Christians claim to be following in the way of Jesus. We can therefore glean hints about Christian standards of moral conduct by referring to the sayings and doings of Jesus in the New Testament. His so-called Great Commandments (Mt 22:37–40)—that we should love God with all our heart, soul, and mind, and love our neighbor as our self—accent the centrality of *agape*, an other-oriented, sacrificial love, in Christian discipleship.[35] We are to love one another as God loves us, unconditionally. As in Islam, this love is to extend beyond family and kin to the larger community, including one's enemies.

Although he was thoroughly Jewish, revered the Hebrew Bible, and participated in Jewish religious rituals, Jesus—like the Jewish prophets of the Bible—often criticized that tradition as it was practiced in his day. His message centered on the kingdom of God, or the prophetic reign of God in relation to the covenant people. This rule included the teachings of the Law (or the "Torah," understood as the first five books of the Hebrew Bible). Christians often appeal to the Ten Commandments (Ex 20:1–17 or Deut 5:6–21) found in the Torah as moral guides. The rule of God also included the Prophets (or those who heard and voiced the admonitions and expectations of God) and the Writings (or psalms, narratives, and practical, commonsense wisdom for everyday life).

In his preaching about the kingdom, however, Jesus shifted the focus from what he perceived as an overly legalistic concern with ritual cleanliness and observance of the Sabbath to the urgency of embodying the two great commandments. In the Sermon on the Mount (Mt 5:1—7:29), Jesus challenges followers to a path of discipleship that lifts up those who hunger and thirst, the merciful, the peacemakers, the pure of heart, and the persecuted. He warns against harboring enmity, jealousy, and lustful thoughts in one's heart, even if one is outwardly righteous. Further, Christians are to love their enemies, pray for their persecutors, turn the other cheek if someone assaults them, and model God's justice. They are to avoid hypocrisy in their observance of rituals and forgive the wrongs others have done to them. They are not to be attached to worldly possessions or overly concerned for their own livelihoods or social status.

Many ethicists have stressed the need to view these so-called hard-sayings of Jesus in the light of the pervasive expectation in first-century Palestine that the old world was coming to an end and that God would bring about a new rule—either through the Messiah, who would lead a military movement and/or facilitate God's seizing direct control of nations, or through a catastrophic end and the creation of a whole new order. Whether or not Jesus himself shared this expectation, he did appear to proclaim a radical, thoroughgoing, challenging obedience to God—that is, he advocated a straight and narrow path and even his closest disciples struggled to keep the discipline.

As a consequence, beyond a very general appeal to the standard of *agape*, today's Christians espouse a wide variety of moral principles. Many evangelical Christians stress adherence to the Ten Commandments (Ex 20:2–17), injunctions from other law codes in Leviticus and Exodus, and warnings about the end time. Thus, they condemn adultery, stealing, murder, lying, and coveting others' possessions. Many Christians also stress Jesus' teachings about reaching out to the poor, joining in solidarity with the marginalized, and working for peace and justice

---

35. In this section, I draw extensively on Wayne A. Meeks, *The Origins of Christian Morality: The First Two Centuries* (New Haven, CT: Yale University Press, 1993).

in social and political affairs. However, a number of what might be termed mainline Christians strive for a "good, middle-class morality," where they uphold the civil laws, attend church services regularly, give tithes and offerings for the needy, and otherwise try to treat one another with loving kindness, but refrain from joining movements for social change or risking the loss of material prosperity.

Hindu Moral Teachings: Living in Harmony with the Dharma

Unlike Islam and Christianity, Hindu moral teachings are not integral to one central text, such as the Qur'an or Bible, both of which are believed to be uniquely authoritative. Also, the term *Hindu*, which is derived from a name applied by foreigners to people living in the region of the Indus River, is not particularly helpful for identifying a religious ethic.[36] A more definitive label is *Sanatana Dharma*. *Sanatana* means "eternal" or "ageless."[37] *Dharma*, frequently translated as "religion," is derived from the root *dhr*, meaning "to sustain."[38] *Dharma* is therefore action that dutifully sustains the cosmic order, including natural law, social welfare, morals, and health.

By the first centuries of the Common Era, there were many treatises in India, called the *dharmashastras*, on the nature of righteousness and moral duty, and these became foundational for later Hindu laws.[39] The most famous of these was the *Manava Dharmashastra*, or Laws of Manu, which specified a caste (or social class) system and recognized four distinct *ashramas*, or stages of life.[40] But the *dharma* was also vividly and dramatically portrayed in great epics, especially in the *Mahabharata* and the *Ramayana*. Thus, we can characterize Hindu ethics as living in harmony with the *dharma*, whether articulated in a law code or dramatized in a narrative.

A second problem the Westerner confronts in understanding Hindu ethics is that there is always a dialectical relationship between two experiences of reality: this world of the senses, in which we have *dharma* duties to fulfill, and *moksha*, or the experience of liberation, where *dharma* duties are superseded.[41] Thus, while focusing on living in accordance to the *dharma*, one must remain conscious that this mode of right conduct is bound up in a world of *karma*, or causation, that one ultimately seeks to move beyond.

But while living within the sensory world of *karma*, where one's present circumstances are determined by one's soul's past deeds and all of one's current actions determine one's future circumstances, one should perform *dharma*, or specific duties, to the best of one's ability. There are two sets of obligations that determine these duties. The first consists of the *sadharanadharma*, or the everyday norms and values applicable to all persons regardless of age or caste, such as honesty, respect for the property and well being of others, patience, selfless action, noninjury, forbearance, and *ahimsa*, or nonviolence.[42] The second, the

---

36. Mary Fisher, *Living Religions*. 6th ed. (Upper Saddle River, NJ: Prentice-Hall, 2005), 69.

37. Ibid.

38. William Theodore de Bary, *Sources of Indian Tradition* (New York: Columbia University Press, 1958), 211.

39. Ludwig, *Sacred Paths*, 109.

40. Heinrich Zimmer, *Philosophies of India*, ed. Joseph Campbell (Princeton, NJ: Princeton University Press, 1953), 152–153. See also, Émile Senant, *Caste in India* (London: Methuen and Company, 1930), 94.

41. I am indebted to Dr. Andrew O. Fort, my colleague in the T. C .U. Religion Department, for this insight about the *dharma* duties.

42. Adams, *Reader's Guide*, 54–55.

varnashramadharma, are prescriptions associated with one's caste and station in life. For example, those in the highest caste, the Brahmans, are priests and philosophers who are responsible for teaching and guidance on spirituality and the good life. As bearers of liberation, they are to model virtues such as purity, wisdom, and inner peace. The *kshatriyas*, or the soldiers and administrators, are responsible for guarding and preserving society. As such, they are expected to exemplify courage and majesty. In an analogous way, there are different obligations for different *ashramas*. If one is at the student stage, one should strive to listen, learn, and develop one's skills and intellectual capabilities. But if one is at the householder stage, then one must provide for one's family and contribute to the community.

Consequently, when asking about standards of human conduct in Hindu religious ethics, one must always inquire about specific cases and the circumstances of the actors involved. It is erroneous to view oneself as an autonomous actor apart from one's social location. Perhaps the most celebrated case is that of the mythical figure Arjuna, in the Bhagavad-Gita,[43] a story within the larger *Mahabharata*. Arjuna is a warrior who questions whether or not he should fight and kill family members in battle. At one point he declares, "I will not fight." But eventually, acting in devotion to Krishna, he enters the battle. And in this instance, service to Krishna becomes a way of acting in accordance with the *dharma* duties associated with his caste.

Learning Exercise

Imagine that you are a parent of a 10-year-old daughter. She wants to see a very violent film, *The Texas Chainsaw Massacre*. It includes graphic scenes of violence and the abuse of women. Based on one of the traditions of the moral teachings outlined above, how would you advise her? Explain how you have drawn on laws, paths, or principles of moral conduct in that tradition in formulating your advice.

Questions for Reflection and Discussion

- Look up the different versions of the Ten Commandments in the Qur'an (17:23–39) and in the Bible (Ex 20:1–17). How are these versions similar to and different from each other?

- What are the strengths and weaknesses of a moral system, such as Hinduism, that is grounded in the performance of duties associated with one's caste and stage of life? How does this differ from Islamic teaching?

---

43. The Gita is an interpolation from the *Mahabharata*, which was compiled between 400 BCE and 400 CE. It is composed mainly of episodes from the *kshatriya* clans. See Creighton Lacy, *The Conscience of India: Moral Traditions in the Modern World* (New York: Holt, Rinehart and Winston, 1965), 20.

RELIGIOUS MORAL TEACHINGS AND CONTEMPORARY ETHICAL ISSUES

Faith and Moral Decision-Making in Modern Societies

Just as each religious tradition understands standards of moral conduct differently, so each tradition has a distinct approach to applying those standards to contemporary ethical issues. Even when reflecting on how religious adherents apply their ethical standards to contemporary issues, we need to be careful about making generalizations. Let us consider a case in point.

A Comparative Illustration: Economic Justice

Looking to the Qur'an and the practices of Muhammad for guidance on economic behavior, Muslims affirm private ownership of property and aspirations for material progress and prosperity.[44] Nevertheless, since Allah is the owner of all creation, humans are to act as stewards, managing Allah's wealth effectively and using surplus wealth for the common good. In particular, *zakat* requires that at least 2.5 percent of all wealth be spent on the needy each year.[45] While recognizing that there will be economic disparity, everyone should get what is rightfully theirs, and there should not be undue concentrations of wealth in the hands of a few. Two distinctive features of Islamic economic justice are the condemnation of usury, especially interest as a source of income, and the belief that those who

are unable to work, or those whose work cannot provide them with their basic needs, have a right to share in the wealth of the community. In some Muslim societies, however, there has been a gap between these ideals of economic justice and realities of poverty and economic oppression imposed by authorities. Nevertheless, the essential egalitarian nature of a massive public ritual such as the hajj, functions in a practical way to let the rich and poor recognize their equal status before God.

Like Muslims, most Christians affirm private property ownership and the value of material prosperity, and many also draw on biblical principles to argue that laissez-faire (meaning, noninterference by the government) capitalism is especially compatible with Christianity because of its association with individual liberty. Yet other Christians who also cite biblical teachings condemn capitalism as a greedy, exploitative system and call for greater government regulation. The former argue that while Jesus challenges us to be charitable to the poor, he also preached that there would always be poverty (Mk 14:7). Max Weber, a German sociologist of religion, stipulated the "Protestant ethic thesis," which argues that Protestant Christianity fueled the spirit of capitalism by emphasizing work as a religious calling, worldly asceticism, rationalism, and virtues such as thriftiness and punctuality.[46] On the other hand, recognizing the growing gap between rich and poor in our times, Pope John Paul II (1920–2005) called for a transformation of the structure of economic life toward the abolition of poverty worldwide.[47] So while some Christians are calling for systemic economic

---

44. William A. Young, *The World's Religions: Worldviews and Contemporary Issues* (Englewood Cliffs, NJ: Prentice Hall, 1995), 377.

45. Ibid.

46. *The Protestant Ethic and the Spirit of Capitalism* (New York: Charles Scribner's Sons, 1958).

47. Young, *World's Religions*, 339.

changes, including changed spending priorities and higher tax rates for businesses and individuals with incomes in the top percentiles, many Christian societies harbor the world's wealthiest individuals while simultaneously tolerating increasing levels of homelessness and the growth of a permanent underclass.

According to traditional Hindu moral teaching, *artha* (wealth or material prosperity) and *kama* (sensual pleasure) were valued and seen as compatible with *dharma* duties, at least for the majority of castes, and especially for persons in the householder stage.[48] People are supposed to live the good life in the sense of worldly attainments. However, wealth or poverty was believed to be a result of one's *karma* or accumulated actions over previous lives. Therefore, while outsiders might perceive large gaps in wealth between rich and poor in India as evidence of social injustice, such gaps would be viewed by traditional Hindu teaching as inevitable outcomes of *karma*. Nonetheless, partly as a result of the movement led by the Hindu reformer Mahatma Gandhi, the modern state of India has outlawed discrimination based on caste.[49] Gandhi and other reformers used the idea of *ahimsa* (noninjury) to inaugurate programs designed to alleviate poverty, hunger, and homelessness. Some religious orders have set up clinics and centers to reduce human suffering. Also, the government's provision of welfare, including food and housing assistance, has reduced the percentage of Indians living in poverty. Nevertheless, India remains a highly stratified society in which a minority enjoys considerable wealth, and Hindu traditionalist movements, though still somewhat marginal, are pressuring against the dismantling of the caste system.

Learning Exercise

Consider a pressing social ethical issue such as war or abortion. Refer to the previous section on "Laws, Paths, and Principles of Moral Conduct" and apply insights from that section to one of those issues. Explain three ways that a Muslim or Christian might view the issue differently from a Hindu.

Questions for Reflection and Discussion

- Do you think there are "natural" gender roles for women and men? Does your religion affect your view on this question?

- What is your view on capital punishment (or state executions)? How can you reconcile or justify your view with your faith tradition?

---

48. Ludwig, *Sacred Paths*, 112.

49. Young, *World's Religions*, 128.

THE QUEST FOR A GLOBAL RELIGIOUS ETHICS

Given the great diversity of systems of religious ethics, the question arises, is it possible to discover a common set of values, rules, or principles that underlie all religious systems? From a monotheistic standpoint, if there is one Creator, should there not also be one set of ethical aims or purposes for humankind? Even if one acknowledges the validity of nonmonotheistic traditions such as Buddhism, cannot humans, reasoning together, find common ground in values that are universally shared?

In 1993, religious leaders from all the major faiths came together at the Parliament of the World's Religions and agreed on a number of core ethical principles, which were published as the *Declaration Toward a Global Ethic*. The *Declaration* reflected the ideas of Hans Küng, a German theologian who had previously argued that all the major faiths expressed a version of the golden rule ("do as you would be done unto").[50] However, this proposal has been criticized as imposing Western values on non-Western religious traditions.[51] In this regard, in 1995, participants in the Commission on Global Governance advocated a "global civic ethic" (*Our Global Neighborhood*)[52] that does not claim to espouse timeless, universal moral truths, but rather outlines lists of values and rights that are needed to live successfully in the modern world.

Other scholars believe that the *Earth Charter*—a set of ethical principles developed in 2000 by the Earth Council, an international nongovernmental organization based in Costa Rica—provides a global ethic that is capable of being widely shared, if not universally accepted. In its emphases on respect for the earth and life in all its forms, love, and the building of just, participatory, and sustainable societies, it provides a set of principles that emerged from an extensive process of worldwide consultation and can be accepted as a practical tool to deal with common problems and threats to human well being.

Questions for Reflection and Discussion

- Identify three or four core ethical values that are shared by all three of the religions discussed in this chapter. Do you think these would be shared by all religions? Why or why not?

- If you were going to engage in interfaith dialogue with people from different faith traditions, what steps might you take to restrain or reduce your own biases prior to the dialogue?

50. In this subsection, I draw on Nigel Dower's article "The Nature and Scope of Global Ethics and the Relevance of the *Earth Charter*," *Journal of Global Ethics* 1, no. 1 (June 2005): 25–43.

51. The recent enterprise globethics.net represents an attempt to expand the range of participants worldwide who contribute to shaping the global ethics discourse. This network of institutions and persons is particularly concerned with including voices from the developing countries of the south and with engaging participants with different worldviews.

52. (Oxford, UK: Oxford University Press, 1995). Cited in Dower, "Nature and Scope."

Additional Resources

An, Ok-Sun. 1998. *Compassion and Benevolence: A Comparative Study of Early Buddhist and Classical Confucian Ethics*. New York: Peter Lang.

Berquist, Jon L., ed. 2002. *Strike Terror No More: Theology, Ethics, and the New War*. St. Louis: Chalice.

Cannon, Katie G. 1988. *Black Womanist Ethics*. Atlanta, GA: Scholar's Press.

Chapple, Christopher Key, and Mary Evelyn, eds. 2000. *Hinduism and Ecology*. Cambridge, MA: Harvard University Press.

De La Torre, Miguel A. 2004. *Doing Christian Ethics from the Margins*. Maryknoll, NY: Orbis Books.

Dorff, Elliot N. 2003. *Love Your Neighbor and Yourself: A Jewish Approach to Modern Personal Ethics*. Philadelphia: Jewish Publications Society.

Elizondo, Virgilio. 2000. *The Future Is Mestizo: Life Where Cultures Meet*. Boulder: University Press of Colorado.

Ellis, Marc. 2004. *Toward a Jewish Theology of Liberation*. 3rd ed. Waco, TX: Baylor University Press.

Ellison, Marvin. 2004. *Same-Sex Marriage?* Cleveland: Pilgrim Press.

Fasching, Darrell J., and Dell DeChant. 2001. *Comparative Religious Ethics: A Narrative Approach*. Malden, MA: Blackwell Publishers.

Harvey, Peter. 2000. *An Introduction to Buddhist Ethics: Foundations, Values, and Issues*. New York: Cambridge.

Hashmi, Sohail H., ed. 2002. *Islamic Political Ethics: Civil Society, Pluralism and Conflict*. Princeton, NJ: Princeton University Press.

Küng, Hans, and Karl-Josef Kuschel, eds. 1993. *A Global Ethic: The Declaration of the Parliament of the World's Religions*. New York: Continuum International Publishing Group.

Newman, Louis, ed. 2005. *Introduction to Jewish Ethics*. Upper Saddle River, NJ: Prentice Hall.

Pinn, Anthony. 2004. *African American Humanist Principles: Living and Thinking Like the Children of Nimrod*. New York: Palgrave/Macmillan.

Sharma, Arvind, and Katherine T. Young. *Feminism and the World Religions*. Albany: State University of New York Press, 1999.

Sideris, Lisa H. 2003. *Environmental Ethics, Ecological Theology, and Natural Selection*. New York: Columbia University Press.

Villafane, Eldin. *The Liberating Spirit: Toward an Hispanic American Pentecostal Social Ethic*. Grand Rapids, MI: Eerdmans, 2003.

Marx, Werner. 1992. *Towards a Phenomenological Ethics: Ethos and the Life-World*. Albany: State University of New York Press.

West, Traci C. 2006. *Disruptive Christian Ethics: When Racism and Women's Lives Matter*. Louisville, KY: Westminster John Knox Press.

Web Resources

Global Ethics

www.globalethics.org, Institute for Global Ethics.

www.globethics.net, international network for sharing values across cultures and religions.

www.wabashcenter.wabash.edu, an expansive listing of resources, including on interreligious dialogue, religion, and violence.

Christianity

http://www.iclnet.org/pub/resources/christian-history.html, "Early Christian Texts," provides full-text versions of creeds and writings of early theologians.

http://goon.stg.brown.edu/bible_browser/pbeasy.shtml, a search tool that allows users to locate words or phrases relating to ethics and morality in numerous versions of the Bible.

http://www.vpm.com/thawes, "Theology on the Web," a collection of links relating to Christianity and ethics.

Continued . . .

Additional Resources

Continued . . .

Hinduism

http://kaladarshan.arts.OH-state.edu/exhib/meetgod/hp.thml, excellent exhibit on elements of Hindu devotion.

http://rbhatnagar.csm,uc.edu:8080/scriptures.html, "The Hindu Electronic Scriptures Reference Center," provides full texts in English translation of several Hindu scriptures including the *Mahabharata*.

http://virtualreligion.net/vri/hindu.html, a good collection of Web sites on Hinduism.

Islam

www.Islamist.org/images/ethicshm.pdf, provides images relevant to study of Islamic ethics.

www.princeton.edu/~humcomp/alkhaz.html, "Al-Khazina: The Treasury," an educational Web site with links to information on the *Qur'an, Hadith*, and *Hajj* databases.

http://wings.buffalo.edu/student-life/sa/muslim/isl/texts.html, different links to the hypertext version of the Qur'an along with sound files of recitations.

VIOLENCE AND RELIGION

Dr. Darlene Fozard Weaver
Villanova University

Preface

Questions about the connection between religion and violence have been prevalent since the inception of studies in religion. What might be different today is a heightened interest in religiously motivated violence. Perceptions of what constitutes violence vary greatly according to religious tradition and understandings of those traditions. For example, for some religious adherents, conversion from one faith to another might be considered an act of violence, for it destroys at the same time as it seeks to provide a place for the creative power of the sacred to take root. Some believers justify violence as necessary to preserve "truth" and root out "falsehood." Since the terrorist attacks of September 11, 2001—and even before this event—people have been made painfully aware that some branches of religion espouse violence to enforce and export convictions about what is right and wrong. Some believers are convinced their deity ordains their activities to cleanse the earth and exert divine will over others. Reasons cited for religious violence range from hermeneutic to economic to social to cultural factors. In this chapter, Darlene Weaver explores various connections between violence and religion.

Chapter Goals

- To explore how religious discourse can lead to moral recoding that facilitates violence
- To consider explanations for the connection between human acts of violence and religious convictions, beliefs, and practices
- To invite readers to examine their own religious and ethical commitments in relation to religion and violence

INTRODUCTION

History provides ample evidence that human acts of violence may be motivated by and justified through appeal to religious beliefs. The terrorist attacks on the United States by radical Islamic fundamentalists on September 11, 2001, and ongoing sectarian violence in the Middle East offer recent examples.

Historical and contemporary examples of religious violence are found in every major world religion. During the Crusades (1096–1270 CE), Christians killed Jews and Muslims. In World War II (1939–1945), Christian anti-Semites aided and abetted the German Nazis' mass slaughter of Jewish people. Hindus and Muslims continue what may be a centuries-old battle in Kashmir. Buddhist-inspired Asahara Shoko and Aum Shinrikyo members released deadly nerve gas in Japanese subway stations in 1995. Some religious adherents fight members of their own traditions — Protestant and Catholic Christians in Northern Ireland, Sunnis and Shi'ites in Iraq. Sadly, we could go on and on. Moreover, these examples refer only to overt forms of violence that inflict bodily harm or kill.[1] Religiously sponsored violence also includes such things as: psychological harm through mechanisms that induce shame, guilt, and social isolation; sexual assault and the beliefs and practices that make people, especially women and children, vulnerable to it; life-threatening economic deprivation; and environmental damage. In short, any sort of violence that human beings can do to themselves, other persons, and creation itself can be motivated by and find some justification through appeals to religion.

Is religion inherently violent? This chapter will seek a nuanced answer to this question. First, we will consider what counts as religion and what counts as violence. As a category, religion is complex. As a phenomenon, religion cannot be separated neatly from other aspects of human culture. Second, we will introduce readers to several theories about religion and violence. Each theory points to a central problem surrounding religious truth-claims and morality. We will argue that there are particular features of religion that can lead to violence. Specifically, religious truth-claims can facilitate violence by morally "recoding" our perceptions to justify violence against persons we think deserve our wrath. To discover what can be done about such moral recoding, we will draw from the theories of religion and violence discussed here.

Questions for Reflection and Discussion

- What has been your experience with religion and violence?

- Is religion inherently violent? Why or why not?

- In what ways might religion "recode" human perceptions about the use or restraint of violence?

---

1. What counts as bodily harm is open to debate. Consider female genital cutting, or other practices of altering human bodies. See *Religion and the Body*, Sarah Coakley, ed. (Cambridge, UK: Cambridge University Press, 2000) and David Hollenbach, SJ, "Human Rights and Women's Rights: Initiatives and Interventions in the Name of Universality," in Maura A. Ryan and Brian F. Linnane, SJ, eds., *A Just and True Love: Feminism at the Frontiers of Theological Ethics; Essays in Honor of Margaret A. Farley* (Notre Dame, IN: University of Notre Dame, 2007).

WHAT COUNTS AS RELIGION?

Anyone beginning the academic study of religion will soon find sharp disagreements about what religion is or involves. When studying religion, one risks treating "religion" as though it is a clearly demarcated human phenomenon that we can scrutinize and dissect independently and objectively, and then connect to other discrete human phenomena like economic life, sexuality, and politics. This way of proceeding risks turning religion into an abstraction, with neat boundaries and tidy explanations. It ignores (1) concrete differences among particular religions, (2) variations within particular religious traditions (for example, Orthodox versus Reformed Judaism, or Theravada versus Mahayana Buddhism), (3) historical development of religious traditions, and (4) complex relationships among religions, politics, economic life, and intellectual and aesthetic cultural trends. Moreover, attempts to reduce the varied and dynamic reality of religions to the single abstraction "religion" inevitably smuggle into the definition various forms of cultural conditioning and bias. Clifford Geertz's view of religion as a "cultural system," for example, is now widely criticized for its uncritical emphasis on private, interior aspects of religious life, which may be typical of Protestantism but do not describe the more communal practices found in other religions such as Islam. By treating certain sorts of religions, however unintentionally, as the basis for what counts as "religion," others are not only neglected but also comparatively stigmatized. They may appear less civilized, for example, or more irrational. As Bruce Lincoln notes in *Holy Terrors: Thinking about Religion after September 11*, "the view of religion as delimited, and therefore definable, is thus itself culturally bound, historically recent, and discursively loaded."[2] Lincoln argues that attempts to define religion need to be flexible enough to accommodate the different forms and the dynamic character of religions. At the least, attempts to define religion should attend to four domains: discourse, practice, community, and institution.

First, Lincoln says that religions involve "a discourse whose concerns transcend the human, temporal, and contingent, and that claims for itself a similarly transcendent status."[3] Lincoln's point is that human discourse becomes religious in character not merely when it is about something that obviously appears spiritual (e.g., "These are the steps to enlightenment" or "God is love") but also when it claims to be true and authoritative on the basis of something or someone greater than humans. In other words, such discourse must claim a transcendental warrant or justification. If, for instance, the Christian Bible is true, it is true because of divine revelation and not human choice, preference, or invention.

Moreover, since human discourse becomes "religious" by appealing to a transcendent authority, any matter or thing can be communicated in religious terms. For example, the book of Exodus in the Hebrew Scriptures (also the Christian Old Testament) discusses how to make reparations when your ox gores someone; the Christian Gospels lay out the genealogy of Jesus; and the 9/11 hijackers follow written instructions that tell them to shave, shower, and wear cologne. These seemingly banal passages are religious because they claim divine authorization. This transforms a rule about ox goring into divine law, an ancestral record into a testament to God's provident

---

2. Bruce Lincoln, *Holy Terrors: Thinking about Religion after September 11* (Chicago and London: University of Chicago Press, 2003), 2.

3. Ibid., 5.

governance in history, and hygiene into a ritual of self-purification.[4] Indeed, "religious discourse can recode virtually any content as sacred[—]ranging from the high-minded and progressive to the murderous, oppressive, and banal"— by framing the content as truths that cannot be made false by mere human proclamation or standards of proof.[5]

Second, religions involve "a set of practices whose goal is to produce a proper world and/or proper human subjects, as defined by a religious discourse to which these practices are connected."[6] That is, religions include practices — like rituals and moral behaviors — that give practical expression to religious beliefs and values. These practices are the tools believers use to build the sorts of people and the sort of world their religion deems proper. Again, religions can "recode" ordinary human practices, turning things that seem morally neutral and religiously irrelevant into expressions of fidelity or violations of the standards and values their religion promulgates. "Thus, for instance, for a man to grow a beard becomes a religious action when he does so in emulation of Jesus or the prophet Muhammad, constituted as the ultimate examples of human perfection. Lacking an argument and motive of this sort, his beard reflects a strictly aesthetic preference."[7]

Third, religions involve a "community whose members construct their identity" in relation to the religion's discourse and practices.[8] Shared devotion to common texts, standards, and practices unite people, even though they may disagree about how to interpret a text or adhere to a moral standard or perform a practice. They distinguish their community from others who do not share their beliefs, standards, or ways of life. At other times, communities fracture because some members deem others have departed too far from the common ground that once united them. For example, following 9/11 many Muslims rejected the brand of Islam upheld by al-Qaeda and the 9/11 hijackers as a perversion of "true" Islam, while Osama bin Laden condemned "hypocritical" Muslims who failed to practice Islam in the sort of political and militant fashion he equates with "true" Islam.[9]

Fourth, religions involve "an institution that regulates religious discourse, practices, and community, reproducing them over time and modifying them as necessary, while asserting their eternal validity and transcendent value."[10] Institutional structures vary considerably in size, power, centralization, hierarchy, and style, but they house leaders responsible for preserving, interpreting, and disseminating the group's discourse, supervising and enforcing its practices, nurturing, defending, and advancing the community.[11]

Any particular religion will accent these four domains to different degrees and realize them in varied ways. Moreover, any particular religion is unavoidably historical and dynamic, so that the relations and degrees of harmony or tension among these domains shift. Finally, any particular religion is internally varied, comprised of smaller communities that place their own

---

4. See Exodus 21:28–32 for rules about what to do when your ox gores someone. For genealogies of Jesus, see Matthew 1:2–16 and Luke 3:23–38. For the text of the instructions for the 9/11 hijackers (found in Muhamed Atta's luggage), see Lincoln's *Holy Terrors*, where he offers a fascinating comparative reading of the instructions and George W. Bush's "Address to the Nation" on October 7, 2001.

5. Lincoln, *Holy Terrors*, 6.

6. Ibid.

7. Ibid.

8. Ibid.

9. See Meghnad Desai, *Rethinking Islamism: The Ideology of the New Terror* (London: I. B. Tauris, 2007).

10. Lincoln, *Holy Terrors*, 7.

11. Ibid.

cultural stamp on the religious tradition in which they participate. It follows that small communities within overarching religious traditions will disagree regarding what sorts of interpretations, practices, relations, and institutional structures are most faithful, authentic, and orthodox.[12]

Sometimes these disagreements occur between those who advocate what Lincoln calls "maximalist" and "minimalist" forms of their common religion. A maximalist form of religion is one characterized by "the conviction that religion ought to permeate all aspects of social, indeed of human existence."[13] Thus, religion would order and infuse all human institutions; political, economic, social, and family life would correspond to the dictates of faith, as would modes of dress, the content of school curriculums, and so forth. Minimalist models affirm the importance of religious concerns and advocate the protection of religion from governmental intrusion but restrict religious "activity and influence" to the realm of private practice.[14] In a minimalist form of religion, I want to be free to practice my faith but I do not seek to translate its moral teachings into civil law or penalize others who do not share my faith. Think of politicians who say, "I am personally opposed to abortion, but I do not think it should be made illegal."

Religious adherents who seek to realize a maximalist form of their religion could employ their religion's discourse to construe themselves as the "faithful" and others as "heathens," and to recode the moral meaning of violent acts against the "heathens," so that killing them, for instance, becomes an act of purification. Lincoln argues that maximalist forms of religions do not end conflict but ensure "that a culture's most bruising conflicts will assume religious . . . character, and in that form they can be more destructive than ever."[15] In other words, there is a contagious quality to religious violence; when I frame my community's conflict with you in religious terms and morally recode your status as a fellow human being to that of an inferior "other," I encourage you to respond by framing the conflict in religious terms as well, ones that invert the moral evaluations I use so that my "just cause" against you is cast instead as "unprovoked aggression" or some such moral reversal.[16]

What does Lincoln's approach to defining religion help us see? That religious discourse combines claims to truth and authority in ways that impact our moral perceptions and judgments. It can recode what is ordinary as special, what is cruel as spiritual zeal, what is violent as purification; strangers can become as brothers and sisters, fellow human beings can become subhuman, and so on. Religious discourse shapes our attitudes toward the moral status of other people and particular acts of violence. Because religious discourse can "recode" moral meanings, and because it does so by claiming a transcendent authority or warrant, religious discourse can facilitate violence by eroding things like respect for another's rights or social disapproval of violence.[17] In this way, religious discourse can affect our moral judgment

---

12. Ibid., 8.

13. Ibid., 5. Osama bin Laden exemplifies a maximalist approach to Islam. Jerry Falwell and Pat Robertson exemplify a maximalist approach to Christianity.

14. Ibid.

15. Ibid., 61.

16. Mark Juergensmeyer, *Terror in the Mind of God: The Global Rise of Religious Violence,* 3rd ed. (Berkeley, CA: University of California Press, 2003). Juergensmeyer acknowledges Lincoln's claim that religious discourse can morally "recode" violence through its symbols and practices.

17. Scholars today often acknowledge that the notion of human rights derives from Western ideas about human worth and equality. For a discussion of human rights in a cross-cultural context, see David Hollenbach, SJ, "Human Rights and Women's Rights: Initiatives and Interventions in the Name of Universality," in *A Just and True Love: Feminism at the Frontiers of Theological Ethics, Essays in Honor of Margaret A. Farley,* Maura A. Ryan and Brian F. Linnane, SJ, eds. (Notre Dame, IN: University of Notre Dame, 2007).

or perception in the same way that a judge can sequester a jury, that is, by isolating it from the influence of other perspectives. And because religious discourse claims transcendent or divine authorization, religious truth-claims can be fairly immune to counterarguments and counterevidence. These particular features of religion factor greatly in religiously sponsored violence.

Questions for Reflection and Discussion

- What does it mean to say that an attempt to define religion should attend to four domains: discourse, practice, community, and institution?

- In what ways do people recognize "divine" law? Can it be discerned?

- What might be identified in your religious experience as a force uniting or dividing others?

- What is "true" religion? Is it always established by adherents?

- What is the difference between maximalist and minimalist forms of religion?

WHAT COUNTS AS VIOLENCE?

Just as we must avoid narrow and rigid definitions of religion, we must not limit violence to the infliction of physical harm, or we would fail to account for important forms of violence that affect human life. Violence is the destructive exercise of power. This destructive power may be aimed against other persons or oneself, and it may also be aimed against property and the environment.

Violence occurs in two forms: interpersonal and structural. Interpersonal violence may occur between individuals or groups, and in more or less direct forms. It includes the deliberate and overt infliction of physical harm, such as killing or maiming another, as well as emotional, psychological, and spiritual harm (which often accompany physical harm). Interpersonal violence further includes harming others through unjustly acquiring or damaging their property, or by restricting or denying their access to resources essential for human life and well being, for instance, food and water. Structural violence occurs through cultural and institutional mechanisms that oppress individuals and groups. Examples of structural violence include economic oppression, racism, sexism, and heterosexism.[18] Structural violence takes shape and is sustained by the choices people make, even as these same structures limit human choice and agency. For example, sexist beliefs and attitudes are institutionalized in laws and customs that govern women's property ownership and employment, as well as choices regarding marriage, divorce, and reproduction. Because oppression occurs through conventional structures, it can be difficult to recognize the violence these structures cause. Structures mask the violence by making it appear benignly conventional, inevitable, natural, and unchangeable, or even necessary and justified. Liberation from structural violence therefore requires a moral (re-)education to unmask the destructive character of social structures,

---

18. For a treatment of structural violence, see Paul Farmer, *Pathologies of Power: Health, Human Rights, and the New War on the Poor* (Berkeley and Los Angeles: University of California Press, 2003). Religiously informed accounts can be found in various liberation theologies.

and to move those who benefit from them toward solidarity with those who are oppressed by them. In any case, by defining violence to include structural as well as interpersonal forms, it becomes clear that religiously sponsored violence extends well beyond war, suicide bombings, or murdering abortionists. By morally recoding and divinely authorizing attitudes, customs, and access to material (e.g., food) and immaterial (e.g., prestige) resources, religions help to mask and warrant structural violence.

IS RELIGION INHERENTLY VIOLENT?

Some religious adherents have wrought considerable harm in the name of their faith and will continue to do so. Some also have provided considerable help and healing to others in the name of their faith and will continue to do this as well. It is easy to list various wrongs — which range from atrocities to blunders — committed by and for the sake of religious communities, but it is important to remember that long lists of good deeds are just as easy to fashion.[19] Religious communities have founded hospitals and schools, played important roles in brokering peace and reconciliation (as in the South African Truth and Reconciliation Committees), provided food for the hungry, companionship for the lonely, and care for the dying. Religion, like any aspect of human culture, whether economic, political, aesthetic, technological, or social, can

be marshaled in ways that destroy or build up, that divide or unite.[20]

Nevertheless, there are particular features of religions, even when we broadly and flexibly define that term, that facilitate destructive and divisive human behavior, especially under the influence of other factors that contribute to conflict, such as economic scarcity. Let us consider three different theories regarding religiously sponsored violence.[21] There are certainly other theories of religion and violence. These three, however, nicely convey a spectrum of answers to the question "Is religion inherently violent?" Moreover, their different positions on that spectrum have to do with the important relation between religious truth claims and morality.

Charles Kimball on Religion and Violence

Charles Kimball is a professor of comparative religion, an expert in Christian-Muslim relations, and an ordained Baptist minister. In his book *When Religion Becomes Evil*, he repeatedly claims, as I did above, that religions can foster good as well as evil. According to Kimball, those who say religions lead to violence are partly right. When particular religions are interpreted and practiced in narrow and rigidly exclusivist ways ("My religion, indeed, my particular understanding of my religion, is the only truth"), or "if religious institutions and teachings lack flexibility, opportunities for growth, and systems of checks

19. See R. Scott Appleby, *The Ambivalence of the Sacred: Religion, Violence, and Reconciliation* (Lanham, MD: Rowman & Littlefield Publishers, 2000).

20. Hector Avalos, whose work is discussed below, takes a different view of religiously motivated "good works," arguing that all apparent acts of altruism are in fact self-interested. See Hector Avalos, *Fighting Words: The Origins of Religious Violence* (Amherst, NY: Prometheus Books, 2005), 369. His argument on this point, and his equation of ethics and determinations of interest, are terribly reductive and uninformed by ethical theory.

21. Two of the theorists discussed here, Hector Avalos and Charles Kimball, were interviewed together on the National Public Radio program *Talk of the Nation*. The program, "Examining the Intersection of Religion and Violence," originally aired on August 22, 2005. As of this writing it can be heard online at *http://www.npr.org/templates/story/story.php?storyId=4810212*.

and balances,"[22] religion may lead more easily to violent conflict. Kimball says that is not a necessary outcome, however.[23] When religion is understood and practiced in ways that are more inclusive and flexible, it can facilitate human quests for meaning and hope without necessarily leading to violence.[24]

Kimball argues that there are five factors in religions that can lead to religiously sponsored violence. First, all religions involve absolute truth-claims, for instance, that Israel is the chosen people of God, that Jesus is the Messiah, that the Qur'an is the Word of God. "While truth claims are the essential ingredients of religion, they are also the points at which divergent interpretations arise. When particular understandings become rigidly fixed and uncritically appropriated as absolute truths, well-meaning people can and often do paint themselves into a corner from which they must assume a defensive or even offensive posture."[25] For instance, insisting on a literal interpretation of religious texts can lead one to deny scientific evidence that seems to contradict it, as some Christians do with biblical accounts of creation.

Second, when religions demand blind obedience to charismatic authority figures (for example, Jim Jones) or particular doctrines, and involve severe physical isolation from the rest of society (again, Jim Jones provides an example), red flags arise.[26] "Beware of any religious movement that seeks to limit the intellectual freedom

and individual integrity of its adherents. When individual believers abdicate personal responsibility and yield to the authority of a charismatic leader or become enslaved to particular ideas or teachings, religion can easily become the framework for violence and destruction."[27]

The third factor Kimball describes is the establishment of an "ideal" time. What Kimball means here correlates with Lincoln's observation (discussed above) that some strands of religious traditions are "maximalist," meaning their adherents seek to implement their religion in every aspect of human life. Remember that for Lincoln all religions entail "a set of practices whose goal is to produce [what the religion judges to be a] proper world and/or proper human subjects."[28] This proper world, inhabited by properly living humans, is an "ideal time," a period in which the religion's ideal form of existence is actualized. Different religions picture the ideal time in different ways (e.g., heaven versus nirvana) and take different positions on whether this ideal time ever has been achieved or to what degree we can approximate it in this life, say, short of some apocalypse that ushers in the fullness of the ideal time. According to Kimball, "When the hoped-for ideal is tied to a particular religious worldview and those who wish to implement their vision become convinced that they know what God wants for them and everyone else, you have a prescription for disaster."[29]

---

22. Charles Kimball, *When Religion Becomes Evil* (San Francisco: HarperSanFrancisco, 2002), 32.

23. Ibid., 28.

24. Ibid., 32.

25. Ibid., 46.

26. Jim Jones (James Warren Jones) was the founder of the People's Temple. His career as a cult leader culminated in 1978 in Guyana. Members of a congressional fact-finding delegation who were investigating Jones and the People's Temple for human rights abuses were murdered at an airstrip as they tried to leave Guyana. Jones then ordered some nine hundred followers to drink a cyanide-laced beverage and apparently shot himself. See David Chidester, *Salvation and Suicide: Jim Jones, the People's Temple, and Jonestown*, 2nd ed. (Indianapolis: Indiana University Press, 2003).

27. Kimball, *When Religion Becomes Evil*, 72.

28. Lincoln, *Holy Terrors*, 6.

29. Kimball, *When Religion Becomes Evil*, 105.

A fourth danger is the notion that the end justifies the means. "Various components of religious life—including sacred space and time, communal identity, and institutional structures—are vitally important. But they are not the ends of religious life. They facilitate the life of faith in community."[30] Religion may become violent when "the end goal of protecting or defending a key component of religion is . . . used to justify any means necessary."[31] An important element in the turn toward violence is the dehumanization of fellow human beings as "others" who do not deserve our respect and whose difference from us justifies our neglect or maltreatment of them. "The most obvious sign of this corruption [coming to believe the end justifies the means] is visible when compassionate and constructive relationships with others are discarded."[32]

Finally, there is the declaration of a holy war. Kimball is initially using "war" metaphorically here, as in a "war on drugs." What he means is that when a religion declares a holy war on something (or someone) it might not at first involve overt violence but rather a commitment to concerted action to resist or overcome the object of one's "warfare." For example, Kimball rightly notes that, post 9/11, the Islamic term *jihad* has for many English speakers become synonymous with religiously sponsored military violence, when in fact it means more broadly the struggle to do what is just and virtuous.[33] Nevertheless, when religious adherents believe the end justifies the means, a holy war that initially does not include overt violence easily comes to include it. "Declaring war 'holy' is a sure sign of corrupt religion."[34]

An imperfect world includes violence and presents us with situations that "may indeed warrant the decisive use of force or focused military action. But such action must not be cloaked in religious language or justified by religion."[35] Because Kimball thinks religions are not inherently violent, but easily become violent when interpreted and practiced as absolute and inflexible, he distinguishes between "corrupt" and "authentic" religion. "Authentic religion engages the intellect as people wrestle with the mystery of existence and the challenges of living in an imperfect world."[36] Recognizing that our understanding of religious truth is both limited and evolving can lead us toward greater humility and openness to other points of view and discourage defensiveness or condescension. Because the world is imperfect, "the pursuit of religious truth is an ongoing process."[37] According to Kimball, "The only intelligent way forward is the route laid out by authentic religion: we must be peacemakers."[38] Indeed, Kimball insists that "at the center of authentic religion one *always* finds the promise of peace, both an inner peace for the adherent and a requirement to seek peaceful coexistence with the rest of creation."[39]

What is unclear is whether this is meant to be a normative claim (only religions that promise

---

30. Ibid., 150–151.

31. Ibid., 129.

32. Ibid.

33. Ibid., 173–178.

34. Ibid., 156.

35. Ibid.

36. Ibid., 72.

37. Ibid., 68.

38. Ibid., 183.

39. Ibid., 156.

peace should count as authentic) or an empirical one (albeit with normative implications). Kimball does not adequately support either version. He may well be correct, but his book does not show him to be.

Essentially, Kimball is saying that "peace" provides a moral criterion for distinguishing authentic religion from inauthentic religion (i.e., the kind of religion on its way to becoming evil or that is already evil). By asking whether a particular religious belief, practice, community, or institution promotes or hinders peace, we can morally evaluate these aspects of essentially peaceful religions and presumably reject wholesale any religion that has hate or violence at its core. On its face, the task of morally denouncing aspects of religion or entire religions when they deviate from peacemaking seems promising, or, if we are duly chastened by the historic persistence and proliferation of religiously sponsored violence, it may simply be the best we can manage. But, as Hector Avalos helps us to see, endeavors to minimize or avoid religiously sponsored violence by differentiating between "authentic" and "evil" forms of religion may very well fuel religious violence.

Hector Avalos on Religion and Violence

Hector Avalos argues that religions are inherently prone to violence. He summarizes his argument this way:

1. Most violence is due to scarce resources, real or perceived. Whenever people perceive that there is not enough of something they value, conflict may ensue to maintain or acquire that resource. This resource can range from love in a family to oil on a global scale.

2. When religion causes violence, it often does so because it has *created new scarce resources*.[40]

Religions create new scarce resources in several ways, according to Avalos. They typically proclaim exclusive access to divine communications, particularly through "inscripturation," creating an authoritative written account about or from supernatural beings or forces. Since some people do not have access to this text or canon, or cannot read, the access to divine communications becomes a scarce resource. Furthermore, those who view the text as authoritative may become aggressive toward those who do not.[41] Sacred spaces are another scarce resource; sacred space is a space that some deem more valuable for purely religious reasons, not because of its market value or strategic political value. It is a scarce resource when some people have access to this space and others do not. Examples range from cities like Mecca and Jerusalem, natural places like Uluru/Ayer's Rock, and intentionally constructed places like mosques, temples, shrines, and churches. Religions also involve group privileges, such as the authority to interpret sacred texts or preside over sacred spaces; the privileges themselves are scarce resources. The ultimate scarce resource that religions create is salvation. Different religions understand salvation in different ways, of course, but salvation always designates some ostensibly valuable benefit for those who receive it. Since not everyone is (or, perhaps, can be) saved, salvation is a scarce resource.

What is important for Avalos is that no one can prove these resources are real. Religion, according to Avalos, is a "mode of life and thought that presupposes the existence of, and

---

40. Avalos, *Fighting Words*, 18. The emphasis is Avalos'.
41. Ibid., 106.

a relationship with, supernatural forces and/ or beings."[42] The scarce resources that religions generate require only belief in order to "exist."[43] I need only believe that the Bible or the Qur'an is the word of God in order to claim a kind of access to God that others do not have and, voila, that access is a scarce resource. For Avalos, humans prove or verify claims only through logic or empirical evidence obtained through our five senses. He calls this "empirico-rational" verification. "Unlike many non-religious sources of conflict, religious conflict relies solely on resources whose scarcity is wholly manufactured by, or reliant on, unverifiable premises. When the truth or falsity of opposing propositions cannot be verified then violence becomes a common resort in adjudicating disputes."[44] In other words, religions create scarce resources, and in doing so contribute to conflict over those resources. "Do we get to occupy this holy land or do you?" "Do you get to determine and apply our sacred texts or do I?" "Who are you to say that I am not saved or that God rejects my lifestyle?" Because we cannot prove one side is right and the other wrong, one interpretation is correct and the other false; because we cannot prove things like salvation are even real, it may seem better, even necessary, to settle our conflict through violence.

Avalos thinks that violence can be morally justified in order to address nonreligious disputes, but religious violence is always immoral because it involves trading bodily harm or causing death for the sake of scarce resources that cannot be proven to exist (and which, therefore, cannot exist).[45] There are those who endeavor to "redeem" religions, whether by ignoring or rejecting violent portions of sacred texts and emphasizing portions that encourage love or peace, by reinterpreting religious doctrines to accord with a "true" or "original" religious message that is peaceable, or by promoting the efforts of peacemakers in their religious traditions. Avalos argues that all such efforts are futile, and in fact are immoral insofar as they still encourage trade-offs of bodily well-being for unverifiable resources. They ignore the fact that what counts as "peace" is usually a state of affairs that serves the interests of those who define what "peace" is. Moreover, any attempt to identify the "true" message or "original meaning" or the "authentic" form of religion is, for Avalos: arbitrary in its selection of what counts as true, original, or authentic; unverifiable in any case; and inevitably creates another scarce resource that can lead to violence, namely, access to the true, original, or authentic meaning of that religion. This means that Kimball's call for moral denunciations of inauthentic religion and an embrace of authentic, peacemaking religion will only contribute to religious violence.

Avalos argues that his "scarce resources" argument is novel and superior to alternative theories about religion and violence. He criticizes Kimball both for overlooking how scarce resources cause religious violence and for helping to create scarce religious resources by urging "authentic" forms of religion based on "true" understandings and practices. Other theories regarding religion and violence fail for similar reasons, argues Avalos. Not only do they overlook the importance of scarce resources for all types of violence, they ignore how religions create scarce resources that do not really exist and foster tragically needless violence for their sake. Moreover, other theories are, like Kimball's, beholden to the "essentialist" view that religion is essentially good

---

42. Ibid., 103.
42. Ibid.
44. Ibid., 18.
45. Ibid., 29.

and religious violence is a deviation from this goodness. "If a new theory of religious violence is to be successful, it will have to directly address the deeply entrenched view that 'true' religion is primarily designed for peaceful and altruistic purposes,"[46] he writes.

To solve the problem of religious violence, argues Avalos, we need to do away with religion. "Since all religious beliefs are ultimately unverifiable, the greatest scarce resource of all is verifiability. And one way to remedy or minimize unverifiability in any decision-making process, especially that leading to violence, is to eliminate religion from human life altogether."[47] To do so requires, among other things, aggressive educational efforts to convince "world citizens that violence about resources that do not exist, or cannot be verified to exist, is against their own interest. Ultimately, such a strategy would be in everyone's best interest."[48] Avalos is not so naive as to think that religious believers will readily abandon their beliefs, but he insists that nonbelievers need to make concerted efforts to show believers the folly, indeed, the immorality of making trade-offs for resources that cannot be shown to be real. Avalos is basically offering a moral rejection of religion by appealing to human self-interest.

The idea that religion could be eliminated from human existence is clearly untenable on its face. But the theoretical flaw in Avalos' argument is that he bases his moral argument against religion on the insistence that no religious claim can be true because none of them can be empirically verified or proven. He doesn't appreciate the force of Lincoln's insight that religious discourse claims for itself a standard of truth and source of authority that transcends humanity. To argue that religious claims cannot be true because they cannot be verified empirically is merely to *say* that they are false, not to *prove* it, since the transcendent authorization religious discourse claims for itself cannot be reduced to human standards for proof. Just as Avalos is committed to restricting knowledge or truth to that which can be verified on narrow empirical grounds, many religious adherents are equally committed to and insistent upon the truth of their religious commitments. Neither side can be argued into agreement with the other. And Avalos' approach may itself fuel religious violence insofar as it can lead to condescending and dismissive attitudes toward religious believers, encouraging them to feel besieged by secularists whom they must oppose.

Despite these problems, Avalos does contribute to our reflection on religion and violence. He brings a healthy skepticism in response to claims like Kimball's that world religions are essentially peaceful. He also offers the insight that attempts to identify some forms of religion as authentic and others as corrupt or evil can actually contribute to religious violence. Partly this is a consequence of the way religious discourse can morally recode our perceptions. But as René Girard helps us to see, violence is a *religious* problem because violence is a *human* problem.

René Girard on Religion and Violence

René Girard is one of the most significant and controversial writers on religion and violence. His body of work brings together literary criticism,

---

46. Ibid., 87.

47. Ibid., 371. Mark Juergensmeyer argues that dissatisfaction with secular authorities is a contributing factor in religious violence; see his book *Terror in the Mind of God: The Global Rise of Religious Violence*, 3rd ed. (Berkeley, CA: University of California Press, 2003).

48. Avalos, *Fighting Words*, 378.

anthropology, history, philosophy, cultural studies, and religious studies. His work is as complex as it is wide-ranging, and here we can offer only a brief and basic overview of his contribution to our thinking about religion and violence.

Girard's theories about the intersection of religion and violence begin with a particular account of how human desire works. Girard argues that human desire is mimetic, or imitative, in a triangular fashion. This requires some explanation. Here in the West, we commonly think of desire in a linear fashion: "I want that" or "He wants her." But Girard's insight is that desire actually works in a triangular fashion, in which we learn to desire according to the desires of another. The "triangle" consists of me, a model of desiring whom I imitate, and the object desired. "I see that you want that, now I want it, too" or "He wants her, so I do, too, or at least someone like her." Consider the way advertisements elicit our desire for something by showing someone else enjoying it—we learn to think of these jeans or those shoes or that hamburger by observing a model's desire for those things. The mimetic character of desire is harnessed in trends or fads (and in our fickle rejection of what once was "in" and is now *so* "out"), in social and economic "dos and don'ts" (shop here, not there; hang out at this place, not that one), and in social hierarchies (we join or leave groups, aspire to be like so-and-so, outfit our Second Life avatars, and collect friends on Facebook according to the cues of others).

Desire in itself is not a problem. Indeed, the mimetic character of desire is crucial to our development; as infants and young children, we learn by observing and imitating our parents. The "self" we become is not something independent, but something that emerges into being according to the desires of our caregivers, who are themselves mimetic reflections of the desires of their various models. Says Girard:

Humankind is that creature who lost a part of its animal instinct. . . . Once their natural needs are satisfied, humans desire intensely, but they don't know exactly what they desire, for no instinct guides them. . . . Truly to desire, we must have recourse to people about us; we have to borrow their desires.

This borrowing occurs quite often without either the loaner or the borrower being aware of it. It is not only desire that one borrows from those whom one takes for models; it is a mass of behaviors, attitudes, things learned, prejudices, preferences, etc. And at the heart of these things the loan that places us most deeply into debt—the other's desire—occurs often unawares.[49]

Although desire itself is not bad, it can and frequently does lead to conflict and violence. Seeing another person desire what we have, for instance, leads us to imitate them in return by increasing our desire; knowing that you want my boyfriend makes me feel more possessive toward him. We become rivals. Or perhaps I admire you and try to become more like you. Eventually, as I copy your style and pattern myself after you, the ego boost you derive from my admiration turns to hostility and a need to distinguish yourself from me. There are many other ways mimetic rivalries play out in human life. Since any desire we have is indebted to the desires of many others and will spawn desires in others, desire and the rivalry that accompanies it are contagious.

As rivalries multiply, conflict escalates. Girard argues that our individual rivalries accumulate in social life, gathering like a snowball or the channeling of streams and creeks into rivers. Together they "create a mimetic crisis, the war of *all against all*. The resulting violence of all against all would finally annihilate the community if it were not transformed, in the end, into a war of *all against one*, thanks to which the unity of the

49. René Girard, *I See Satan Fall like Lightning* (Maryknoll, NY: Orbis Books), 15.

community is reestablished."[50] What Girard is saying here is that mimetic rivalry threatens the social order, and in order to defuse the threat, the members of a community come to affirm their unity against a victim or scapegoat in the way a group of girlfriends smooth over their competitive tensions by making fun of another girl. The same plot line plays out every day in small and large scenarios—we regain some measure of stability and peace in our shared antagonism toward a scapegoat or victim. Of course, this stability doesn't last. We soon find ourselves caught again in mimetic rivalry. We require strategies for minimizing or managing this rivalry, and if these prove inadequate, we return to the scapegoating mechanism that brought peace before.

Where, for Girard, does religion enter the mix? By examining the myths of archaic religions, Girard comes to the conclusion that the evolution of human beings from animals, the emergence of human desire and mimetic rivalry, and the mechanism of sacrificing a victim to resolve that rivalry unfolded together. Archaic religious myths show us that religious and cultural systems took shape in the earliest periods of human history in response to the problem of mimetic rivalry. Religion is therefore both an effect of mimetic violence and a means to control that violence through rules against violence and rituals of sacrifice. "Archaic religions are essentially combinations of prohibitions and sacrifices. Prohibitions forbade violence directly, but they often failed and, when they did, archaic communities fell back upon their second line of defense, sacrifice. The paradox of archaic religion is that, in order to prevent violence, it resorted to substitute violence."[51] What makes sacrificial violence so effective as a response to mimetic rivalry is that it deludes the mob who attacks the

victim into believing that they are innocent and the victim is guilty. Therefore, violence against the victim is justified. The community's relative peace and cohesion deflect members away from the truth, that it is their own anger that needs to be appeased, rather than the anger of the gods. The religious myths they create only shore up and partake in the community's mimetic violence by concealing it in the lie of their innocence vis-à-vis a guilty victim.

In short, Girard's study of religious myths leads him to conclude that religion and violence are deeply entangled. As a human phenomenon, religion is a result of mimetic violence and at times restrains us from violence. Of course, because the real root of human violence lies not in "religion" but in human beings, religion, like anything else we humans touch, can facilitate mimetic violence. Indeed, the sort of exclusivism that worries Kimball (our religion is true, not theirs), which Avalos rightly sees as creating a scarce resource (access to the truth) to battle over, easily feeds into the lie of "our" innocence and "their" guilt.

While Girard's arguments about desire and scapegoats meet with much agreement, there are also plenty of folks who argue against him on historical, anthropological, or philosophical grounds. But the real controversy surrounding Girard's approach concerns the next step of his argument, namely that the Christian Bible reveals the truth about mimetic violence. The Christian Gospels proclaim Jesus the victim to be innocent and the mob that kills him guilty. The Gospels thus reverse the way we ascribe innocence and blame. They reveal that we are complicit in the violence that creates the fragile peace human communities periodically attain. Moreover, the Christian Gospels do not reveal a God who requires bloody sacrifice in order to be appeased. Instead, they reveal

---

50. Ibid., 24.

51. René Girard, "Violence and Religion: Cause or Effect?" *The Hedgehog Review* 6, no. 1 (2004): 8–13, *http://mimetictheory.net/bios/articles/Girad_Violence_and_religion.pdf.*

a God who is willing to undergo mimetic violence in order to show that God has nothing to do with our fatal rivalries and that we do not need to live enslaved to them any longer.[52] We can instead live as disciples of Jesus, whose example will harness our mimetic desire in peaceful rather than violent ways. Christianity thereby makes us aware of how we victimize innocent persons and gradually makes the sacrificial order ineffective. Girard argues that the historical effects of Christianity's exposé are slow to unfold but real. He also grants that these effects are muddled. We are so caught up in mimetic violence that people can use Christ as another weapon in that violence, attacking those who do not believe in him, enlisting him to warrant the domination of fellow Christians, and on and on. Avalos criticizes Girard on this score: "Contrary to Girard's theory, the belief in sacrifice can create new rationales for violence rather than result in the final overthrow of mimetic or scapegoating violence. The supposed uniqueness of the sacrifice of Christ" relates to ideas about salvation that generate new scarce resources over which to fight.[53] Girard already knows this, but our aim here is not to vindicate Girard or Christianity. We can take insights from Girard and see the difference they make for our study of religion and violence.

What does Girard contribute to our reflection on religion and violence? He shows how important it is to acknowledge our own complicity in violence. He shows that our complicity is also a sign of our dependence on one another. And he shows that we need to rehabilitate desire through dedication to peaceful models of desire. We do not need to endorse Girard's entire approach to appreciate

that violence is facilitated by moral perceptions of fellow human beings as inferior or threatening "others," a point Kimball and Avalos also make. By acknowledging our own complicity in violence we mitigate these perceptions. Moreover, when we appreciate Girard's insight that our complicity in violence is a sign of our interdependence (a point he makes by arguing that our desires are indebted to others and in turn indebt others), we come to see that we depend upon each other to learn what to desire and how to desire in peaceful ways. This interdependence means we are implicated in one another's violence *and* one another's peacemaking, a point that can energize us to work toward more peaceable ways of living together, but only if we pursue a rehabilitation of our own desire through dedication to models who are just peacemakers. In short, we need to learn to want peace. But, we should not settle for *any* peace, not the sort of peace that consists in suppressing violence through domination and control. We need to learn to want a peace that does justice to others.[54] And we need to learn to want it more than we want to be right, more than we want to horde scarce resources, and more than we want to win.

CONCLUSION

This chapter has argued that religious discourse can facilitate violence by claiming a transcendent authorization that allows it to recode the moral status of people and practices. Hence, we need moral commitments and interpretive standards that expose and prevent this "recoding." Can these commitments and standards come from religious

---

52. See James Alison, *On Being Liked* (London and New York: Crossroad, 2004). Alison's Christian theology is indebted to Girard. In this volume, Alison offers a Girardian response to the sort of claims Avalos makes regarding the "supposed uniqueness of the sacrifice of Christ" as a scarce resource.

53. Avalos, *Holy Terrors*, 205.

54. Kimball makes this point, as we noted. But we acknowledge or address objections like Avalos', that distinguishing "authentic" and "corrupt" forms of religion can feed religious violence rather than ameliorate it.

traditions themselves? If so, do we merely continue to create unnecessary and unverifiable scarce resources that lead us to conflict? Do we forgo building common ground in favor of trying to sustain and defend our respective religious traditions? If, instead, we subject religions to moral and interpretive norms that are foreign to them, do we violate their integrity, court condescension, and stir up religious opposition? These are important questions to consider in future reflection on religion and violence. For the moment, we can learn from the theorists whom we have engaged.

In their own ways, both Kimball and Avalos call for moral criticisms of religion. Kimball suggests that good work can be done within particular religious traditions, that we can reinterpret and rehabilitate various aspects of a tradition, like a doctrine or institutional arrangements, by testing them against the tradition's essential moral commitment to a just peace. Avalos points out several difficulties that vex efforts to morally revise religious traditions from within. The commitments and standards we endorse as true or better seem to him to be arbitrary, unverified, and unverifiable; moreover, efforts to identify better and worse forms of religious life can lead to violence. But Avalos confines us all to a narrow standard of empirical proof and reduces the complexity of human desire and moral motivation to self-interest. Girard, however, helps us to see two things. First, working with religious traditions is more a task of interpretation than verification. Second, morally motivating people to denounce religious violence is less a matter of convincing them not to make trade-offs for unverifiable resources and more about changing what they want by presenting them with an attractive alternative.

In sum, the problem is not that *religions* are ambivalent or hypocritical about violence but that *we* are. That one and the same religious tradition would endorse violence and peace, fellowship and xenophobia, equality and hierarchy should neither surprise us nor lead us to the conclusion that we must abandon religious traditions altogether. We need to engage in such rehabilitative efforts because *we* are the ones who may be rehabilitated in doing so. The point is not to "redeem" religious traditions for the sake of the tradition itself, but to clarify our own complicity in violence and cultivate our own commitment to just peacemaking.

Questions for Reflection and Discussion

- Do you think religion is inherently violent? Why or why not?

- What might be some examples of violence in religion not identified in this chapter?

- Could teaching religion be an act of violence? Why or why not?

- In what ways do you agree or disagree with the idea that when religion causes violence, it often does so because it has created new scarce resources?

- Does a religion negate itself if it does not advocate or pursue peace? Why?

- Which of Kimball's points above do you find to be most helpful? Why?

- Which of Kimball's points above do you find to be the most disturbing? Why?

- In what ways is religion either essentially good or flawed?

- How does mimetic rivalry encourage or reduce religious violence?

- What might happen to the world if religion ceased to exist?

Additional Resources

Adams, Carol J., and Marie M. Fortune. 1995. *Violence Against Women and Children: A Christian Theological Sourcebook*. New York: Continuum.

Alison, James. 2004. *On Being Liked*. London and New York: Crossroad.

Appleby, R. Scott. 2000. *The Ambivalence of the Sacred: Religion, Violence, and Reconciliation*. Lanham, MD: Rowman and Littlefield Publishers.

Avalos, Hector. 2005. *Fighting Words: The Origins of Religious Violence*. Amherst, NY: Prometheus Books.

Bellinger, Charles K. "Religion and Violence: A Bibliography." *http://www.wabashcenter.wabash.edu/resources/article2.aspx?id=10516*. This bibliography is an expanded version of one originally published in the *Hedgehog Review* 6, no. 1 (2004).

Chidester, David. 2003. *Salvation and Suicide: Jim Jones, the People's Temple, and Jonestown*. 2nd ed. Indianapolis: Indiana University Press.

Coakley, Sarah, ed. 2000. *Religion and the Body*. Cambridge, UK: Cambridge University Press.

Cobb, Kelton. 2002. "Violent Faith." In *11 September: Religious Perspectives on the Causes and Consequences*. Ian Markham and Ibrahim M. Abu-Rabi, eds. Oxford, UK: Oneworld. *http://www.hartsem.edu/centers/cobb_article1.htm*.

Collins, John J. 2005. *The Bible after Babel: Historical Criticism in a Postmodern Age*. Grand Rapids: Eerdmans.

Desai, Meghnad. 2007. *Rethinking Islamism: The Ideology of the New Terror*. London: I. B. Tauris.

De Vries, Hent. 2002. *Religion and Violence: Philosophical Perspectives from Kant to Derrida*. Baltimore and London: Johns Hopkins University Press.

Ellis, Marc H. 1997. *Unholy Alliance: Religion and Atrocity in Our Time*. Minneapolis: Fortress.

Esposito, John L. 2002. *Unholy War: Terror in the Name of Islam*. New York: Oxford University Press.

Girard, René. 2006. *I See Satan Fall Like Lightning*. Maryknoll, NY: Orbis Books.

Girard, René. 2004. "Violence and Religion: Cause or Effect?" *Hedgehog Review* 6, no. 1: 8–13. This entire volume of the *Hedgehog Review* considers religion and violence. Girard's essay is also online at *http://mimetictheory.net/bios/articles/Girad_Violence_and_religion.pdf*.

Hollenbach, David, SJ. 2007. "Human Rights and Women's Rights: Initiatives and Interventions in the Name of Universality." In *A Just and True Love: Feminism at the Frontiers of Theological Ethics, Essays in Honor of Margaret A. Farley*. Maura A. Ryan and Brian F. Linnane, SJ, eds. Notre Dame, IN: University of Notre Dame.

Juergensmeyer, Mark. 2003. *Terror in the Mind of God: The Global Rise of Religious Violence*. 3rd ed. Berkeley, CA: University of California Press.

Kimball, Charles. 2002. *When Religion Becomes Evil*. San Francisco: HarperSanFrancisco.

Lawrence, Bruce B. 1998. *Shattering the Myth: Islam beyond Violence*. Princeton, NJ: Princeton University Press.

Lincoln, Bruce. 2003. *Holy Terrors: Thinking about Religion after September 11*. Chicago and London: University of Chicago Press.

Markham, Ian, and Ibrahim M. Abu-Rabi, eds. 2002. *11 September: Religious Perspectives on the Causes and Consequences*. Oxford, UK: Oneworld.

Schwartz, Regina M. 1997. *The Curse of Cain: The Violent Legacy of Monotheism*. Chicago and London: University of Chicago Press.

Sells, Michael. 1998. *The Bridge Betrayed: Religion and Genocide in Bosnia*. Berkeley and Los Angeles: University of California Press.

Web Resources

Center for Advanced Holocaust Studies, *http://www.ushmm.org/research/center/*.

Children of Abraham Institute, *http://etext.lib.virginia.edu/journals/abraham/*.

Colloquium on Violence and Religion, *http://www.uibk.ac.at/theol/cover/*.

Continued . . .

Additional Resources

Continued . . .

Interfaith Youth Core, *http://www.ifyc.org/*.

Scriptural Reasoning, *http://www.scripturalreasoning.org/*.

South African Truth and Reconciliation Commission, *http://www.doj.gov.za/trc/*.

Speaking of Faith, "Religion and Violence"; host Krista Tippett interviews Miroslav Volf, *http://speakingoffaith. publicradio.org/programs/volf/index.shtml*.

United States Institute of Peace, *http://www.usip.org/ aboutus/index.html*.

SOCIAL ACTIVISM AND ENGAGEMENT

Dr. Swasti Bhattacharyya
Buena Vista University

Preface

The thread of social engagement runs through many religions. Giving alms or gifts to alleviate suffering of the poor, for example, is found in many religions of the world. Many hospitals, clinics, and social service agencies can trace their foundations to religious traditions or beliefs. Social activism has often been the work of inspired believers whose ideas and actions are motivated by their faith: Alcoholics Anonymous, homes for victims of domestic violence or poverty, political candidates whose platform reflects their faith convictions—the list of examples goes on and on. In this chapter, Swasti Bhattacharyya considers three examples of religiously motivated social activists: Rev. Dr. Martin Luther King Jr., Malcolm X, and Vinoba Bhave. This chapter also invites readers to reflect on how religion positively influences social, cultural, and political actions.

Chapter Goals

- To introduce links between social activism and religion
- To promote critical reflection that may contribute to the development of social activism

INTRODUCTION

Religion is difficult to define. Karl Marx claimed, "Religion is the sigh of the oppressed creature, the heart of a heartless world, just as it is the spirit of a spiritless situation. It is the opium of the people."[1] As Marx examined society, he saw religion as a force that pacifies the poor and the oppressed, enabling them to accept their lower status in this life and to hope for a better future

---

1. As quoted in Daniel L. Pals, *Seven Theories of Religion* (Oxford: Oxford University Press, 1996), 141; quoted from Karl Marx, "Contribution to the Critique of Hegel's Philosophy of Right: Introduction," in *Karl Marx and Friedrich Engels on Religion* (New York: Schocken Books, 1964), 41.

in an afterlife, in heaven. According to Marx, Freud, and others, it is by promulgating false beliefs that religion allows the poor to accept their lot, the privileged to ignore the needs of the poor, and both to refrain from revolt or the fight for justice.[2] Religion is thus a passive force whose "otherworldly" focus allows individuals to ignore the needs of others.

Other definitions of religion lead to quite different conclusions regarding how we are to act in this world. Religion can be a powerful force for change that challenges the status quo. Desmond Tutu, former archbishop of the Anglican Church of South Africa, grounds his successful fight against apartheid in his religious commitments. As Tutu proclaimed in accepting the Nobel Peace Prize in 1984:

> There is no peace in Southern Africa. There is no peace because there is no justice. There can be no real peace and security until there be first justice enjoyed by all the inhabitants of that beautiful land. The Bible knows nothing about peace without justice, for that would be crying "peace, peace, where there is no peace." God's Shalom, peace, involves inevitably righteousness, justice, wholeness, fullness of life, participation in decision-making, goodness, laughter, joy, compassion, sharing and reconciliation.

Tutu continued:

> God created us for fellowship. God created us so that we should form the human family, existing together because we were made for one another. . . . When will we learn that human beings are of infinite value because they have been created in the image of God? Let us work to be peacemakers, those given a wonderful share in Our Lord's ministry of reconciliation. If we want peace, so we have been told, let us work for justice. Let us beat our swords into ploughshares.[3]

It is through his religious faith that Tutu gains the strength to fight without violence for justice, peace, and social change. According to him, all people, regardless of color, are children of God, and so oppressive structures such as apartheid must be challenged and corrected. Religion for Tutu is not a drug to pacify, as Marx saw it, but a motivating force for active resistance and social involvement. It is this latter understanding of religion that we will explore in this chapter.

People's religious convictions, whether connected to an organized religious group or a philosophical, spiritual commitment,[4] have been and can be powerful motivators for action. Here we examine the lives of three religiously motivated individuals: the Rev. Dr. Martin Luther King Jr., Malcolm X, and Vinoba Bhave. King and Malcolm X were both African American civil rights activists. While King explicitly anchored his actions for civil rights in his Protestant Christianity, Malcolm X's life and message were informed and motivated by two Islamic contexts, the Nation of Islam and traditional Arab Islam. The Indian activist Vinoba Bhave was a disciple, friend, confidant, and spiritual successor to Mahatma Gandhi. He and the group of women who followed him acted from within

---

2. Daniel Pals, *Seven Theories of Religion* (Oxford: Oxford University Press, 1996), 140–143.

3. Desmond Tutu, "Nobel Lecture" (acceptance speech upon receiving the Nobel Peace Prize on December 11, 1984), *http://nobelprize.org/nobel_prizes/peace/laureates/1984/tutu-lecture.html.*

4. In this chapter, the term *religion* is used in two ways. It may refer to an individual's faith commitment to an organized religious group, such as King's commitment to the Southern Baptists. It may also refer to a commitment to a metaphysical, spiritual ideal, not necessarily connected to an organized religion. The latter distinction is important to a few of the women of the Brahma Vidya Mandir. For them, their commitment to nonviolence and purposeful action is not tied to specific doctrinal religious teachings, but rather to their beliefs in something they term "spiritual" that is beyond an organized religious group.

spiritual traditions often associated with Hinduism. By examining the lives of these people, we will explore the power of religion as a motivator for making positive change in the world.[5]

The methodology used in this chapter is "ethnographic." Rather than examine theoretical aspects of the religious motivation for social engagement, we look at the lives of individuals for whom religion was a powerful driving force. King was not a civil rights leader who happened to be a Baptist minister; he was a Baptist minister compelled to engage in the civil rights movement, with a commitment to nonviolence based on his interpretation of the teachings of Jesus. Malcolm X is often juxtaposed to King and portrayed as a radical, violent African American activist. While by no means a pacifist, Malcolm X was similarly motivated by his religious convictions, in his case his conversions to Islam. Finally, Vinoba Bhave acts out of a spiritual commitment to a belief in the underlying unity of all life, a perspective shared by many within Hinduism. Through his life, we find yet another example of how faith can motivate individuals to social action.

Questions for Reflection and Discussion

- What role do you think social activism plays in global religions, and how is religion tied to social issues?

- In what ways have you been socially active? Has your social activism been tied directly to religious commitment? If so, what was the connection and why was it important?

THE REV. DR. MARTIN LUTHER KING JR.

I have a dream that one day down in Alabama, with its vicious racists, with its governor having his lips dripping with the words of "interposition" and "nullification," one day right there in Alabama little black boys and black girls will be able to join hands with little white boys and white girls as sisters and brothers. I have a dream today. I have a dream that one day *every valley shall be exalted, and every hill and mountain shall be made low; the rough places will be made plain, and the crooked places will be made straight, and the glory of the Lord shall be revealed, and all flesh shall see it together.*[6]

Through these words, delivered on the steps of the Washington Monument in Washington, DC, the Rev. Martin Luther King Jr. anchors his dream of unity between black and white in the Hebrew Bible and New Testament. King recalls the cry of John the Baptist in the Gospel of Luke 3:5, a passage that itself recalls words from Isaiah 40:3–5. King's commitment to biblical texts and Christianity are not surprising given the environment from which he came.

Born January 15, 1929, Martin Luther King Jr. grew up in a loving, stable, financially secure, and deeply religious family of educated ministers in Atlanta, Georgia. In the face of discrimination and segregation, King's mother, Alberta Williams King, instilled in him a sense of "somebodiness."

---

5. The lives of the individuals we examine in this chapter are complex. None is perfect, and sometimes their actions contradicted their words. The purpose here is not to comprehensively examine all aspects of their lives, but rather to discover the ways in which religion motivated them to publicly act for social justice.

6. Martin Luther King Jr., "I Have a Dream," in *A Call to Conscience: The Landmark Speeches of Dr. Martin Luther King Jr.*, eds. Clayborne Carson and Kris Shepard (New York: Warner Books, 2001), 85–86. Emphasis added.

The only daughter of a successful minister, Alberta grew up sheltered from many aspects of discrimination, attending the best high schools and then college. She never adjusted to the segregation in the South. While she tried to explain the divided societal system to her young son, she also made it clear that he should never allow the system to make him feel inferior; that he was as good as anyone else.[7]

Martin Luther King Sr., a son of a sharecropper, began high school at age 18 and eventually graduated from Morehouse College (an all-male historically black college). He went on to become president of the National Association for the Advancement of Colored People (NAACP) and pastor of Ebenezer Baptist Church. Highly respected by both black and white communities, King Sr. provided for the family in such a way that his namesake could pursue his education and goals without ever having to worry about basic needs.

At age 14, King Jr. won a contest with a speech entitled, "The Negro and the Constitution," in which he said, "We cannot be truly Christian people so long as we flout the central teachings of Jesus: [loving one another][8] and the Golden Rule."[9] King Jr. further developed his philosophical ideas while attending seminary and graduate school. This higher education provided King with an understanding of and appreciation for religious and philosophical ideas that later became the foundation for his work in civil rights.

As King studied Marx, Reinhold Niebuhr, and other philosophers and theologians, he strengthened his understanding of and commitment to the Christian theology he was learning. While moved by the pacifist teachings of Dr. A. J. Muste (a leading early-twentieth-century nonviolent social activist in the United States),[10] King was at first convinced that Jesus' ethic of love was to be lived out in the context of individual relationships. He did not see how this nonviolent ethic of love could address the societal conflicts of his day. However, upon examining Gandhi's writings on love, King began to envision how Jesus' call to love one another could be applied on a societal level. King says,

> My study of Gandhi convinced me that true pacifism is not nonresistance to evil, but nonviolent resistance to evil. Between the two positions, there is a world of difference. Gandhi resisted evil with as much vigor and power as the violent resister, but he resisted with love instead of hate. True pacifism is not unrealistic submission to evil power, as Niebuhr contends. It is rather a courageous confrontation of evil by the power of love.[11]

Through Gandhi's example, King began to see Jesus' primary teaching of love as the basis for action. King finished graduate school convinced that the most powerful weapon for the oppressed against social injustice is nonviolent resistance, or

---

7. Martin Luther King Jr., *The Autobiography of Martin Luther King, Jr.*, ed. Clayborne Carson (New York: Warner Books, 1998), 1–5.

8. In this specific example, King said "brotherly love." In the context of his comments, he is referring to a love among the followers of Jesus; he is not speaking exclusively to men. When it is appropriate, or will not disrupt the flow of a quotation, I edit in favor of inclusive language. Similarly, when appropriate, I use gender-inclusive language when referring to God or the Divine. In keeping with protocol, all such changes are in brackets. The reader should keep in mind that though a quotation may refer to "men," the speakers are often addressing all people regardless of gender.

9. Ibid., 9.

10. A. J. Muste is another excellent example of an individual whose active involvement in the struggle for peace and justice is steeped in religious commitment. To learn more about his life go to *http://www.ajmuste.org*.

11. Ibid., 26.

noncooperation and passive resistance. He saw these commitments as epitomized by Christian love as modeled in the Sermon on the Mount. This intellectual commitment became the foundation for his actions as a civil rights leader.[12]

Just as King's commitment to nonviolence was based on the teachings of Jesus, so the rest of his participation in the civil rights movement was grounded in his Christian faith. According to King, nonviolence is simply Christianity in action, a way of life and not just a technique to fight social injustice. During the Montgomery bus boycott in early 1956, discouraged, weakened, and ready to give up, King prayed, "I am at the end of my powers. I have nothing left. I've come to the point where I can't face it alone." In his kitchen at midnight, he found reassurance and strength. King writes, "I heard the voice of Jesus saying still to fight on. He promised never to leave me alone. At that moment I experienced the presence of the Divine as I had never experienced Him before. Almost at once my fears began to go. My uncertainty disappeared. I was ready to face anything."[13]

King's speeches demonstrate again and again his reliance on faith. After Rosa Parks was arrested for refusing to give up her seat on a bus, King was invited to speak to the crowd gathered for the first Montgomery Improvement Association (MIA) mass meeting. King had less than twenty minutes to prepare the "most decisive speech of my life."[14] In the heart of his talk, King proclaims:

> [W]e must keep God in the forefront. Let us be Christian in all of our actions. But I want to tell you this evening that it is not enough for us to talk about love, love is one of the pivotal points of the Christian faith. There is another side called justice. And justice is really love in calculation. Justice is love correcting that which revolts. The Almighty God is not the only, not the God just standing out saying through Hosea, "I love you, Israel." [God is] also the God that stands up before the nations and said, "Be still and know that I'm God, that if you don't obey me I will break the backbone of your power and slap you out of the orbits of your international and national relationships." Standing beside love is always justice, and we are only using the tools of justice.[15]

According to King, love is the central teaching of Christianity and justice is inseparable from it. By going forward with the tools of love and justice, King sees the possibility of victory in his fight for civil rights.

In another speech, "Give Us the Ballot," King again emphasizes the importance of working for freedom nonviolently.

> [W]e must be sure that our hands are clean in the struggle. We must never struggle with falsehood, hate or malice. We must never become bitter. . . .
>
> We must meet hate with love. We must meet physical force with soul force. There is still a voice crying out through the vista of time, saying: "Love your enemies, bless them that curse you, pray for them that despitefully use you."[16]

Here again King quotes from the New Testament to explain his response to injustice. His faith clearly dictates how he ought to respond, even to those who are the cause of his and others'

---

12. Ibid., 32, 67.

13. Ibid., 78.

14. *A Call to Conscience*, 11–12.

15. Martin Luther King Jr., "Address to the First Montgomery Improvement Association (MIA) Mass Meeting," in *A Call to Conscience*, 11–12. This speech was delivered at Holt Street Baptist Church, Montgomery, Alabama, December 5, 1955.

16. Martin Luther King Jr., "Give Us the Ballot," in *A Call to Conscience*, 51–52.

pain. As a Christian, he is fighting for freedom for all people, all of God's created beings.

King's faith enables him to see that there is a place for suffering; Jesus after all was beaten and crucified. However, King's belief also indicates that though righteousness and justice may seem dead, crucifixion is followed by resurrection and eventual victory. King's speeches are filled with biblical imagery and Christian hymns. As he addressed the marchers who walked from Selma to Montgomery, Alabama, he recalled the story of Joshua and the children of Israel's march around Jericho. His speech ended with words from the hymn "Glory Hallelujah": "My eyes have seen the glory of the coming of the Lord." His "I Have a Dream" speech and his talk at the Freedom Rally in Cobo Hall in Detroit ended with words from an old, Negro spiritual, "Free at last! Free at last! Thank God Almighty, we are free at last!"

One of King's last speeches, "The Birth of a Nation," demonstrates his continuing firm faith and commitment to nonviolence in the fight for justice. Recalling the biblical story of the Exodus of the Hebrew people from slavery in Egypt, King discussed the universal human

struggle for freedom. According to King, to "rob a man of his freedom is to take from him the essential basis of his manhood. To take from him his freedom is to rob him of something of God's image." He continued, "There is something deep down within the very soul of man that reaches out for Canaan."[17] King answered this cry for freedom with boycotts, sit-ins, and other nonviolent actions.

In this same speech, King described the benefits of nonviolent resistance: "The aftermath of nonviolence is the creation of the beloved community. The aftermath of nonviolence is redemption. The aftermath of nonviolence is reconciliation. The aftermath of violence [is] emptiness and bitterness."[18] As he closed this speech, reflecting that freedom, fought for nonviolently, is never easy, he again turned to the narratives of the Hebrew Bible and the New Testament. He recalled the stories of the Exodus, of Isaiah's hills and valleys, of Moses, Joshua, John, and other biblical figures. Through them he painted a picture of a world where all see God at the head and all of humanity living together as brothers and sisters.[19]

Questions for Reflection and Discussion

- If you had been a young adult in the 1950s and 1960s, how, if at all, would you have participated in the struggle for civil rights?
- In what ways might the sacred texts of Christianity be used to support or restrict civil rights?

- Have you experienced racism or bigotry? If so, how did you respond to it?
- What social systems exist today that might be addressed through social activism?
- Would you become involved with a social activist group if asked? Why or why not?

17. Martin Luther King Jr., "The Birth of a Nation," in *A Call to Conscience*, 20.
18. Ibid., 32.
19. Ibid., 39–41.

MALCOLM X

Unlike King, who enjoyed a relatively comfortable and secure family life, Malcolm Little was born into a family thrown into chaos when his father was killed, his mother was put in a mental institution, and he and his siblings were split up among different foster families and orphanages. While King was raised by loving, nurturing parents and supported financially and emotionally through college, Malcolm X was raised by several foster parents, lived in a group home for delinquent children, and had little support from the adults around him. While Protestant Christianity provided a firm religious foundation and consistent base for King, religion was anything but a stabilizing force within the early years of Malcolm X's life. Only later, during his time in prison, did certain forms of Islam become the driving force in his life. Specifically, the Nation of Islam and traditional Arab Islam brought about two dramatic changes for Malcolm X, not only transforming his life but also redefining his world and his activity in it.

From early childhood, Malcolm X's experiences with white people and people claiming to be Christian were largely negative. Ku Klux Klan members burned crosses in his yard; white men burned his home and may have killed his father. His mother struggled to keep the family together, but members of her local church and white social workers finally had her institutionalized and his family dispersed.

In grade school, Malcolm was the only African American and one of the school's top students. He would later recall a conversation with a white English teacher whom he trusted and respected as a major turning point in his life. When asked by this teacher what career he would like to pursue, Malcolm said he wanted to be a lawyer. This same teacher encouraged his white students to follow their dreams, but his advice to Malcolm was to be "more realistic. You need to think about something you *can* be. You're good with your hands — making things. Everybody admires your carpentry shop work. Why don't you plan on carpentry?"[20] Though people like this teacher may have meant the best for Malcolm, he realized he did not fit into that white Christian world. After completing eighth grade, he wrote to his older half-sister, Ella, and asked to move to Boston to live with her.

THE NATION OF ISLAM

The Nation of Islam (NOI) began as one of many African American Muslim groups focusing on the experience of African Americans. (See article by Curtis.) The NOI was primarily under the leadership of Elijah Muhammad, who claimed to be a messenger of Allah. As with most groups, its membership and the teachings they espoused were not monolithic. Upon Elijah Muhammad's death, the NOI underwent major changes and splits. While many followed his sixth son, W. D. Muhammad, others sought the leadership of Louis Farrakhan. W. D. Muhammad brought many changes, among them he renounced a number of teachings seen as heretical by most Sunni Muslims, he allowed white people to join the group, and he changed the name of the group to World Community of Al-Islam in the West. In 1980 he changed the name again, this time to American Muslim Mission. Currently, NOI is under the leadership of Louis Farrakhan.

20. Malcolm X, *The Autobiography of Malcolm X*, as told to Alex Haley (New York: Ballantine Books, 1965), 43.

Looking back, Malcolm X described this move as life changing. If he had not moved to Roxbury, "I'd probably still be a brainwashed black Christian," he said.[21]

In his autobiography, Malcolm X describes his early involvement in a world of crime. Beginning as a shoe shiner at the Roseland State Ballroom, he entered into a world of nightclubs, big bands, hustling, gambling, pushing and doing drugs, womanizing, drinking, and violence. In 1946, Malcolm was convicted of carrying firearms and breaking and entering and sentenced to ten years in prison. While in prison, his brothers and sisters converted to the Nation of Islam (NOI) and slowly introduced him to their new faith and the teachings of Elijah Muhammad. Through the guidance of Elijah Muhammad and visits from his siblings, Malcolm began following the practices and beliefs of the NOI.

Elijah Muhammad taught that blacks were the original human beings and that whites were the devil. According to him, this devil had been oppressing the black race long enough, and it was time for blacks to stand tall and claim their rightful place. These teachings helped Malcolm X make sense of his life as a black man. He wrote:

> Here is a black [person] caged behind bars, probably for years, put there by the white [people]. Usually the convict comes from among those bottom-of-the-pile Negroes, the Negroes who through their entire lives have been kicked about, treated like children—Negroes who never have met one white [person] who didn't either take something from them or do something to them. . . . You let this caged-up black [person] start realizing, as I did, how from the first landing of the first slave ship, the millions of black [people] in American have been like sheep in a den of wolves. That's why black prisoners become Muslims so fast. . . . "The white [person] is the devil" is a perfect echo of that black convict's lifelong experience.[22]

While sitting in prison, Malcolm reflected upon his life. He saw many instances where the white person indeed had been a "devil." It was this devil who had burned his home, killed his father, institutionalized his mother, separated his family, encouraged him to abandon his dreams, and ultimately thrown him in prison. The teachings of Elijah Muhammad made sense to him.

By the time Malcolm was paroled in 1952, he had been studying the teachings of Elijah Muhammad for four years. His criminal days were over and through his conversion to the NOI, his whole life had been transformed. Later he wrote, "Any fornication was absolutely forbidden in the Nation of Islam. No Muslim who followed Elijah Muhammad could dance, gamble, date, attend movies, or sports."[23] While Malcolm was once a hustler, womanizer, and thief who looked out only for himself, he was now a devout student of Elijah Muhammad. He stopped smoking, doing drugs, even eating pork. He was celibate from the time of his conversion until he married his wife, Sister Betty X. Following a tradition established by Elijah Muhammad, Malcolm and Betty replaced their last names of "Little" and "Sanders," respectively, with "X." This signified their unknown, original African surnames and their rejection of their slave masters' last names.

Once out of prison, Malcolm X devoted his life to Elijah Muhammad, a man who had saved his life—both literally and spiritually. This conversion directly influenced the path and focus

---

21. Ibid., 46.
22. Ibid., 211–212.
23. Ibid., 255.

of his life. Malcolm X rose within the leadership of the NOI. He traveled the country speaking, recruiting members, and opening NOI temples. Under his leadership, the NOI grew from about five hundred members to a powerful force of black people numbering in the thousands.

Malcolm X's new faith propelled him onto the national stage with a message that differed from that of other African American leaders of the time. While Martin Luther King Jr. advocated equality among white sand blacks, Malcolm X argued that equality is impossible and preached the "sharp truth" that he thought could cure and save the African American man and woman. He wrote that he wanted to begin to help them see the truth about the white man. "I know you don't realize the enormity, the horrors, of the so-called Christian white man's crime." Malcolm X exhorted. "Every time you see a white man, think about the devil you're seeing! Think of how it was on *your* slave foreparents' bloody, sweaty back that he built this empire that's today the richest of all nations—where his evil and his greed cause him to be hated around the world!"[24] As Malcolm X spread this message, he was convinced it spoke truth to the experience of many African Americans like himself.

The teachings of Elijah Muhammad redefined how Malcolm X understood the world: whites were the devil; salvation or freedom was gained by fighting and overcoming these white, Christian devils. Malcolm X felt compelled to enlighten his fellow brothers and sisters with his new faith. It became the ground upon which he spoke:

A QUOTE ABOUT HATE

Shortly after President John F. Kennedy's assassination on November 22, 1963, reporters asked Malcolm X what he thought about the assassination. His now famous (infamous) response: "Without a second thought, I said what I honestly felt—that it was, as I saw it, a case of 'the chickens coming home to roost.' I said that the hate in white men had not stopped with the killing of defenseless black people, but that hate, allowed to spread unchecked, finally had struck down this country's Chief of State." (Malcolm X, *The Autobiography of Malcolm X*, as told to Alex Haley [New York: Ballantine Books, 1965], 347.)

Brothers and sisters, the white man has brainwashed us black people to fasten our gaze upon a blond-haired, blue-eyed Jesus! . . . The white man has taught us to shout and sing and pray until we *die*, to wait until *death*, for some dreamy heaven-in-the-hereafter, when we're *dead*, while this white man has his milk and honey in the streets paved with golden dollars right here on *this* earth![25]

Malcolm X called for blacks to come out from under the burden of oppression and stand on their own, to separate from their former white, Christian oppressors. Whereas Malcolm X's early experience of Christianity led him to an attitude of acceptance and passivity, he found the teachings of Elijah Muhammad to be life affirming and a call to action and reform. No longer, as an African American man, would he accept the enslavement of white Christianity.

Today, many think of Malcolm X as the black, radical instigator of violence against

---

24. Ibid., 244–245.
25. Ibid., 253.

whites. While Malcolm X's early messages called African Americans to reject discrimination and subjugation using all means necessary, including violence, he actually ended most of his meetings saying: "Do nothing unto anyone that you would not like to have done unto yourself. Seek peace, and never be the aggressor—but if anyone attacks you, we do not teach you to turn the other cheek."[26] Clearly Malcolm X was not a pacifist or a nonviolent activist like King, but he did not instigate violence either. As Malcolm X saw it, he was simply a messenger of Elijah Muhammad, passing on the truth that saved his life.

In 1954, while preparing to speak at the Harvard Law School Forum, Malcolm X happened to look out the window and see the apartment building where he and his burglary gang used to hang out. He later wrote, "Awareness came surging up in me—how deeply the religion of Islam had reached down into the mud to lift me up, to save me from being what I inevitably would have been."[27] For Malcolm X and others, Elijah Muhammad was a father, he was the NOI. According to Malcolm X, "We Muslims regarded ourselves as moral and mental and spiritual examples for other black Americans, because we followed the personal example of Elijah Muhammad."[28] He wrote, "I *loved* the Nation, and Mr. Muhammad. I *lived for* the Nation, and for Mr. Muhammad."[29]

That admiration and love were challenged at the end of 1962 and 1963. Malcolm X learned of Elijah Muhammad's adulterous relationships with three former secretaries. Elijah Muhammad

also silenced Malcolm X for his "chickens come home to roost" comment, and the previously life-sustaining relationship between the two began to crumble.[30] During his painful split with Elijah Muhammad and the NOI, Malcolm X was keenly aware of his unique position of leadership. While he could command the microphones of major news media, speak at Harvard and other universities, and talk with middle-class African Americans, he was one of the few leaders who could also communicate with the "ghetto blacks." He had lived in that world and never strayed far from it. His frequent NOI rallies in Harlem, Chicago's inner city, and other cities earned him the respect and trust of poor urban blacks: Malcolm X was their leader and spokesperson. He felt challenged to create an organization that "could help to cure the black man in North America of the sickness which has kept him under the white man's heel." The African American black person was psychologically and spiritually sick, he said, "because for centuries he had accepted the white man's Christianity."[31]

While he left the NOI, Malcolm X did not abandon his commitment to free his fellow African Americans from such crippling bonds. His dream was to create an organization different from the NOI that "would embrace *all* faiths of black [people], and it would carry into practice what the Nation of Islam had only preached."[32] He founded the Muslim Mosque Inc. Organization of Afro-American Unity (OAAU). While he accepted the support of whites for his new organization, membership was limited to African Americans. This organization formed

26. Ibid., 246.

27. Ibid., 330.

28. Ibid., 332.

29. Ibid., 337.

30. Ibid., 332–365.

31. Ibid., 360–361.

32. Ibid., 363 (emphasis added).

the base for "an action program designed to eliminate the political oppression, the economic exploitation, and the social degradation suffered daily by twenty-two million Afro-Americans."[33] In establishing this organization, Malcolm X retained Elijah Muhammad's teachings that white Christians were the oppressors. However, his new message broke from Elijah Muhammad's teachings in two primary ways. First, membership was open to African Americans of all faiths (not just members of the NOI), and second, there was a focus on political action.

Malcolm X did not belittle the words of the NOI or Elijah Muhammad, as they had saved his life and shaped how he engaged the world once he was released from prison. However, the break with the NOI ultimately lead Malcolm X to a second conversion experience that was just as transformative as his first. After establishing the OAAU, Malcolm X had another pressing desire: to go on his hajj, his pilgrimage to Mecca.[34] In April 1964, Malcolm X embarked on a journey that led to a religious experience that again redefined his world.

From the beginning of his pilgrimage to the Middle East, Malcolm X was repeatedly amazed by how he was treated—and how he was received by white people. On the flight to Saudi Arabia, in the airports, in Cairo, Jedda, and Mecca, Malcolm X was welcomed and honored. When asked by a group of fellow Muslims on their hajj what impressed him the most, he answered: "The *brotherhood*! The people of all races, colors, from all over the world coming together as *one*! It has proved to me the power of the One God."[35] On this journey, Malcolm X was experiencing Islam in a way he never had as a member of the NOI. He felt he was coming to understand the oneness of God on a different level.

In a letter he wrote home to Betty, he said,

Never have I witnessed such sincere hospitality and the overwhelming spirit of true brotherhood as is practiced by people of all colors and races here. . . . There were tens of thousands of pilgrims, from all over the world. They were of all colors, from blue-eyed blonds to black-skinned Africans. But we were all participating in the same ritual, displaying a spirit of unity and brotherhood that my experiences in America had led me to believe never could exist between the white and the non-white.[36]

Malcolm X continued:

What, I have seen, and experienced, has forced me to re-arrange much of my thought-patterns previously held, and to toss aside some of my previous conclusions. . . .

During the past eleven days here in the Muslim world, I have eaten from the same plate, drunk from the same glass . . . with fellow Muslims, whose eyes were the bluest of blue, whose hair was the blondest of blond, and whose skin was the whitest of white. And in the *words* and in the *actions* and in the *deeds* of the "white" Muslims, I felt the same sincerity that I felt among the black African Muslims of Nigeria, Sudan, and Ghana.

We were *truly* all the same (brothers).[37]

---

33. Ibid., 365.

34. The hajj is one of the five pillars of Islamic faith, the central teachings of orthodox Islam. For more basic information on traditional Islam, see Fredrick Mathewson Denny's *Introduction to Islam* (Upper Saddle River, NJ: Pearson Prentice Hall, 2006), or John L. Esposito, *Islam: The Straight Path* (New York: Oxford University Press Inc., 2004).

35. Ibid., 390–391.

36. Ibid., 391.

37. Ibid., 390–391.

In the above letter, we see how Malcolm X's experience was causing him to reassess what he was taught and was teaching about white people. His experience transformed his understanding of the world around him: a white person could now be his brother or sister, not the devil.

In his speech, "After the Bombing," delivered at the Ford Auditorium on February 14, 1965, Malcolm X said:

> When I was in the Black Muslim movement, I wasn't—they didn't have the real religion of Islam in that movement. It was something else. And the real religion of Islam doesn't teach anyone to judge another human being by the color of his skin. The yardstick that is used by the Muslim to measure another [person] is not the [person's] color but the [person's] deeds, the [person's] conscious behavior, the [person's] intentions. And when you use that as a standard of measurement or judgment, you never go wrong.[38]

This is a long way from what Malcolm X preached under the tutelage of Elijah Muhammad. Malcolm X's hajj had introduced him to what he termed "real" and "true" Islam. Through his conversion to traditional Arab Islam, Malcolm X again found a way to understand the world, one that coincided with what he was experiencing.

Throughout Malcolm X's life, the powerful influence of religion is evident. His conversion to the NOI had transformed his life and how he engaged the world. Where he once stole, pimped, and got high, his conversion to the NOI and commitment to Elijah Muhammad

TRADITIONAL ARAB ISLAM

Traditional Arab Islam does not support a number of Elijah Muhammad's teachings, including that white people are the devil and the original humans were black (Yacub's History). Central to most, if not all, Islamic traditions are the five pillars of faith:

1. *Shahada*: witnessing, a statement of faith (creed), "There is no God but God, and Muhammad is the messenger of God"
2. *Salat*: formal prayer five times a day
3. *Zakat*: almsgiving, an act that sustains the community and cares for those who are less fortunate
4. *Sawm*: fasting during the month of Ramadan
5. *Hajj*: one's pilgrimage to Mecca

put his lawless days behind him. He became an outstanding leader of the NOI and worked to better the lives of others. Later his experiences during his hajj were in part responsible for his second conversion, to traditional Arab Islam. Upon discovering the teachings of what he called "real" Islam, his understanding of the world again changed: no longer was it white against black. Now his fight was against the oppressor without regard to color, race, or religious conviction. Where he once rejected the offer of a young white woman to assist in his fight, he now welcomed the assistance of all who were willing to fight oppression—black or white.

Malcolm X's experiences within these two aspects of Islam dramatically transformed his life and influenced how he perceived and acted in the world. As with Dr. King, Malcolm X's life is a testament to the power behind religious motivation for social engagement.

---

38. *http://www.malcolm-x.org/speeches/spc_021465.htm*. This speech was delivered the day after his house had been bombed.

Questions for Reflection and Discussion

- Have you ever experienced what it is like to be a minority? If so, what did it feel like and in what ways did religion or religious commitments help or hinder you?

- How does religion influence how one might think about one's life and life-choices?

- What roles might religion play in fostering or fighting oppression?

- How might a religious pilgrimage influence one's understanding of religion?

VINOBA BHAVE

During his long-awaited 1959 visit to India, Dr. King Jr. met Vinoba Bhave, a follower, friend, confidant, and spiritual successor to M. K. Gandhi. While most in the United States and the world know of Gandhi and Dr. King, few have heard of Vinoba Bhave. Though Vinoba[39] is considered a saint by many, he says of himself, "I am just one individual; I wear no label, I am not a member of any institution, I have nothing to do with political parties. . . . People like what I say because my work is rooted in compassion, love, and thought."[40] Here Vinoba claims no particular religious affiliation. However, in his discourses on the Bhagavad-Gita and in his memoir, *Moved by Love*, as well as in many other writings, he speaks from a position that finds firm footing in the religious traditions of India. His ability to embrace any number of traditions, his abiding commitment to nonviolence, and his work rooted in compassion and love all comfortably fall within Hindu religious traditions.

As a student of Gandhi, Vinoba writes, "I not only studied his ideas and writings, I lived in his company, and spent my whole time, in my youth, in the various forms of service which he started.

HINDUISM

Hindu, as a religious label, is a late term originally applied to people living east of India's western border who were not Jewish, Christian, or Muslim. While there are no central leaders, religious texts, or practices, there are many common threads that permeate a number of religious traditions categorized as Hindu. Here are but four:

- a belief in the underlying unity of all life;
- a belief that an all-pervading Reality (*Brahman*) and one's soul or Self (*Atman*) are one and the same;
- a belief in certain rules and values concerning social order, duty, responsibility, and so on (*dharma*);
- a belief in a cosmic law of cause and effect (*karma*).

According to persons such as Gandhi and Vinoba, these beliefs presume a commitment to no-harm and nonviolence (*ahimsa*).

---

39. In academics, it is common to refer to an individual by last name. However, Vinoba Bhave has traditionally been referred to by his first name. Thus, out of respect for him and his followers, I follow this convention and refer to him as Vinoba, a name given to him by Gandhi.

40. Vinoba Bhave, *Moved by Love: The Memoirs of Vinoba Bhave*, trans. Marjorie Sykes from a Hindi text prepared by Kalindi (Hyderabad: Sat Sahitya Sahayogi Sangh, 1994), 17.

His presence, his ideas, and the opportunity to put them into practice—I had the benefit of all three."[41] Of particular importance to Vinoba were Gandhi's teachings on nonviolence. While living and working in one of Gandhi's ashrams,[42] Vinoba learned that the basis of nonviolence was fearlessness. According to Gandhi, "There could be no non-violence without fearlessness. . . . [I]t follows from that that the most important aspect of non-violence is inward non-violence, which is not possible without fearlessness."[43] Vinoba was intrigued by this idea of nonviolence and began a correspondence with Gandhi.

Vinoba understood nonviolence as a religious vow often taken by individuals; however, Gandhi's call went beyond personal religious commitment, it was a vow necessary for national freedom. Gandhi called for the entire nation of Indians to rise up and nonviolently resist the British occupation of India. This challenged Vinoba's ideas regarding an individual's commitment to nonviolence. Vinoba writes:

> [H]ere is someone who insists that [vows of nonviolence] are necessary for national service too. That was what drew me to Bapu [Gandhi]. Here was a man, I felt, who aimed at one and the same point at both political freedom and spiritual development. I was delighted. He said "Come," and I went.[44]

While a personal commitment to nonviolence continues to be an important belief for many, Gandhi's work of bringing it into the public, political sphere extended that value to a great many people.

The same nonviolence that characterized Gandhi's fight for Indian independence from Britain also inspired and influenced Vinoba's writings and actions—especially his social reform efforts.

Vinoba's commitment to nonviolence in everyday life is evident in his explanation of whether the Bhagavad-Gita, a key text within Hinduism, provides clear teachings on what one should or should not do. In his well-loved and well-read text, *Talks on the Gita*, Vinoba writes:

> Some say that the Gita enjoins us to act with renunciation of the fruit; it does not suggest which actions should be done. It does appear so, but it is not true. When it is said that one should act and renounce the fruit of action, it becomes clear what actions should be done and which should not be done. Actions intended to harm others, actions full of falsehood, actions like stealing can never be done if their fruit is to be renounced.[45]

According to Vinoba, the Gita does indeed teach people how to act. People should behave in such a way that they do not hold on to the results or consequences of their actions—that is what is meant by "renunciation of the fruits." People are not to get too excited when they win or lose. While it is true that this teaching in and of itself does not provide specific instructions regarding how people ought to act, Vinoba argues that if followed faithfully, this teaching clearly calls all people to nonviolent actions. When people intend to harm, lie, or steal, they are, by the very nature of these activities, tied to the results of their actions. Thus, according to Vinoba, the

---

41. Ibid., 19–20.

42. An ashram is an intentional community where members are usually brought together by a particular religious leader for a common purpose. The focus of Gandhi's ashrams was "constructive work": to implement programs of basic social reform in India. Gandhi's fight for Indian independence emphasized education and political and social reform. Vinoba worked for social reform.

43. Vinoba, *Moved by Love*, 64.

44. Ibid., 65.

45. Vinoba Bhave, *Talks on the Gita*, 16th ed. (Wardha: Paramdham Prakashan, 2005), 263.

Gita clearly instructs individuals how to act. According to him, it teaches nonviolence.

Following Gandhi's example, Vinoba develops his understanding and application of nonviolence far beyond a personal vow. In *Moved by Love*, he writes,

> During the course of my work, both in Ashrams and outside them, I have aimed at finding out how difficulties of every kind in the life of a society, and in the life of the individual, may be overcome by non-violence. . . . After Gandhi passed away I was therefore trying to discover how a non-violent social order might be built.[46]

To this end, Vinoba works to bring about a nonviolent revolution that infuses the everyday life of every individual. His writing, life, and many projects demonstrate his commitment to bring about this nonviolent society.

In his commentary on the Bhagavad-Gita, Vinoba defines what he means by nonviolence: "Compassion for all creatures, gentleness, forgiveness, serenity, freedom from anger and malice—all these are different terms for non-violence. In fact all the virtues are contained in truth and nonviolence; truth and nonviolence are the essence of all of them."[47] Nonviolence for Vinoba is more than simply not fighting; it is having compassion for others and living truthfully. Coupled with this compassion and freedom from anger is the powerful force of fearlessness espoused by Gandhi.

Vinoba's fearlessness and confidence in the power of compassion is evident in one of his best-known projects: the *Bhoodan Yatra* (land gift) movement. In 1951, Vinoba was approached by a group of poor, landless people from the village of Pochampalli in Andhra Pradesh in

southeastern India. They told Vinoba that if they could get just eighty acres of land, then they could live, farm, and sustain themselves and their families. Vinoba agreed to assist them under one condition; they had to promise to work the land together, as a cooperative, not as individual farmers. They agreed and Vinoba promised to send their petition to the proper state authorities.[48] Vinoba was well aware that his promise was limited. Though this petition might be accepted by a government official and might bring life and a livelihood to a particular set of families, it would not answer the devastating poverty that engulfed so many of India's landless poor.

During that meeting, after Vinoba had promised to do what he could, a man from the village of Pochampalli, Ramachandra Reddy, offered to give the poor families one hundred acres of his own land. Vinoba reflects on this event:

> There in my presence he gave them his word: "I will give you one hundred acres." What was this? People murder for land, go to court over land, yet here it comes as a free gift. This was something so completely out of the ordinary that it must surely be a sign from God! All night long I pondered over what had happened. It was a revolution—people may be moved by love to share even their land . . . for my part I believe that any problem can be solved in a non-violent way, provided only that the heart is pure.[49]

Vinoba saw Reddy's act as a nonviolent, noncommunist answer that could actually diminish, if not eradicate, the problems of poverty in India. This act of love for one's fellow human beings compelled Vinoba to act, and he established the Bhoodhan Yatra.

46. Vinoba, *Moved by Love*, 18–19.
47. Vinoba, *Talks on the Gita*, 233.
48. Vinoba, *Moved by Love*, 129.
49. Ibid.

According to Vinoba, this new movement had one main purpose: "to get land for the poor. Mother Earth must no longer be separated from her sons [and daughters], she and they must be brought together again."[50] Earlier, Vinoba said,

> Every human being has as much right to land as he has to air, water and sunlight; so long as there are people with no land at all it is wrong for an individual to keep more than he needs. When he gives it away it should be because he wants to right the wrong. That is the spirit of the land-gift movement.[51]

Vinoba made clear that this revolution would not be successful unless the land given was a gift to redress a wrong, not a handout that entitled the giver and obligated the recipient.

After some calculations, Vinoba decided to ask landowners to give one-sixth of their land to the poor. He based this on the idea that an average Indian family of five could accept one poor, landless individual as a "sixth member of the family." With the planning done, Vinoba set out on foot asking people to give land as a gift in the name of "God in the form of the poor." He said, "I am not asking alms. I am asking [people] to accept an initiation into a new way of life."[52] For fourteen years, Vinoba walked throughout India. He would come into a village, gather its members, deliver a lecture on *sarvodaya* (the word implies "the wholistic [sic] growth and all around development of all the sections of global humanity"),[53] talk with the villagers, and encourage them to act as a family and care for the needs of all their members. He taught about the fearlessness required to act nonviolently, and

he invited those with land to give a portion to those who had none.

In 1959 during a visit to a village, Vinoba was approached by a number of women who worked with him in the Bhoodan Yatra. These women sought the opportunity to pursue a "spiritual life" rather than the standard life of wife and mother. Upon their insistence, Vinoba established the Brahma Vidya Mandir, an ashram for women. He writes, "With Truth and non-violence in our armoury, we should march ahead fearlessly. We ought to move freely over the whole expanse of the vast and extensive life.... We can then fearlessly move ahead, carrying out experiments in truth and non-violence."[54] One such experiment was this ashram for women.

When establishing the Brahma Vidya Mandir, Vinoba wrote,

> The spiritual achievements of women have always remained hidden; and while they have certainly influenced individuals, it is needful that their sadhana [spiritual development] should now be openly seen. Without the women, men alone cannot bring about the world peace which is the crying need of our present times.

Reflecting historically, he continued:

> In former days women tried to realize their spiritual strength as individuals, and their efforts bear fruit today, by inspiring us to believe that they may also realize themselves in community. The coming age will be one in which women play a major role, and their spiritual strength must therefore be called out.[55]

50. Ibid., 133.

51. Ibid., 130.

52. Ibid., 134–135.

53. Acharya Dada Dharmadhikari, *Philosophy of Sarvodaya* (Delhi: Tarun Enterprises, 2000), vii.

54. Vinoba, *Talks on the Gita*, 233

55. Vinoba, *Moved by Love*, 197–198.

The women today living in the Brahma Vidya Mandir live a simple life focusing on spiritual development as a community. According to one sister, it is the community aspect that enables them to develop spiritually on a different level. She could live by herself in a cave, isolated from others, but it is in her struggles to work and live with the other members that her shortcomings come to light; it is in this process that she is shown the areas in her own life on which she needs to work.

The Bhoodan Yatra, a movement grounded in Vinoba's belief in the goodness of humankind, God being "in the poor," and *sarvodaya*, is one of his most widespread legacies. His teachings and efforts are continued today by countless *sarvodaya* workers throughout India. A second legacy is the Brahma Vidya Mandir. As a beacon on a hill, this community of women helps Vinoba's vision to continue today. According to the women currently living in this ashram, the purpose of the Brahma Vidya Mandir is "to offer women the possibility of living a deeply contemplative life overflowing in fruitful activities for the good of society."[56] In their own words, they are

> diligently committed to *samuhik sadhana* (collective spiritual devotion for the realization of the Self). This collective spiritual *sadhana* is a central theme of the ashram. In short, this means surrendering all of one's capacities at the feet [of] the Lord, abiding in the group, and seeing the inter-union of all aspirants as different organs of one body.[57]

Together the sisters live, work, and pray as a community. They run the day-to-day business of the ashram by dividing the labor and working together. Decisions are made by the group, and they do not move forward on an issue without unanimous consensus. The ideal, or goal, is that every member, regardless of age, is given an equal vote. They worship the divine while living in solidarity with the poor, owning little, working with simple tools, and living close to the earth. They spin the cotton thread for their own *khadi* (hand-spun cotton fabric) clothing. By doing so, they circumvent the market economy that suppresses and oppresses the poorest and most vulnerable women and children in the world. As they produce most of their food and have cows for milk and biofuel, their carbon footprint is negligible — demonstrating a commitment to nonviolence that extends from all people to the earth itself. Again, it is in the struggle to live with such ideas that the women of the Brahma Vidya Mandir believe they are growing and developing spiritually. Their work and their very lifestyle are grounded in spiritual or religious convictions.

Questions for Reflection and Discussion

- Are religion and nonviolence natural allies? Why or why not?
- Do religions and religious practices teach fearlessness? If so, how? If not, why not?
- If you ascribe to a particular religion, how does it influence how you interact in political, public, and social sectors of life?
- Do you need religion in order to effectively engage social and political problems? Why or why not?

---

56. Quote from a Brahma Vidya Mandir handout for English-speaking visitors and guests to the ashram.

57. Ibid.

e been describing a particular
on in the society he was examin-
alled it an opiate. However, Marx's
u.... / no means captures the transformative, mot.ating power of religion as demonstrated in the lives of the individuals discussed
here. Dr. King, Malcolm X, and Vinoba Bhave
spoke and acted on behalf of peace and justice.
Their fights against discrimination, racism,
injustice, and poverty grew directly out of their
commitments to religious teachings, ideologies,
and traditions.

Sam Harris in *The End of Faith: Religion,
Terror, and the Future of Reason* and Jack Nelson-
Pallmeyer in *Is Religion Killing Us?* contend that
religion is either "dead" or not helpful, and perhaps even dangerous. According to these authors
and others, the September 11 terrorist attacks
rendered religion outdated and irrelevant.

But Daniel L. Smith-Christopher takes
a different view of the challenge that many
bring to religion in our "post-9/11" world. In an
introductory chapter to *Subverting Hatred: The
Challenge of Nonviolence in Religious Traditions,*
Smith-Christopher questions the belief that
"everything is different now." He asks: "Different for whom? Can we be so narrow in our perspective, so self-centered, so ill-informed? This
popular phrase . . . can be interpreted to imply
that the times are 'different' because now *we* are
the ones who have suffered; *I* am the one who
feels vulnerable."[58] The destruction of the Twin
Towers in New York City along with a large portion of the Pentagon in Washington, DC, and
the crash of Flight 93 in a Pennsylvania field
was unquestionably the worst act of terrorism

the people of the United States have ever experienced. However, Smith-Christopher argues that
the idea that everything is different now "presents
a questionable claim that some peoples ought to
be somehow exempt from the innocent suffering
of humanity throughout history."[59] According
to him, "The faithful of all religious traditions
are called upon to reflect on the truth that our
suffering is a comparative suffering because there
have been so many others." He continues,

> In truth, people of faith ought to be the last ones
> taken in by the notion that "everything is differ-
> ent now." We know better. Some things change.
> But there is something deeply embedded in
> centuries of religious wisdom that remains true,
> remains the same, and remains the guiding light
> for our lives, even in the twenty-first century.[60]

Smith-Christopher sees religions as a
repository of the wisdom of the past. It is through
reflecting on this past, drawing from the wisdom
and experience of those who have come before,
that humanity can participate in a deep, thought-
ful conversation that can address human suffering.
For King, Malcolm X, Vinoba, the women of the
Brahma Vidya Mandir, and all those these persons
affect, religion is not outdated. It is a repository
of some of the most successful "weapons" against
violence: peace, justice, and nonviolence.

There are many other examples of people
whose choice to act for good in this world are
based on religious convictions. Kathy Kelly, the
cofounder of Voices for Creative Nonviolence,
firmly grounds her nonviolent, peace-activist work
in the tradition of the Catholic Worker movement.
In her attempts to stand for peace, Kelly works
toward embracing all with unconditional love.

---

58. Daniel L. Smith-Christopher, ed., "Everything Is Different Now," in *Subverting Hatred: The Challenge of Nonviolence in
Religious Traditions,* 10th ed. (New York: Orbis Books, 2007), xviii.

59. Ibid.

60. Ibid., xxiii.

Dorothy Day, the founder of the Catholic Worker Movement, worked with the poor and homeless in New York and throughout the United States. As a Christian, she was an antiwar activist and a voice and advocate for the poor. Catholic Sister Helen Prejean, in her book, *Dead Man Walking: An Eyewitness Account of the Death Penalty in the United States*, chronicles her now-famous experience of working with death row inmates and the families of their victims. The Dalai Lama and Thich Nhat Hanh, both world-renowned Buddhists, speak out for peace, justice, and nonviolence. Dedicated, young Muslim men and women have been working under the banner of UMMA (University Muslim Medical Association) over the past dozen years to better the health of people living in South Central Los Angeles. Their mission "is to promote the well-being of the underserved by providing access to high quality healthcare for all, regardless of ability to pay."[61] The medical clinic they have established is a direct result of the Muslim commitment to *Zakat*, or almsgiving, one of the Five Pillars of Islam. Examples abound of fearless persons standing for peace and justice in the world. While not all claim a religious grounding for their efforts, many do.

Questions for Reflection and Discussion

- How do religious convictions influence your interactions with the world?
- Would you risk anything to serve your religion or your religious commitments? Explain.

- What else might be said about the link between religion and social activism?

Additional Resources

DeYoung, Curtiss Paul. 2007. *Living Faith: How Faith Inspires Social Justice.* Minneapolis, MN: Fortress Press.

Kelly, Kathy. 2005. *Other Lands Have Dreams: From Baghdad to Pekin Prison.* Petrolia, CA: CounterPunch Books.

Wink, Walter. 2000. *Peace Is the Way: Writings on Nonviolence from the Fellowship of Reconciliation.* Maryknoll, NY: Orbis Books.

References

Bhave, Vinoba. 2005. *Talks on the Gita.* 16th ed. Wardha: Paramdham Prakashan.

Bhave, Vinoba. 1994. *Moved by Love: The Memoirs of Vinoba Bhave.* Translated by Marjorie Sykes from a Hindi text prepared by Kalindi. Hyderabad: Sat Sahitya Sahayogi Sangh.

Curtis, Edward E. 2005. "African-American Islamization Reconsidered: Black History Narratives and Muslim Identity." *Journal of the American Academy of Religion* 73, no. 3 (September): 659–684.

Continued . . .

61. To learn more about UMMA, their free clinic and other projects, see *http://www.ummaclinic.org*.

Additional Resources   *Continued . . .*

King, Martin Luther, Jr. 2001. "Address to the first Montgomery Improvement Association (MIA) Mass Meeting." In *A Call to Conscience: The Landmark Speeches of Dr. Martin Luther King, Jr.* Clayborne Carson and Kris Shepard, eds. New York: Warner Books. This speech was delivered at Holt Street Baptist Church in Montgomery, Alabama, on December 5, 1955.

King, Martin Luther, Jr. 2001. "The Birth of a Nation." In *A Call to Conscience: The Landmark Speeches of Dr. Martin Luther King, Jr.* Clayborne Carson and Kris Shepard, eds. New York: Warner Books.

King, Martin Luther, Jr. 2001. "I Have a Dream." In *A Call to Conscience: The Landmark Speeches of Dr. Martin Luther King, Jr.* Clayborne Carson and Kris Shepard, eds. New York: Warner Books.

King, Martin Luther, Jr. 1998. *The Autobiography of Martin Luther King, Jr.* Edited by Clayborne Carson. New York: Warner Books.

Malcolm X. 1965. *The Autobiography of Malcolm X.* As told to Alex Haley. New York: Ballantine Books.

Marx, Karl. 1964. "Contribution to the Critique of Hegel's Philosophy of Right: Introduction." In *Karl Marx and Friedrich Engels on Religion.* New York: Schocken Books.

Pals, Daniel L. 1996. *Seven Theories of Religion.* Oxford, UK: Oxford University Press.

Smith-Christopher, Daniel L., ed. 2007. *Subverting Hatred: The Challenge of Nonviolence in Religious Traditions.* 10th ed. Maryknoll, NY: Orbis Books.

Web References

Malcolm X. *http://www.malcolm-x.org/speeches/spc_021465.htm.* This speech, "After the Bombing," was delivered the day after his house had been bombed.

Tutu, Desmond. "Nobel Lecture." Acceptance speech for the Nobel Peace Prize, December 11, 1984. *http://nobelprize.org/nobel_prizes/peace/laureates/1984/tutu-lecture.html.*

http://www.ummaclinic.org. This is the Web site for the UMMA clinic in south central Los Angeles. It provides information regarding the organization, their mission, and the work that they do.

http://www.vcnv.org. This is the web site for Voices for Creative Nonviolence. Begun in 2005, Voices is committed to "active nonviolent resistance to U. S. war-making," according to its web site.

WORLD RELIGIONS: ENVIRONMENTALLY ACTIVE

Dr. Daniel G. Deffenbaugh
Hastings College

Preface

In an age that is witnessing global warming, the overconsumption of natural resources, chemical pollution, the dwindling of safe drinking-water supplies, forest clear-cutting, holes in the ozone layer, genetic engineering, overcrowded feedlots and monoculture agriculture, and on and on, various religions of the world are responding in a host of ways. In this chapter, Daniel Deffenbaugh explores religiously motivated environmental activism. Why do some religions consider environmental issues imperative and others treat them with indifference? How do religious perspectives inform, motivate, or incline people toward care of the environment? While exploring these and other questions, this chapter encourages students to reflect on how their own environmental convictions may be rooted in religious belief.

Chapter Goals

- To introduce a subdiscipline of religious studies concerned with the environment
- To promote critical reflection on links between religious convictions and attitudes toward nature
- To encourage critical reflection on personal convictions regarding the environment

INTRODUCTION

In *Last Child in the Woods*, Richard Louv writes that children have begun manifesting symptoms of what appears to be a new disease, what he calls "nature-deficit disorder." This malady would have been inconceivable to most Americans as few as twenty years ago, argues Louv. Until recently, children's free time allowed them to become intimately acquainted with the bugs, birds, and other creatures living in their backyards, vacant lots, and nearby open fields. Nowadays children no longer wade in creeks to search for frogs and crayfish. They don't climb in trees and build forts in the woods. Asked where their dinner peas and carrots come from, many kids today can't think of anywhere other than the local supermarket.

The situation is perhaps best illustrated by the example of a young boy who was asked by Louv if he preferred playing indoors or outdoors. "I like to play indoors better," the boy said, "cause that's where all the electrical outlets are."[1]

These days, children see anything short of an action-packed video game or television program as boring and a waste of time. With this new perspective, Louv suggests, comes the loss of something integral to our very being. Without interactions with nature, especially in the earliest stages of our physical and psychological development, our sense of what it means to be connected to the greater web of life cannot be cultivated. When this happens, we lose sight of what it means to be truly human.

So how have we come to this and what might we do to reverse this trend? If what Louv suggests is true—that a burgeoning nature-deficit disorder is contributing to a rising tide of personal and social malady—then it makes sense to search for the source of the problem. The list of potential culprits is certainly impressive.

Many blame technology, the tools we have developed and used over the centuries to make our work less tedious and more efficient. Some say we have allowed our contraptions to get the better of us and now work ever harder just to keep up with the increasingly burdensome demands of our "laborsaving" devices. Some even advocate eliminating many of our gadgets and toys because "you can't be green and love the machine." Their solution is simple: get rid of the video games and lock the kids outside until it's time for supper, then afterward turn off the television and put a book in front of them. But most of us realize that responses like these usually fall short of answering a question as complex as how we might regain a sense of our natural identity. The way we use and abuse technology is merely a symptom of our ecological alienation; it is not the disease.

Others when confronted with this issue accuse the ideas that produced technology. Science, they say, is the problem. The argument often goes like this: By definition, science is a "value-free discipline." The scientific method requires observers of natural phenomena to depersonalize their experience and look only for "facts." Using their observations, scientists search for patterns of order and formulate hypotheses to test and refine. Their objectives are to unveil laws of nature and to better understand how the phenomenon observed could be used for the greater good. The force of water falling over a precipice, for example, could be harnessed to produce electricity so that 12-year-old children can play video games on their large-screen televisions. What is too often lost in the end, however, are such human experiences as awe, beauty, and fear, the kinds of emotions that overcame Meriwether Lewis when he first beheld the great falls along what is now called the Missouri River. In light of this, some say the scientific method is to blame for our children's alienation from the natural world. Science has taken what was once value-laden and personal and treated it as something unworthy of moral consideration. As a result, we now live in a disenchanted cosmos.

Yet whatever the virtues of this argument, it is also true that science could not have emerged in isolation from the fundamental values and ideas of the societies in which it developed. For example, many of us take for granted the notion that nature works according to certain principles that can be observed and tested. There is an order to things. There is consistency. We can trust that what we see is in fact real and worth observing.

1. Richard Louv, *Last Child in the Woods: Saving Our Children from Nature-Deficit Disorder* (Chapel Hill, NC: Algonquin Books, 2006), 10.

These assumptions preceded the advent of the scientific method in the middle of the seventeenth century.

But where did these ideas come from? The answer to this question brings us into the realm of philosophy and religion. We would not expect science as we know it to have emerged in parts of the world where the observable cosmos is regarded as merely an illusion. No one wants to spend time studying an object that is ultimately unreliable. Early European scientists were only able to pursue their enterprise because they were working within a paradigm that framed the world we live in as real and ordered. The same can be said of the Muslim natural philosophers in Baghdad in the eighth and ninth centuries. This paradigm has at its core a belief shared by nearly every culture that affirms a theistic understanding of the divine, namely, that it was God's will to create a cosmos that reflects the very being of God.

So if we follow the thread back from our technology through our science, we arrive at the place from which many would begin to fashion a constructive response to the perceived nature-deficit disorder among many children today. Our *worldview*—that is, the cultural lens through which we establish a sense of what is true, good, and beautiful—is ultimately responsible for how we understand our relationship to the natural world. To explore this, we will turn to religion. It is through the structures of religion—myths, rituals, worship, artifacts—that humans first began to seek answers to their questions of ultimate concern. What is the good? Who is my neighbor? What happens when I die? Or, more to the point for our purposes, *how should I relate with the natural world?*

Questions for Reflection and Discussion

- Does Richard Louv overstate his thesis that most children today suffer from a kind of nature-deficit disorder? Can you offer examples from your own experience that support or challenge his claim?

- What does religion say about human identity in relation to the natural environment?
- How should we relate with the natural world? Why?

A HUGE BURDEN OF GUILT

Humans are by nature storytellers. Though our scientific knowledge offers us extraordinary insights into *what* we are—complexes of carbon, hydrogen, oxygen, and other elements configured into tissues, organs, and bones—our stories tell us *who* we are. We recount personal tales, of course, but our identity is more often shaped by the much broader narratives that we carry with us: a recollection of losing the family farm, or the story of a grandfather's emigration from Russia in the 1930s. We feel centered when we situate ourselves securely within the context of a narrative that is shared with other people—it gives us a sense of meaning and purpose. What is true of individuals is also true of entire cultures: they are in many ways fashioned by the grand stories—the myths—that are told of their origins and journeys into the present. Think, for example, of the pride and emotion that many U.S. war veterans display when saluting the flag. For them, the stars and stripes are a symbol of the national narrative that has helped shape their identity. This story lends purpose and meaning to their lives.

Religious traditions provide the mythic structure within which social groups attempt to answer their collective questions of ultimate concern. Thus the religious myths that are kept alive among a particular group of people can tell us much about their unique system of values.

In the 1960s, when many people in the United States were becoming increasingly alarmed about the rising number of environmental crises, it was an analysis of our grand stories that helped some religious communities come to terms with their relationship to the natural world. This was the era that provided a new word for our environmental lexicon: *smog*, that brown mixture of hydrocarbons and nitrogen oxides from vehicular exhaust that still hangs like a wet blanket over many cities. Rivers were showing signs of severe degradation: in 1969 the Cuyahoga River in Cleveland, Ohio, was so heavily polluted it actually caught fire. Garbage was piling up along the nation's roadsides, and populations of some animal species were on a steep decline, among them the bald eagle, the quintessential symbol of American strength and character. While some critics blamed technology or blind faith in science, social historian Lynn White Jr. offered the novel suggestion that the problem lay in our worldview, more specifically in the stories that have been told for centuries among Jews, Christians, and Muslims—all spiritual descendants of Abraham—about how the world was created and where human responsibility lay within this creation. White argued that Christianity in particular bore "a huge burden of guilt" for the ecological problems besetting communities the world over.[2]

White's thesis focused on one of the two creation accounts featured in the early chapters of Genesis, where Adam is commissioned by God to subdue the earth and have dominion over it (Gen 1:28). White claimed this story created a clear qualitative hierarchy between humans, who bore the image of God (Gen 1:26), and the rest of creation, which was conceived as containing all the resources necessary for meeting human needs. As soon as this perspective joined with the Western notion of human progress, White argued, the stage was set for the ecological tragedies that most of the world was just beginning to experience in the 1960s. So the stories that had been recounted over time by untold numbers of Jews, Christians, and Muslims set values that, when acted upon, led finally to the degradation of the nonhuman world by men and women who believed they were doing what God had commanded. The faithful, having been singled out as the source of the problem, responded that if there were any issue that truly needed to be addressed it lay in their inability to be good stewards of the world God had entrusted to them.

Before long other critics raised their voices. Some pointed out that the peculiar notion held by a few Christian sects that the world would eventually come to a cataclysmic end did little to engender care and concern for the nonhuman world. And if this grand finale was going to come sooner rather than later, as some believed, then it actually made *more* sense to make liberal use of the natural resources that had been entrusted to our care. The evangelical Christian James Watt, secretary of the interior during the Reagan administration, endorsed such an attitude. Others noted that the enthusiasm many Christians demonstrate for their "home in heaven" only detracts from affirming—and protecting—the goodness of their home on earth. So perhaps White was right: Christianity bore, and still bears, a huge burden of guilt for our environmental crisis.

---

2. Lynn White Jr., "The Historical Roots of Our Ecological Crisis," *Western Man and Environmental Ethics,* ed. Ian G. Barbour (Reading, PA: Wesley-Addison Publishing, 1973), 24.

These perceived shortcomings of the Abrahamic religious traditions, and Christianity in particular, led many in the United States to turn their attention elsewhere. The received notion of a God in heaven overseeing events on the stage of creation, a perspective that appeared to acknowledge nature as merely a prop for the real drama of human sin and redemption, no longer seemed viable to many who once affirmed this worldview as their own.

As more and more examples of human excess and greed played themselves out, many men and women began to look to other religions whose myths and philosophies seemed more earth-friendly. This interest in ecology and other religions has continued to grow right up to the present and has made itself evident among individuals and groups in three basic ways that we will consider next: going native, going east, and coming home.

Questions for Reflection and Discussion

- Do you believe that developing a closer relationship with the natural world, and especially with one's local ecology, is essential for realizing a fuller sense of our humanity?

- We are dependent on our biotic communities for our physical needs, but does nature provide us with psychological and spiritual sustenance as well? Explain.

- What are some of the family or community stories, as well as larger cultural or religious myths, that inform your sense of identity? How significant a role does your relationship to a natural place play in these stories? How have these stories helped define your sense of responsibility with respect to the care and preservation of the natural world?

GOING NATIVE

In the United States, many who became disenchanted with the ecological shortcomings of their inherited theistic traditions turned first to Native American cultures to address environmental degradation. An early marketing campaign to raise awareness of pollution—specifically, the distressing amount of trash being strewn across the nation's thoroughfares—featured the image of an Indian man standing on the side of a highway surveying a landscape that was ostensibly once his. Then, as if to wake him from his reverie, a passing motorist hurls a bag of trash at the Indian's feet, the contents exploding into a gooey mess onto his buckskin leggings and moccasins. The commercial ends with the image of a tear running down the man's rough face.

Nearly anyone who grew up in the late sixties remembers this ad, as it joined two symbols of the American past that seemed to so naturally go hand in hand: the beauty of nature and the integrity of the Native American way of life. Where just a century earlier white settlers had done their level best to eradicate native tribes from the Great Plains, referring to them as "savages," now the image of Native Americans was being lauded as the hope of the nation. Indians had become paragons of ecological virtue.

Much of this idolization was accomplished to the detriment of the indigenous peoples themselves. The myth-crafters on Madison Avenue who created the "crying shame" commercial cared little about the immense variety of myths, rituals, and ceremonies practiced by cultures such as the Cherokee, Lakota, Navajo, and many others. It didn't matter to them that their ad featured a man in Plains Indian dress paddling a canoe through an eastern woodland habitat. What mattered was the effect their imagery had on the American populace. So while the ecological movement gained a poignant and effective symbol, the cause of celebrating unique indigenous identities was undermined by a kind of cultural homogenization suggesting that all Indians basically believed the same thing, especially when it came to nature and their place in it. This was not the case among Native peoples prior to European contact, and it behooves us to acknowledge the vast differences that still exist among the First Peoples of North America.

Despite this variety, however, most Native Americans do share the characteristic of being informed in a holistic way by their unique mythologies. Many of us today are used to compartmentalizing our day-to-day lives—separating religion and science, church and state, public and private. This worldview would have been altogether foreign to the indigenous groups of this continent prior to European contact. This is because the stories that were told and ritually enacted among these people clearly established the structure of their society. Every aspect of an Indian's life was tethered, as it were, to a story that imparted a sense of meaning and purpose to that person's existence. Particularly important about this is that the myths Indians recounted ritually at various times of the year seemed to view human beings as but one group of actors, and not necessarily the most important group, among a panoply of creatures who all bore the same life-giving spirit within them. In contrast to the creation account found in the book of Genesis, in which humans are special and set apart, in most Native American creation myths

all creatures participate in demonstrating the deep mystery of the world's creative spirit, and each in its own valuable and inimitable way.

Consider, for example, what sort of ecological worldview is engendered in the minds of a culture wherein a creation story known as the *emergence myth* is ritually recounted on a regular basis.[3] This myth, varied as it is among diverse native peoples, features humans and other creatures passing through a series of stages, beginning in a "time before time," where they reside in nascent form in the womb of the earth, and arriving in the present world, where they are fully formed beings. In the first level of the world, there appears to be little differentiation among all the creatures; they share a kind of amorphous existence. Through a series of heroic gestures by a few mythic heroes, the people are able to ascend through various planes of existence, all the time gaining their distinctive identities in developmental stages. Finally they emerge to inhabit the present world. Usually some geographical feature in the local environment of a cultural group represents the hole from which this "birth" took place and thereby represents the sacred center of their cosmos.

What is critical in this myth is the specific manner in which the term *people* is used. The reference here is not to human beings exclusively but to all creatures who once shared the primordial womb and eventually made their way into the present world. Nonhuman creatures, therefore, are recognized by most indigenous North American cultures with emergence myths as fellow travelers who have shared with human beings the long, arduous journey into a specific geographical location. In most emergence accounts certain animals are even credited with heroic acts that rival those of their human counterparts. In Hopi mythology, for example, the eagle is able to fly from one world

---

3. Emergence myths are found most commonly among agricultural groups and are especially prominent in the desert Southwest among certain Pueblo groups, including the Hopi and the Zuni. For an excellent introduction to Hopi culture, see the National Geographic documentary, *Hopi: Songs of the Fourth World*, as well as a special feature in *National Geographic* magazine, "Hopi Pottery" and "Inside the Sacred Hopi Homeland" (November 1982): 593–630.

into the next and give an account of what is to be found in the realm above, thus giving assistance to the people in their upward odyssey. The bonds of kinship, then, are clear; the same spiritual energy flows through all things and should therefore be acknowledged and affirmed ritually. In other words, all things are sacred, and every aspect of the world, no matter how small, plays a role in manifesting sublime energy. Native Americans therefore live in what Howard Harrod refers to as a "Great Society," a "sacred ecology" in which all people, human and nonhuman, are affirmed as an integral and necessary part of the whole.[4] For Native American societies, as with most indigenous groups around the world, a perception of the cosmos as a sacred ecology accentuates the interconnected nature of all things and fosters a sense of moral responsibility toward other creatures whose life spirit is akin to one's own.

Maintaining balance between the visible and invisible cosmos lies at the center of this Native worldview. Harmony is sustained by observing the rituals prescribed by the unique mythological structure of the group. Among the Blackfeet of Montana, for example, the buffalo hunt could not take place without a series of ceremonies and dances to appease the Keeper of the Buffalo so that he might allow a few of his number to be sacrificed for the welfare of the people. Upon completion of the rituals, the hunt could then proceed with a posture of respect and gratitude and with the confidence that if the ceremonies were properly performed, the hunt would be successful. Similarly, among the agricultural Hopi, the spring planting of corn could not commence without a proper acknowledgment of the people's dependence on and indebtedness to the "cloud spirits," or *kachinas*, whose presence in their midst brought much-needed rain to their desert habitat. Further examples of this

heightened awareness of ecological interdependence abound, not just among the First Peoples of North America but among indigenous groups around the world, from Africa to Australia to South America to New Guinea. The point is that the stories told among various Native American groups instilled in every man, woman, and child the sense that their world was indeed one of dynamic power, of spirit; its balance was maintained by acknowledging and affirming people's kinship with all living things. The cosmos was rife with personality; all creatures were worthy of moral consideration.

Scholars of religion usually refer to this sense of living in a world in which the sacred includes all living things as animism, from the Latin *animus*, a spirit that enlivens a body. For the First Peoples of North America, all creatures, not just humans, possessed a soul and therefore embodied qualities above and beyond what could be attributed to them; in other words, they possessed intrinsic—as opposed to instrumental—value. Once this is established, the foundation for a thoroughgoing relationship of care and reciprocity follows. By contrast, in a world where a consideration of the inherent value of an object only gets in the way of one's disinterested investigation, establishing an ethic of concern becomes difficult if not impossible. In short, while Indians seemed to live in a Great Society replete with beings possessing intrinsic value, most of contemporary Western society merely acknowledged impersonal objects, and too often this objectification was applied not only to nonhuman creatures but also to humans. Perhaps this is the reason for the attraction that some have to Native American religious traditions and their reverence for nature: they long to live once again in an enchanted cosmos where mystery is regarded not as a problem to be solved using reason but as a presence to behold with awe.

---

4. See Howard Harrod, *The Animals Came Dancing: Native American Sacred Ecology and Animal Kinship* (Tucson: University of Arizona Press, 2000), and *Renewing the World: Plains Indian Religion and Morality* (Tucson: University of Arizona Press, 1987).

Questions for Reflection and Discussion

- Many suggest that Native American traditions offer ecological insights our culture would be wise to model. Do you agree? If so, how could our culture begin to incorporate some of these ecological insights? If you do not agree, why not?

- How might geographical place be associated with religion?
- Is there a sacred dimension to the natural world that many religions affirm? If so, how might it be described?

GOING EAST

A belief in human interdependence with the rest of nature seems also to motivate the interest many have shown for the varied religious traditions from India, China, and Japan, especially in the last forty years. When we survey the worldviews represented here, we can make some connections with the animistic traditions that we just considered, but the differences demand our attention. Suffice it to say that Hinduism, Buddhism, Taoism, and Shinto display a spectrum of beliefs that extend from the purely animistic—where spirits are consulted and appeased by daily and yearly rituals—to the purely philosophical, where discussions of animism seem only to divert the seeker's attention from the ultimate nature of reality.

An example of a more purely philosophical approach to reality is the Vedantic school of Hinduism, whose primary text is the Upanishads. Vedantic Hinduism may seem at first to adhere to a worldview not unlike those of the indigenous cultures of North America, but on closer inspection we find that this is not entirely the case. A central tenet of the metaphysical Vedantic worldview is that the concrete reality we observe on a daily basis, a reality marked by diversity and change, is in fact an illusion or *maya*. This holds true even for what we perceive to be our individual "self," or what is referred to in Hinduism as *atman*. The essence of enlightenment in this school of thought lies in the realization that the material world is not real and the notion that we possess individual souls is false. Rather, these aspects of our experience are merely sources of desire that distract us from our pursuit and realization of the truth. The only reality that can be affirmed is *Brahman*, the ultimate source of unity underlying all things, "that which is above heaven and below earth, which is also between heaven and earth, which is the same through the past, present, and future—that is woven, warp and woof, in space."[5]

What are the ecological implications of a worldview in which metaphysical unity is valued over physical diversity, where the rising and passing away of forms—as discussed by Krishna and Arjuna in the second chapter of the Bhagavad-Gita—is incidental to the ultimate, unchanging truth that is *Brahman*? According to this perspective, as the *Brihardaranyaka Upanishad* makes clear,

> A wife loves her husband not for his own sake, dear, but because the Self (*Brahman*) lives in him.
>
> A husband loves his wife not for her own sake, dear, but because the Self lives in her.
>
> . . . The universe is loved not for its own sake, but because the Self lives in it.

---

5. "Brihadaranyaka Upanishad," *The Upanishads,* trans. Eknath Easwaren (Tomales, CA: Nigli Press, 1987), 40.

. . . Creatures are loved not for their own sake but because the Self lives in them.

Everything is loved not for its own sake but because the Self lives in it.[6]

Could such a philosophical religious view be subject to the same critique that some have leveled against the Abrahamic religious traditions, that is, that aspects of this material world of multiplicity and change are valued only inasmuch as they are associated with some transcendent principle? Are we seeing here another religious worldview that focuses its attention somewhere beyond the ordinary realm of everyday life? Do nonhuman creatures and landscapes have value in and of themselves, or does their value derive from their link to a higher reality?

In the Native American traditions just considered, there is no indication that individual creatures, human or nonhuman, were regarded as illusions masking a more worthwhile unified principle of the cosmos, the Great Spirit, as it were. On the contrary, each creature possessed intrinsic value and was recognized as a unique being. The Upanishads, however, seem to step away from affirming the material world and direct our attention to something that lies beyond it. Could this be the philosophical move, present in other religious traditions as well, that has had disastrous results for the world's ecology? Is there a devaluing of the material world here? Does this perspective offer us less incentive to preserve our natural environment?

The trouble with any discussion of Hinduism is that there is no *one* Hinduism, but rather a multitude of religious traditions that emerged on the Indian subcontinent. So any sweeping statement about Hinduism must be accompanied by a host of exceptions and caveats. However, one principle that does seem to connect the religious worldviews of India—whether it be Hinduism, Jainism, or Buddhism—is a belief in the interconnectedness of all things. This principle has vital implications for how people understand their relationship with, and impact on, the natural world.

For centuries Indians have believed that a person's daily actions not only affect others but also affect the actor by creating beneficial or harmful results (good or bad *karma*). Awareness of karma informs how individuals perform their *dharma* or duty. The focus on action is also directed toward a result that will be enjoyed in one's *samsara* or rebirth. Jains, for example, are acutely aware of the implications of their deeds and seek to practice *ahimsa* or nonviolence in all things. This commitment sometimes appears extreme, as when Jain monks sweep the path before them so as not to step on a living creature, no matter how small. *Ahimsa* is also observed in the Jains' vegetarian diet containing no meat or animal byproducts such as eggs, milk, or cheese. The Jain's guiding principle seems to be a belief that one's acts of violence—no matter how small—only perpetuate the pain, disruption, and suffering of the world. Consequently, the truth (*satya*) remains obscured. Jains' lifestyle signals their ecological perspective: "In everything I do, I will choose not to be a conduit for the world's violence; rather, my actions will engender peace."[7]

This same sense of a profound interconnectedness among all life can also be found in Buddhism, especially in the Zen tradition. The Vietnamese Zen monk, Thich Nhat Hanh, for example, has been an eloquent but gentle critic of the classical scientific notion of the detached observer of phenomena. In Zen Buddhism,

6. Ibid., 36.

7. For an excellent introduction to Jainism and ecology, see Nathmal Tatia, "The Jain Worldview and Ecology," *Jainism and Ecology: Nonviolence in the Web of Life*, ed. Christopher Key Chapple (Cambridge, MA: Harvard University Press, 2002), 3–18.

detachment is purely illusory, and its danger lies in the notion that our individual actions have little effect on those around us. Many of us are familiar with the image of the Buddhist monk sitting cross-legged on the floor in quiet meditation, and often we think that the objective of this practice lies in a desire to be removed from the world, as if this goal somehow epitomizes the highest form of spirituality. This is perhaps a reflection of our own Western bias, living as we do in a scientific era where detachment is often lauded as the ideal. But for Zen Buddhists, the opposite is in fact true: the end to be achieved is a kind of radical "attachment," or what is more appropriately referred to as mindfulness. Awareness of the profound interdependence of all things lies at the heart of Zen meditation. The discipline, in other words, is not about being somewhere else; it is about being here now. It is not about detachment; it is about being "attached" through the practice of mindfulness, a perspective that informs everything a Zen Buddhist does, from praying to eating to washing dishes. One can get a sense of this radical awareness of the interdependence of all things in Thich Nhat Hahn's reflection on a simple piece of paper.

> Just as a piece of paper is the fruit, the combination of many elements that can be called non-paper elements, the individual is made of non-individual elements. If you are a poet you will see that there is a cloud floating in this piece of paper. Without a cloud there will be no water; without water the trees cannot grow; without trees you cannot make paper. The existence of this page is dependent on the existence of a cloud. . . . And if you look more closely, with the eyes of a bodhisattva, with the yes of those who are awake, you see not only the cloud and the sunshine in it, but that everything is here: the wheat that became the bread for the logger to eat, the logger's father—everything is in this sheet of paper.[8]

Given this profound co-inherence of all things, it is easy to see why Zen Buddhists like Thich Nhat Hanh live by the ideal of compassion. When they consider how they should relate with the natural world, the word *engagement*, an active form of mindfulness, is often the focus. Guided by the fundamental principle of *karma*, Zen Buddhists move toward empathy, practicing a "being with" that informs every moment of their waking day. The most important precept, as Hanh suggests, is simply to know what is going on, "not just here, but there."[9]

Know that when you eat a piece of meat that has been produced by means of violence—whether to the environment or to the animal itself—you are partly responsible for this violence. Know that when you buy vegetables that have traveled an average of thirteen hundred miles to your dinner plate you are partly responsible for the frivolous use of the earth's natural resources. Know that your consumer choices have an effect on the health of the planet. It is a misunderstanding of the true nature of reality to suggest that the world can be observed objectively. Buddhism reminds us that we must be living mindfully and compassionately. We must be engaged. It is for this reason that many modern Buddhists—among them His Holiness the Dalai Lama—find themselves at the forefront of environmental causes, admonishing many, and particularly those in the West, to reconsider their commitment to the values of detachment and instrumental reason that are so central to the classical scientific worldview.

---

8. Thich Nhat Hanh, *Being Peace* (Berkeley, CA: Parallax Press, 1987), 45–46. See also Thich Nhat Hanh, *Peace Is Every Step: The Path of Mindfulness in Everyday Life* (New York: Bantam Books, 1991).

9. Hanh, *Being Peace*, 65.

In sum, there is a direct link between how we discern value in our world and our attitudes concerning nature and nonhuman creatures. If we affirm that reality and truth lie solely beyond the horizon of the material world—as we have seen in the Vedantic school of Hindu philosophy—then our tendency is to be less concerned with our responsibilities toward this tangible world where we eat, drink, and breathe. By contrast, if we recognize that each entity in the universe has intrinsic value—as we have seen in Native American traditions—then concern for the nonhuman becomes more likely.

Taoism, a religious tradition indigenous to China, shares much in common with perspectives that see intrinsic value in all created matter. In Taoism, "the way" of ultimate reality—the *tao*, which cannot be rationally comprehended—is nevertheless evident in the creative interplay of *yin* and *yang* in every facet of creation. Nature moves and transforms itself without will, without desire, and this, according to the *Tao Te Ching*, is the model that we should adopt as our own. It is the essence of wisdom.

> The Tao never does anything,
> yet through it all things are done.
>
> If powerful men and women
> could center themselves in it,
> the whole world would be transformed
> by itself, in its natural rhythms.
> People would be content
> with their simple, everyday lives,
> in harmony, and free of desire.
>
> When there is no desire,
> all things are at peace.[10]

Whereas the universe acts without acting—what Taoists refer to as *wu-wei*—most of us are guilty of acting according to our individual desires, "grasping at the moon" as the literal translation of *yu-wei* suggests. One cannot stop the waxing or waning of the moon anymore than one can completely harness the power of a river, yet we continue to delude ourselves into believing that we can. We consult our thoughts within instead of the wisdom without, in nature, and the *tao* remains obscured to us. The sage, however, is able to "act without acting" by conforming his or her will to the way of the cosmos. While so many of us seek to swim against the current, as it were—remaining true to our best-laid plans while fighting the *tao* all the way—the sage knows that enlightenment lies in following the example of water, which over time, by its gentle nonaction (*wu-wei*), can smooth over even the roughest of river rocks. Thus Taoism offers an insight that seems to have been all but lost in the modern world. While many Westerners tend to think about environmental challenges as "problems" that need to be solved through instrumental reason, it is perhaps more appropriate to refer to these as "embarrassments," indications of an inability, or an unwillingness, to consult the way of the cosmos as a guide. Nature is not the enemy in this endeavor, "red in tooth and claw,"[11] but a teacher. An affirmation of this truth, so evident in the wisdom of philosophical Taoism, might serve as a corrective for how Westerners have typically sought to address their environmental shortcomings with so much "new and improved" gadgetry.

The ecological deterioration in the last few decades has led many in the United States to seek alternative ways of knowing and living in the world, and the religious traditions of Asia seem to have filled this void to a certain extent. At the heart of the search has been a longing for a reconnection with nature, which has long been

---

10. *Tao Te Ching*, ch. 37, in Stephen Mitchell, *Tao Te Ching: A New English Version* (New York: HarperPerennial Modern Classics, 2006).

11. Alfred, Lord Tennyson, *In Memoriam: Authoritative Text: Criticism*, ed. Erik Gray (New York: Norton, 2004).

perceived as "out there" or "other." Hinduism, Jainism, Buddhism, and Taoism have attracted the attention of many primarily because each appears, in its own way, to offer a worldview in which the line between humanity and the rest of creation is not so clearly defined. In a scientific world where certainty is held up as the ideal, these traditions also seem to leave open the possibility of mystery, the sense that, as Hamlet once opined, "there are more things in heaven and earth . . . than are dreamt of in your philosophy" (*Hamlet*, Act 1, Scene 5). But for some the prospect of "going East," while attractive initially,

has shown itself to be more complicated than anticipated. We cannot easily just "believe as a Buddhist" by assenting to certain philosophical claims, especially when our day-to-day lives are so deeply influenced by the theistic religious worldviews that have shaped much of Western culture. For this reason there have been many who have decided to work constructively within their inherited spiritual tradition and address questions of the human-nature relationship that have not been posed or considered creatively in the past. They have chosen, in other words, to "come home."

Questions for Reflection and Discussion

- What aspects of the traditions of Asia considered here most attract you? Does one tradition in particular offer compelling insights into the human-nature relationship? Explain.

- Do any of the insights gathered so far challenge the way that you live? Explain.

- Explain any significance you see in what we choose to consume.

- Do your religious convictions shape your consumer choices? Explain.

COMING HOME

We have seen how the Abrahamic religious traditions, and especially Christianity, have been criticized for less-than-positive attitudes regarding the human relationship with the natural world. In short, these traditions have been denounced as too anthropocentric, too enamored of the notion that *Homo sapiens* lies at the center of God's plan for creating the cosmos. According to this perspective, creation is little more than a backdrop or a stage on which the human drama of sin and redemption takes place. Indeed, in parts of the world where the Abrahamic traditions have flourished, the realm of nonhuman creatures tends to be perceived as foreign, "out there," or "wholly other." This point is brought home clearly in Louv's book, *Last Child in the Woods*, in the example of a primary school teacher

who asked her students to "draw nature." The result was a series of pictures that included birds and bunnies, trees and flowers, and happy suns smiling from the corners of the pages, but not one of the drawings featured a man or a woman or even a child. The implication, of course, is that humans are somehow outside of nature, living in a different world than that inhabited by the myriad creatures in fields, streams, and forests that are largely beyond our personal and social experience. If this is how children illustrate the human-nature relationship, what does this say about the perspective of American culture? As we have seen, many blame the Abrahamic traditions for this state of affairs, but there are others who are not so quick to make this judgment. On the contrary, they find there is much in Judaism, Christianity, and Islam that distinguishes them from other religious worldviews, and it is in these differences that they find hope for the future of our planet.

The one feature distinguishing the Abrahamic religions from other faith traditions is the belief in a personal God who is one and wholly good. The Creator, in other words, is not an abstract power that lies hidden beneath the ordinary, but a personal reality who calls human beings—people like Adam and Eve, Noah, Abraham and Sarah, Moses, and Muhammad—to act as God's messengers on earth, admonishing them to seek the truth and live abundantly in relationship with their Creator and with Creation. Christians even take the extent of God's association with the world one step further by claiming that God actually became incarnate—took on human nature and form—in the person of Jesus of Nazareth.

Implicit in all this is an affirmation that can be easily overlooked: God created the world, not out of compulsion or necessity, but freely, as an act of will. And it is through the created order that God's purposes can be known. As the Psalmist proclaims, "The heavens are telling the glory of God; and the firmament proclaims his handiwork" (Ps 19:1). Further, creation reflects the being of God, though the material world must not be confused with the divine. Creation is not an illusion. It is not evil, as some Gnostic sects of early Christianity claimed. On the contrary, the world is good and can be trusted, to such an extent that those patient enough can discern complex laws to record and test their observations of particular phenomena.

It was this affirmation of the inherent order of the material world that led the first Muslim scientists to "read the book of nature" and develop the discipline of "natural philosophy." Those in the Christian tradition regard God's incarnation—literally, God's "enfleshment"—in the person of Jesus Christ as the ultimate assertion of the value of creation itself. After all, God would not become that which is contrary to God's nature; the goodness of the cosmos is affirmed by the very notion of the divine becoming corporeal. To those who have committed themselves to "coming home" as they seek out an ecologically viable spirituality, this starting point—the recognition of the inherent value of creation—has been both an inspiration and a comfort.

Central to the notion of God choosing to enter into a relationship with the cosmos itself is the fact that God makes provisions for the continued care of the natural world. Much has been made of the theological assertion that humans are created exclusively in the image of God (*imago dei*) and thereby enjoy a position of power and privilege among all creatures. This was central to Lynn White's critique of Christianity more than four decades ago. Unfortunately, this is a misguided interpretation of the Bible that reflects only half the story, focusing as it does on just one of Israel's creation accounts. The second chapter of Genesis features a narrative that, when compared to the imagery of the preceding chapter in which God speaks the world into being, is much more pastoral in its setting. Here God walks in the Garden of Eden in the cool of the day. Here Adam is formed out of the earth itself (as is implied by his very name: *adamah* is the Hebrew word for "earth") and receives his spirit as God breathes the breath of life into his nostrils. Some have suggested that this narrative has certain affinities with the emergence myths of various Native American cultures and might therefore instill in those who claim the story a sense of kinship and reciprocity with nature similar to that found in most Native American worldviews. The fact that Adam shares with all other creatures an earthly origin could serve as a foundation for a peculiarly Abrahamic "sacred ecology."[12] But even apart from this observation, it is important to note that the tradition

---

12. See, for example, chapter 4 of my book *Learning the Language of the Fields: Tilling and Keeping as Christian Vocation* (Cambridge, MA: Cowley Publications, 2006).

associated with the Genesis creation myth indicates that humans are placed in Eden, not as overlords who are justified in the profligate use of the resources placed at their disposal, but as caretakers, "tillers and keepers." Their charge is one of responsibility, not privilege. Humans are God's representatives on earth, entrusted with the task of ensuring that the movement of God's creative spirit in the world will continue. Humans' creation in the image of God merely emphasizes the fact that they are God's cocreators, called to reflect in all things, in each of their actions, God's love for the world.

This concern for creation is underscored as God enters into a series of covenants or agreements with individuals like Sarah, Abraham, Jacob, and Moses. While it is commonly assumed that these special relationships consist exclusively of a bond between God and a specific person or group of people, this is in fact a misreading of the tradition. It is instructive to remember that the first covenant, recorded in the Book of Genesis, is made between God and Creation itself, shortly after the flood. God promises that the world will never again be destroyed by water, and then offers a special sign: "When the bow is in the clouds, I will see it and remember the everlasting covenant between God and every living creature of all flesh that is on the earth" (Gen 9:16). This sacred connection between Creator and Creation is also implied in the covenants later initiated with Abraham and Moses. As the biblical scholar Walter Brueggemann notes, the covenant itself can only be properly observed when the people are established in the land; apart from this, the agreement between God and God's people is only an abstraction. Why? Because in the books of Exodus, Deuteronomy, and Leviticus—where the details of the covenant are enumerated—there is a list of

provisions made not only for nurturing sacred relationships between humans and God, men and women, parents and children, "haves" and "have-nots," but also for the appropriate care of nonhuman creatures and the land itself.[13] The Book of Leviticus, for example, requires that every seventh year the agricultural fields be allowed to enjoy a season of rest: "Six years you shall sow your field, and six years you shall prune your vineyard, and gather in their yield; but in the seventh year there shall be a sabbath of complete rest for the land, a sabbath for the Lord: you shall not sow your field or prune your vineyard" (Lev 25:3–4). Similarly, there are prescribed means for showing respect for the animals that have been entrusted to one's care, even to the point of ensuring for them a death that is free of pain or undue anxiety.

Even today among Jews and Muslims, there are very specific laws that govern the slaughter of specific animals for food. Only when proper practices are carefully observed can a creature be regarded as ritually pure (*kosher* in Judaism; *halal* in Islam). People often make the mistake of assuming that the concern here is primarily for health and sanitation; it is perhaps more accurate to say that the final objective is holiness and sanctification—that is, in recognizing that all life comes from the Creator and should therefore be treated with gratitude and respect. In all things, humans are called to be good stewards of God's creation; to neglect this calling is indeed a refusal to be the human creatures that God created them to be.

One of the problems that many Jews, Christians, and Muslims have had to address over the centuries is the temptation on the part of some believers to rely too heavily on the word of God as it is revealed in a particular text, in its most basic form a practice known as *proof-texting*. While

---

13. See Walter Brueggemann, *The Land* (Minneapolis: Augsburg Fortress Press, 1987).

these traditions are "religions of the book," too often the book—and more specifically the letter of the law—takes precedence over the wisdom of God that can be found in the face of the other or in the intricacies of the natural world. Though each of these traditions affirms that the essence of God is ineffable—that like the *tao* God cannot be comprehended by the rational mind—many of the faithful find they are uncomfortable living with the uncertainties that accompany seeking God's wisdom in the world. So they turn to words and precise definitions instead. As a result, division and strife have often marked these three religious traditions, so much so that the "religions of the word" have come to be known also as the "religions of the sword." Often the conflict is most violent between two sects of the same faith, as the violence in Iraq between Sunni and Shiite Muslims so tragically demonstrated.

This interfaith conflict based on a reading of scripture then begs the question of whether a reliance on sacred texts, and on the rational faculties required to comprehend them in all their complexity, has contributed in part to the nature-deficit disorder that we have been considering here. Though the Bible and the Qu'ran speak of a God who becomes present to humans in a very real way, the more prominent tradition among these three religions features a God who is utterly transcendent, existing beyond the realm of the comprehensible. Therefore, any knowledge of God coming in and through the natural world is by virtue of its very medium incomplete. In order truly to comprehend the mystery of the divine, God must reveal Godself to humans in a unique, "supernatural" manner. It is indeed unfortunate that these special revelations have come to be identified with the texts that were originally meant only to bear witness to the events themselves. When the focus turns to the word alone, it is easy to see how beholding the divine in nature can fade to irrelevance. And when Creation becomes irrelevant, the next step cannot help but be its neglect and abuse.

Questions for Reflection and Discussion

- Does monotheistic belief in a personal God hinder or enhance one's perceived moral obligations toward the natural world?

- Do you agree with Lynn White that the Christian tradition bears a "huge burden of guilt" for our current environmental crisis? Explain.

- In relation to the natural environment, what might it mean for human decision-making to be aware of our elemental connection to the earth—clay, molecules, and so on?

THE FINAL RELIGION

We find among the world's faith traditions a variety of approaches to understanding the human-nature relationship, with some approaches appearing more promising than others. The sad fact, however, is that regardless of where one travels in the world today—whether it be to the forests of China, the Indian reservations of the desert Southwest, or the oceans separating the continents—one does not have to look far to find examples of ecological exploitation. It seems reasonable to expect that if one religious tradition were indeed more ecofriendly than the rest, we could encounter in those regions under its influence a pristine landscape free from the blemishes of industrial excess.

We will look in vain to find such a utopia, however. Today, wherever an ecosystem is marked by human habitation, there is at least some evidence of severe environmental degradation. Can we conclude from this, then, that none of the world's religions is capable of instilling in its adherents a commitment to valuing and preserving the biotic communities in which they live? Perhaps this is too strong a statement, but it does raise the concern that perhaps religion itself has become inconsequential in stemming the tide of ecological destruction. This could be because another faith tradition, one with a global reach, has superseded all the rest: the tradition of unrestrained consumer capitalism. The popularity of this tradition has grown leaps and bounds over the past century, and its gurus are quickly becoming an elite minority who control the lives of billions of people the world over. The fundamental tenets of this new religion are unconcerned with matters of ecological justice; these only serve to distract its devotees in their pursuit of material happiness and salvation.

CONCLUSION

As we conclude this discussion, it will be timely to consider whether the religious traditions of the world can stand up to the global reach of unfettered capitalism. In China, where nature is seen as revealing most clearly the wisdom of the *tao*, the wholesale destruction of mountain habitats moves on apace in the search for coal to meet the increasing energy demands of its population. Christianity has shown itself to be ineffectual in addressing the ecological embarrassments evident across the planet; indeed, some have even suggested Christianity is the source of the problem. The sacred river of India, the Ganges, was until recent cleanup efforts among the most polluted in the world. Japan, whose Buddhist heritage runs deep, consistently violates international conservation laws by "harvesting" more whales from the ocean every year than the species can sustain.

Where is the commitment of the faithful—whether Buddhist, Taoist, Hindu, or Christian—in the midst of this environmental annihilation? Have religiously informed values become irrelevant, paling compared to the lust for material acquisition and economic expansion? Has consumerism finally succeeded in unifying the world in a way that faith traditions could not? Such are the tidings of the new prophets of profit. But who loses in this equation? Certainly the world's poor, who for pennies a day are conscripted into being fodder for the production game. But a larger loser is nature itself, the source of the raw materials that keep the wheels of commerce turning. Richard Louv suggests that many children in the United States today suffer from a nature-deficit disorder, and he could be right. But this, too, may be only a symptom of a much more alarming disease. How long will it be before the world itself begins to suffer from a total deficit of nature?

Questions for Reflection and Discussion

- Do you prefer the phrase "ecological embarrassment" or "environmental problem"? Explain.
- Should we be concerned about the language we use to address certain human experiences? Explain.

- Is consumerism a religion? Why or why not?
- If consumerism is a religion, what are its rituals, sacraments, and assumptions about nature and what it means to be human?

Additional Resources

References

The definitive series on this topic, *Religions of the World and Ecology*, is edited by Mary Evelyn Tucker and John Grim and distributed by Harvard University Press for the Harvard University Center for the Study of World Religions (1997–2003). Though the volumes provide a wealth of information on the ecological sensibilities and challenges of each of the world's major religions, the texts are perhaps not as accessible to the introductory student. Each volume is included under the appropriate heading below.

Buddhism

Badiner, Allan Hunt, ed. 2002. *Mindfulness in the Marketplace: Compassionate Responses to Consumerism*. Berkeley, CA: Parallax Press.

Hanh, Thich Nhat. 1987. *Being Peace*. Edited by Arnold Kotler. Berkeley, CA: Parallax Press.

Hunt Badiner, Allan, ed. 1990. *Dharma Gaia: A Harvest of Essays in Buddhism and Ecology*. Berkeley, CA: Parallax Press.

Tucker, Mary Evelyn, and Duncan Ryūken Williams, eds. 1997. *Buddhism and Ecology: The Interconnection of Dharma and Deeds*. Religions of the World and Ecology Series. Cambridge, MA: Harvard University Press.

Christianity

Deffenbaugh, Daniel G. 2006. *Learning the Language of the Fields: Tilling and Keeping as Christian Vocation*. Cambridge, MA: Cowley Publications.

Hessel, Dieter T., and Rosemary Radford Ruether, eds. 2000. *Christianity and Ecology: Seeking the Well-Being of Earth and Humans*. Religions of the World and Ecology Series. Cambridge, MA: Harvard University Press.

Rasmussen, Larry. 1998. *Earth Community, Earth Ethics*. Orbis Ecology and Justice Series. Maryknoll, NY: Orbis Books.

Earth-Based Religious Movements

Albanese, Catherine. 1991. *Nature Religion in America: From the Algonkian Indians to the New Age*. Chicago History of American Religion Series. Chicago: University of Chicago Press.

Starhawk. 2005. *The Earth Path: Grounding Your Spirit in the Rhythms of Nature*. New York: HarperOne.

Hinduism and Jainism

Chapple, Christopher Key, and Mary Evelyn Tucker, eds. 2000. *Hinduism and Ecology: The Intersection of Earth, Sky, and Water*. Religions of the World and Ecology Series. Cambridge, MA: Harvard University Press.

Chapple, Christopher Key, ed. 2002. *Jainism and Ecology: Nonviolence in the Web of Life*. Religions of the World and Ecology Series. Cambridge, MA: Harvard University Press.

Indigenous Traditions

Callicott, J. Baird. "American Indian Land Wisdom? Sorting Out the Issues." *Journal of Forest History* 33, no.1 (January 1989): 35–42.

Callicott, J. Baird. "Traditional American Indian and Western European Attitudes toward Nature: An Overview." *Environmental Ethics* 4, no. 4 (1982): 304–329.

Grim, John A., ed. 2001. *Indigenous Traditions and Ecology: The Interbeing of Cosmology and Community*. Religions of the World and Ecology Series. Cambridge, MA: Harvard University Press.

Harrod, Howard. 2000. *The Animals Came Dancing: Native American Sacred Ecology and Animal Kinship*. Tucson: University of Arizona Press.

Islam

Foltz, Richard C., Frederick M. Denny, and Azizan Baharuddin, eds. 2003. *Islam and Ecology: A Bestowed Trust*. Religions of the World and Ecology Series. Cambridge, MA: Harvard University Press.

Hope, Marjorie, and James Young. "Islam and Ecology." *CrossCurrents* 44, no. 2 (Summer 1994): 180–192.

Judaism

Bernstein, Ellen, ed. 2000. *Ecology and the Jewish Spirit: Where Nature and the Sacred Meet*. Woodstock, VT: Jewish Lights Publications.

Tirosh-Samuelson, Hava. 2002. *Judaism and Ecology: Created World and Revealed Word*. Religions of the World and Ecology Series. Cambridge, MA: Harvard University Press.

Continued . . .

Additional Resources

Continued . . .

Waskow, Arthur, ed. 2000. *Torah of the Earth: Exploring 4,000 Years of Ecology in Jewish Thought*. Woodstock, VT: Jewish Light Publications.

Taoism and Confucianism

Adler, Joseph A., Peter K. Bol, Chung-ying Cheng, and Julia Cheng. 1998. *Confucianism and Ecology: The Interrelation of Heaven, Earth, and Humans*. Religions of the World and Ecology Series. Cambridge, MA: Harvard University Press.

Girardot, N. J., James Miller, and Liu Xiaogan, eds. 2001. *Daoism and Ecology: Ways Within a Cosmic Landscape*. Religions of the World and Ecology Series. Cambridge, MA: Harvard University Press.

Watts, Alan W. 1991. *Nature, Man, Woman*. New York: Vintage.

Other General Resources

Gotlieb, Roger. 2006. *The Oxford Handbook of Religion and Ecology*. Oxford, UK: Oxford University Press.

Tucker, Mary Evelyn, and John A. Grim. 1994. *Worldviews and Ecology: Religion, Philosophy, and the Environment*. Ecology and Justice Series. Maryknoll, NY: Orbis Books.

Videos and DVDs

Baraka. Directed by Ron Fricke. Orland Park, IL: MPI Home Video, 1993. 104 minutes.

Baraka, a Sufi word meaning "blessing" or "breath," is an appropriate title for this elaborate film. The viewer is taken through ecological habitats found on six continents and is left with an overwhelming sense of the world's incredible biodiversity, as well as the tragedy of its destruction at the hands of humans. Other films in this genre featuring high-quality images of the natural world include *Koyaanisgatsi* and *Microcosmos*.

Hopi: Songs of the Fourth World. Produced and Directed by Pat Ferrero. San Francisco: Ferrero Films, 1989. 58 minutes.

An excellent complement to the 1982 *National Geographic* issue on Hopi religion and society, this documentary considers Hopi creation myths, history,

art, agriculture, domestic life, and social customs. It is one of the best videos available on the cultural nuances of a specific Native American group.

Sacred Wildness: Zen Teachings of Rocks and Water. Directed by Sean Murphy. Mount Tremper, NY: Dharma Communications, 1996. 31 minutes.

Zen Mountain Monastery is the setting for this short video featuring insights from a series of workshops led by abbot and founder John Daido Loori. Wisdom from the abbot's teachings is accompanied by images of the surrounding countryside of upstate New York, which serves to emphasize the interconnectedness of humans and the natural world. For more information on Zen Mountain Monastery and its programs, go to *http://www.mro.org/mro.html*.

Visions of Eden: A Jewish Perspective on the Environment. New York: Jewish Theological Seminary of America and the Coalition for the Environment and Jewish Life, 1999. 60 minutes.

Introduced by Senator Joseph Lieberman of Connecticut, this film explores insights from various activists, academics, and religious leaders on the unique perspective that Judaism brings to the environmental movement.

Web Resources

The Forum on Religion and Ecology, sponsored by Harvard University's Center for the Environment, seeks to establish religion and ecology as an area of research and study in colleges, universities, and seminaries. The Web site offers valuable references and resources for educators. See *http://environment. harvard.edu/religion/religion/index.html*.

Religious Studies in Secondary Schools is a coalition of private and public school teachers committed to the academic study of world religions and the values, literature, and cultures associated with them. The Web site features a section on religion and ecology, with brief overviews of each religious tradition, as well as bibliographic and teaching resources. See *http://www. rsiss.net/rsissfore.html*.

ASCETICALLY AND MYSTICALLY REMOVED AND ENGAGED

Dr. Bernadette McNary-Zak
Rhodes College

Preface

Many religions have mystical and ascetic expressions. The deprivation of human wants and needs in order to gain enlightenment, enhance piety, or for some other spiritual end is found in most religions. Many traditions seek mystical engagement with that which is "other," divine, or holy. Some in the Buddhist tradition actively seek nonactivity or non-seeking with the aim of approaching nirvana. Some Christian mystics seek union with God through prayer, self-negation, and other spiritual practices. Native American holy men and women might ingest peyote to induce visions of truth hidden from the naked eye. Many different believers direct their lives by the insights gleened from mystical and ascetic engagement. In this chapter, Bernadette McNary-Zak lifts up examples of religious exercises and life choices aimed at self-negation or mystical encounter. She highlights the human desire to engage in mystical and ascetic practices as a consequence of religious convictions.

Chapter Goals

- To explore the history of mysticism among various religious traditions
- To consider ideas related to mystical practice
- To investigate the role of ascetic discipline in religious experience

INTRODUCTION

In the late fourth century, the Christian bishop Theodoret of Cyrrhus recorded his observations of the lives of holy men and women in his region. In *A History of the Monks of Syria,* Theodoret writes of their poverty and seclusion, their vigilant discipline and steadfast prayer, their extended fasts and the depths of their piety. He includes an account of Symeon Stylites, the "pillar saint" who lived atop a tall pillar for decades because "he yearns to fly up to heaven and to be separated from this life on earth."[1] Symeon's actions deeply impressed the bishop:

> More than all this I admire his endurance. Night and day he is standing within view of all. . . . [H]e is exposed to all as a new and extraordinary spectacle—now standing for a long time, and now bending down repeatedly and offering worship to God. Many of those standing by count the number of these acts of worship. Once one of those with me counted one thousand two hundred and forty-four of them, before slackening and giving up count. In bending down he always makes his forehead touch his toes—for his stomach's receiving food once a week, and little of it, enables his back to bend easily.[2]

While the spectacle of Symeon on his pillar attracts many onlookers, Theodoret is most struck by the throngs who seek Symeon's counsel, healing, and wisdom, with the belief that these are ordained by and reflect the will of God. In Theodoret's account, such gifts are noteworthy not in themselves but rather for their salvific impact on others. Theodoret explains that because God works through Symeon, those "who were enslaved . . . to the darkness of impiety, have been illuminated by his standing on the pillar. For this dazzling lamp, as if placed on a lampstand, has sent out rays in all directions, like the sun."[3]

All religious traditions have stories of holy men and women. How do such persons come by their profound holiness, and how is that holiness defined and validated? What purpose and function do such persons serve in a religious tradition? How do scholars of religion make sense of their lives? In this chapter, we will consider these questions by examining the religious convictions that lead individuals to engage in ascetic and mystical practices.

Like Symeon, many holy men and women encounter the sacred in and through the body. They espouse awareness of the body, including its physical form, the senses, mind, and in some cases the soul, as the site of encounter with the sacred. Often, ascetic or mystical engagement provides a means to this awareness. It is an awareness based on and shaped by an experiential, rather than intellectual or theoretical, understanding of the sacred, and it provides knowledge and insight through self-discipline and directed action. Mystical and ascetic practices, common to all religious worldviews, emerge from and are supported by a distinct theological anthropology: they emphasize knowing the sacred through experience.

Questions for Reflection and Discussion

- How might Symeon's actions be interpreted in terms of religious experience?

- How might the body be understood as a site of encounter with the divine?

---

1. Theodoret of Cyrrhus, *A History of the Monks of Syria*, translated with an introduction and notes by R. M. Price (Kalamazoo, MI: Cistercian Publications, 1985), 165.

2. Ibid., 170.

3. Ibid., 166.

SELF-NEGATION

The Greco-Roman world used the Greek verb *askein*, meaning "to practice, exercise, train," to refer to the physical, mental, and emotional preparation an athlete would undergo in training for a contest or competition. Such *askesis* involved acts of renunciation and self-denial, rigorous exercise and training, and abstinence from certain foods, drink, and sexual activity. In the religious worldview, asceticism retains this meaning while emphasizing the concomitant discipline or training of the mind through such practices as prayer, contemplation, and meditation. Thus, for religious persons physical and mental *askesis* is performed for a spiritual end determined by the specific religious tradition; for example, asceticism may be cultivated in order to acquire virtue, do penance, prepare for encounter with the divine, or gain a heightened consciousness.

Ascetic practices are found in every religious worldview, although emphasis and form vary. Individual practitioners may cultivate asceticism voluntarily in order to enhance piety. In Hinduism, fasting and sexual continence accompany the practice of yoga as techniques to redirect the mind. The sitting practice of Zen Buddhists serves a similar aim. In Judaism on Yom Kippur (Day of Atonement), Jews abstain from many regular activities and fast in order to mourn sinfulness, a practice embedded in the tradition's history. In Islam, during the holy month of Ramadan, the period in which the sacred Qur'an was revealed to Muhammad, Muslims cultivate fasting and abstinence from dawn to sunset. This practice, one of the Five Pillars of Islam, is ordained in the Qur'an. Some Christian denominations cultivate similar ascetic practices during the forty days of Lent, in imitation of Jesus during his temptation in the wilderness. Christianity teaches that self-discipline practiced in seclusion and solitude can serve as an act of penance and purification. In all of these examples, the ascetic practice of fasting is intended to facilitate prayer and self-purification, evoke solidarity with those who are impoverished and suffering, and heighten awareness of the divine as the source and provider of life.

In several religious traditions, ascetic practices are institutionalized to the extent that they are cultivated as a permanent vocation, as in the monastic life. A monk (cf. the Greek, *monachos*, meaning "solitary one") renounces or "leaves the world" of material ties and possessions to focus on a spiritual journey. That journey, taken in a state of internal solitude and seclusion and cultivated in a spirit of humility and compassion, is shaped by various forms of physical and spiritual discipline that may include fasting, chastity, poverty, and contemplation.

Siddhartha Gautama was a practicing non-Vedic, Hindu *samana*, a wandering monk, when he realized the nature of existence as interdependent. Gautama founded an order of monks (*bhikkus*) and an order of nuns (*bhikkunis*), who later settled to cultivate detachment and live in voluntary poverty and chastity. In the Theravadan tradition, these orders constituted the *sangha*; the laity and the monks are distinct, yet codependent. In the Mahayana tradition, the *sangha* came to comprise all lay and monks who are striving on the bodhisattva path. Bodhisattvas are "beings striving for enlightenment."[4] They seek "to realize the emptiness (*shunyata*) of self and world. They seek to dissolve the self that separates and alienates them in the life-flow. To dissolve self is to dissolve the distinctions that separate things and persons and cause suffering; it is to be one with each moment of life-flow

---

4. Robert C. Lester, *Buddhism: The Path to Nirvana* (San Francisco: Harper & Row, 1987), 43.

as it occurs and, therefore, it is to experience the essential unity of life, the bliss of oneness."[5] By realizing the emptiness of self and world, a bodhisattva strives to attain full enlightenment, which has been referred to as "a thorough and complete understanding of the nature and meaning of life, the forces which shape it, the method to end it, and the reality which lies behind it."[6] The distinctive characteristic of the bodhisattva ideal is the rejection of nirvana in order "to be born again and again for the sake of releasing others from suffering."[7] In one sense, the return to samsara is a feature of the bodhisattva's compassion; it is the decision to be "one with each moment of life-flow as it occurs."[8] Compassion, governing conduct, involves self-sacrifice and service to all beings.

Christian monasticism arose as a distinct vocation in the deserts of Egypt, Palestine, and Syria during the early fourth century. As many Christians came to believe that the Christian life required a more visible renunciation of the world, they sought more isolated areas, including the desert regions surrounding their towns and villages, to practice a more rigorous discipline. This is the case for the fourth-century Egyptian hermit Antony, who sought a life in response to the call: "Jesus said to him, 'If you wish to be perfect, go, sell your possessions and give the money to the poor, and you will have treasure in heaven; then come, follow me.'"[9] The conclusion to the fourth-century Christian work, *Life of Antony*, claims that a broad, far-reaching audience can be affected by the ascetic practices of Antony.

Therefore, read these things now to the other brothers so that they may learn what the life of the monks ought to be, and so they may believe that our Lord and Savior Jesus Christ glorifies those who glorify him, and not only leads those who serve him to the end into the Kingdom of heaven. . . . And if the need arises, read this to the pagans as well, so they may understand by this means that our Lord Jesus Christ is God and Son of God—and, additionally, that the Christians who are sincerely devoted to him and truly believe in him not only prove that the demons, whom the Greeks consider gods, are not gods, but also trample and chase them away as deceivers and corrupters of mankind, through Jesus Christ our Lord, to whom belongs glory forever and ever. Amen.[10]

This explicit call to share *Life* with others highlights the author's belief that Antony had an experience of the presence and power of the divine and that it was the task of the text to relay this and to invite a response from the reader. In many stories of holy persons, the delineation of stages in which ascetics had mystical experiences of the divine allows their stories to serve as guides for the reader. As witnesses, or testimonies, to the action of the divine, these stories uphold ascetic practice as a legitimate form of spirituality and mystical union as a viable end. It is telling that, decades later, Augustine of Hippo would appeal explicitly to the model of spirituality in *Life of Antony* in recounting his own conversion experience in *Confessions*.

5. Ibid., 45.

6. Edward Conze, "Buddhism: The Mahayana," in *Encyclopedia of the World's Religions*, R. C. Zaehner, ed. (New York: Barnes & Noble Books, 1997), 300.

7. Lester, *Buddhism*, 43.

8. Ibid., 45.

9. See Mt 19:21, *New Oxford Annotated Bible*.

10. *Athanasius: The Life of Antony and the Letter to Marcellinus*, translation and introduction by Robert C. Gregg (New York: Paulist Press, 1980), *Life of Antony*, section 94.

After spending some time as a hermit, Benedict of Nursia (480–547 CE) founded a small Christian monastic community at Monte Cassino near Rome. He wrote a guide for the monks, the *Rule of Benedict,* to aid them in their effort to "establish a school for the Lord's service."[11] The *Rule of Benedict* retains its appeal today as a program for monastic practice. Monks take vows of poverty, chastity, obedience, and conversion of manners. In Benedictine monasticism, division of labor, as well as common meeting times for prayer and meals, enforce the principles of equality and unity that underlie these self-sufficient communities. Hospitality figures prominently. In most Benedictine communities, the monastic schedule has some slight variation to accommodate the type of labor and the season of the year. For the most part, however, it includes time for personal prayer, Opus Dei (or the divine office), manual labor, *lectio divina* (reading, studying, and meditating on Scripture), eating and sleeping. It is intended to create a balanced, moderate asceticism; thus regulating the practice also establishes an external and internal rhythm that facilitates a freeing of the mind and enables a life of continuous prayer.

A Psychological View of Ascetics

Ascetic practices continue to be studied from a variety of methodological approaches, including historical, phenomenological, psychological, and theological. Each methodology uses a specific set of operating assumptions and provides a specific framework for interpretation, thereby yielding a distinct understanding. Each methodology also works within the parameters of study defined by its discipline. These may change as the discipline itself changes.

To illustrate, we might consider the theories of two psychologists, William James and M. Scott Peck. In his nineteenth century work, *The Varieties of Religious Experience,* James writes that any motive for asceticism is based on a "general good intention."[12] As part of his assessment of ascetic behavior, James poses two psychological considerations as applicable to all proposed motives for asceticism. First, he claims that there is a natural tendency for individuals to define a balance of inner dispositions in order to realize a personal potential level of efficiency within society. It is also natural for individuals to maintain this level of efficiency by undertaking, in moderate degrees, things that are difficult.

> For in its spiritual meaning asceticism . . . symbolizes, lamely enough no doubt, but sincerely, the belief that there is an element of real wrongness in this world, which is neither to be ignored nor evaded, but which must be squarely met and overcome by an appeal to the soul's heroic resources, and neutralized and cleansed away by suffering. . . . The real deliverance . . . must be of universal application. Pain and wrong and death must be fairly met and overcome in higher excitement, or else their sting remains essentially unbroken.[13]

James further maintains that the practice of world-renunciation evidences a desire to achieve detachment through self-expulsion from society, for "only those need renounce worldly actions who are still inwardly attached thereto. If one really be unattached to the fruits of action, one may mix in the world with equanimity."[14]

11. Benedict of Nursia, *The Rule of St. Benedict,* preface by Thomas More, edited by Timothy Fry, OSB (New York: Vintage Books, 1998), prologue, 5.

12. James, *The Varieties of Religious Experience: A Study in Human Nature* (New York: Macmillan, 1961), 287.

13. Ibid., 287. James refers to asceticism in the context of a twice-born philosophy.

14. Ibid., 286.

The contemporary psychologist M. Scott Peck provides a different theory for the motivation and action of asceticism. Assuming no distinction between the mind and the spirit, Peck maintains that the processes of achieving spiritual and mental growth are synonymous. Both are attained through discipline. Here, discipline refers to the "techniques of suffering, means by which we experience the pain of problems in such a way as to work them through and solve them successfully, learning and growing in the process."[15] Techniques of suffering include delaying gratification, accepting responsibility, dedication to the truth, and "balancing."

Understanding "balancing" as a process of renunciation and rebirth, Peck writes that "it is in the giving up of self that human beings can find the most ecstatic and lasting, solid, durable joy of life. And it is death that provides life with all its meaning."[16] Here, Peck interprets asceticism as a dying to the self, which is a sign of spiritual and mental growth; it is incomplete and psychologically unsound unless it is accompanied by service. "Spiritually evolved people, by virtue of their discipline, mastery and love, are people of extraordinary competence, and in their competence they are called on to serve the world, and in their love they answer the call."[17]

Questions for Reflection and Discussion

- Why might James and Peck interpret the role of ascetic discipline differently?
- In what ways might ascetic practices help or hinder religious experience and expression?
- Should ascetic practices be monitored by religious authorities if any are present? Why or why not?
- What dangers might be associated with ascetic practices?

MYSTICAL UNION

The thirteenth-century Jewish mystic Rabbi Abraham Abulafia instructed:

> Be prepared for God, oh Israelite! Make thyself ready to direct thy heart to God alone. Cleanse the body and choose a lonely house where none shall hear thy voice. Sit there in thy closet and do not reveal thy secret to any man. . . . Cleanse thy clothes, and, if possible, let all thy garments be white, for all this is helpful in leading the heart toward the fear of God and the love of God.[18]

Ascetic practice may result in mystical union. "Mystical union is the unmediated, transforming experience of the unification of man or man's soul with the highest reality. Such union represents the supreme and most authentic elevation of the human spirit as it reaches a fusion with, or at least a living cognition of, God or of

---

15. M. Scott Peck, *The Road Less Traveled: A New Psychology of Love, Traditional Values and Spiritual Growth* (New York: Simon & Schuster, 1978), 17.

16. Ibid., 72.

17. Ibid., 75.

18. Arthur Goldwag, *The Beliefnet Guide to Kabbalah*, introduction by Rabbi Lawrence Kushner, the Beliefnet Guides (New York: Three Leaves Press), 1.

the transcendent ground of being."[19] Mystical union is predicated on love by and for the self and the Other.

The word *mystic* derives from the Greek verb *muein* ("to remain silent"). This root indicates a silence that is qualitatively distinct. "[M]onasticism and mysticism in their most profound forms manifest something far more interesting than the literal practice of silence and solitude: monks and mystics often understand solitude as the climate and silence as the language of liberation, enlightenment, or union with God."[20] Mysticism is possible for those who are no longer able to think or act from self-will; a mystical experience can occur when self-will is in complete accordance with the divine or sacred. Thus, mysticism is hardly void of human effort. "Mystics insist that direct confirmation of the oneness of reality is possible through a unitive experience—an experience of dying to the ego-self and becoming one with the ultimate."[21]

In Islam, mystical experience, if only momentary, can be cultivated through a highly ritualized dance by the whirling dervishes, one of a number of groups of Muslim Sufis (cf. *suf*, meaning "wool"). The eighth-century Muslim mystic Rabi'a al-Adawiyya was a prominent female Sufi whose teachings were formative. As one observer writes: "Over the centuries the Sufis have provided the profoundest metaphysics, cosmology, angelology, psychology, and eschatology to be found in the Islamic tradition and one of the most complete metaphysical expositions found in any religious tradition."[22]

Contemplation figures prominently in the mystical experience of many Christian mystics. The twelfth-century Christian monk and mystic Bernard of Clairvaux delineated stages of ascent and rest on the path to mystical union. In his sermon on Song of Songs, Bernard used the body of Christ as a symbolic template for the movement of mystical ascent. He described being led by Christ from the kiss of repentance on Christ's feet, to the kiss of continence on his hand, to the kiss of union on his mouth. Of this final kiss, he writes: "But if anyone once receives the spiritual kiss of Christ's mouth he seeks eagerly to have it again and again. I think no one can know what it is except he who has received it. It is a hidden manna (Rv 2:17), and he who eats it hungers for more (Sir 24:23)."[23]

The Buddhist forest monk Achaan Chah describes the transformation of understanding and knowledge attained one day as he was sitting in meditation. He describes the one-pointed focus of his mind, as it turned inward peacefully and completely. "The third time the mind went in, the whole world broke apart: the earth, grass, trees, mountains, people, all was just space. Nothing was left. When the mind had gone in and abided as it wished, had stayed for as long as it could, the mind withdrew, and returned to normal. I do not know how it abided; such things are difficult to see and to speak about. There is nothing to compare it with."[24]

In some religious worldviews, mystical union is an experience of salvation. In the Buddhist tradition, such is the case with nirvana, which results in freedom from future rebirth. Gautama

---

19. Ileana Marcoulesco, "Mystical Union," in *Encyclopedia of Religion*, Mircea Eliade, ed. (New York: Collier Macmillian, 1987), 239. William James found in mystical experience the essence of religiosity. "Personal religious experience has its root and center in mystical states of consciousness"; James, *The Varieties of Religious Experience*, 308–309.

20. John F. Teahan, "Solitude: A Central Motif in Thomas Merton's Life and Writings," *Journal of the American Academy of Religion* 50, no. 4 (December 1982), 521.

21. Roger Schmidt, *Exploring Religion*, 2nd ed. (Belmont, CA: Wadsworth Publishing, 1988), 491.

22. Seyyed Hossein Nasr, "Islam," in *Our Religions*, Arvind Sharma, ed. (San Francisco: HarperSanFrancisco, 1993), 470.

23. Bernard of Clairvaux, *Selected Works*, Classics of Western Spirituality, 55, trans. G. R. Evans (New York: Paulist Press, 1987), Sermon 3, p. 221. Biblical passages cited are Rv 2:17 and Sir 24:23.

24. *A Still Forest Pool: The Insight Meditation of Achaan Chah*, compiled and edited by Jack Kornfield and Paul Breiter (Wheaton, IL: Theosophical Publishing House, 1987), 185.

Buddha's insight that freedom from suffering (*dukkha*) comes from a renunciation of all attachments and recognition of impermanence led to his enlightenment. "Self-denial (refusing to lie or steal, to commit violence or engage in sexual misconduct) and meditation will result in enlightenment (*bodhi*)—waking up to life as it really is—and [thereby to] the cessation of suffering (*nirvana*)."[25]

In other religious worldviews, mystical union is interpreted as a divine response gifted by grace. The Christian mystic Julian of Norwich prays for union with the divine through suffering.[26] It is in a state of mystical union that she admits her desire to suffer with Christ and receives her first revelation, a sight of "the red blood running down from under the crown, hot and flowing freely and copiously, a living stream, just as it was at the time when the crown of thorns was pressed on his blessed head."[27] Through this revelation, she begins to understand God's direct impact on all things.

Language often proves inadequate for describing the mystical experience. For many mystics, there is a cessation of speech, as the mystical experience transcends the limits of language. In his work *The Celestial Hierarchy*, Pseudo-Dionysius observes that the universe is an emanation from a God who is above every being and knowledge. Because mystical union produces a way of seeing and understanding that has a cognitive dimension, many mystics use symbolic or poetic language to speak and write about the Other, as in the case of the Chinese mystic, Lao-tzu:

> The Way that can be told of is not an Unvarying Way; the names that can be named are not unvarying names. It was from the Nameless that Heaven and Earth sprang; the named is but the mother that rears the ten thousand creatures, each after its kind. Truly, "Only he that rids himself forever of desires can see the Secret Essences"; He that has never rid himself of desire can see only the Outcomes. These two things issued from the same mould, but nevertheless are different in name. This "same mould" we can but call the Mystery, or rather the "Darker than any Mystery," the Doorway whence issued all Secret Essences.[28]

Such language is also used to express the ineffability of mystical experience itself. The collapse of finite in the Infinite, the release of the self to be taken over by the Other, and the return of the wayward creature to the Created are common themes in mystical discourse, as evidenced in these words from the Muslim mystic, Ibn al-Farid:

> With my Beloved I alone have been,
> When secrets tenderer than evening airs
> Passed and the Vision blessed
> Was granted to my prayers,
> That crowned me, else obscure,
>   with endless fame,
> The while amazed between
> His Beauty and His Majesty
> I stood in silent ecstasy
> Revealing that which over my spirit went
>   and came.
> In His face commingled
> Is every charm and grace;
> The whole of Beauty singled
> Into a perfect face
> Beholding Him would cry,
> "There is no God but He and He is
>   most High."[29]

---

25. Lester, *Buddhism*, 12.

26. See Julian of Norwich, *Showings*, E. Colledge and J. Walsh, trans. (New York: Paulist Press, 1978).

27. Ibid., 129.

28. Arthur Waley, trans., *The Way and Its Power* (New York: Evergreen, 1958), 144.

29. R. A. Nicholson, trans., *The Mystics of Islam*, as quoted in Margaret Smith, *An Introduction to Mysticism* (New York: Oxford University Press, 1977), 9.

Here, Ibn al-Farid offers insight into an intuitive, nondiscursive knowledge of the divine based on his experience. It is the mark of the mystic that experience of the divine is individual; that is to say, it cannot be replicated or transferred to another.

As in the case of asceticism, mysticism has been studied and interpreted from a variety of methodological approaches, including historical, philosophical, and theological. For some, the fundamental relatedness between experience and doctrine in their religious worldview becomes the basis for understanding mystical experience. That is to say, the ascetic/mystical engagement is interpreted from the perspective of the religious worldview in which it occurs. This usually entails consideration of many teachings including those related to the human body. In the doctrinal system of some religious worldviews, the body is interpreted as a gift intended precisely for the purpose of reaching an awareness of the sacred; in other religious worldviews, the body is interpreted as an extension of the cosmos and so exists in interconnectedness to all things that can be realized. So, for example, a theological foundation may be given for the value of ascetic acts and mystical experience. Because both occur in the context of normative claims in a tradition or in the context of a specific understanding of sacred texts, neither practice is an end in itself, as illustrated by the example of this fourth-century Christian:

> She had a stool on which she would rest when the time to sleep came; it measured three and a half cubits by one. Sometimes she would throw herself down on the ground, neglecting her body in order to subdue it. When she happened to be tempted by the devil by hallucinations at night she would get up straight away and beseech God, amid abundant tears, to remove the tempter Satan from her; then she would open the Bible and lovingly meditate on its living and spiritual words.[30]

This ascetic's return to the Bible provides a response to her suffering and trial as well as a hope for deeper understanding. Some religious persons feel called or drawn to this type of encounter in their quest for religious meaning and mystical union as "direct experiences of ultimate reality mediated by literate, scriptural traditions."[31]

Questions for Reflection and Discussion

- Do you think you could live a life of renunciation? Why or why not?

- To what might you be attached that you could not easily give up? Why is this attachment important to you?

FUNCTION OF ASCETIC AND MYSTICAL PRACTICES IN A RELIGIOUS TRADITION

Ascetic and mystical practices make possible an experience of the divine. What is the function of holy persons and their practices within a religious tradition? As Lawrence Cunningham has observed, such persons evidence the continuity of the religious tradition and of the religious quest. By and through their practices, these holy men and women have a specific relationship to society and the world that enables them to serve

---

30. Susan Ashbrook Harvey and Sebastian Brock, eds., *Holy Women of the Syrian Orient* (Berkeley, CA: University of California Press, 1987), 179.

31. Denise Lardner Carmody and John Tully Carmody, *Mysticism: Holiness East and West* (New York: Oxford University Press, 1996), 275.

others in a variety of ways.[32] Theirs is a transformative experience with ramifications that extend beyond the individual ascetic or mystic. For the individual, this experience of the divine brings a state of tranquility and single-mindedness. This state necessarily affects relationships with others through service and thereby serves as a public assertion of the radically distinct identity realized in and enabled by the experience of the divine. For example, the ecstatic experience of the shaman, which some would deem a mystical experience, has a public benefit. Shamans "acquire their extraordinary powers from spirit beings, including the power to heal and to divine the significance of the past, present, and future events. As mediators of salvation, they diagnose the causes of disease and misfortune and perform the proper ritual action to restore the well-being of their clients. In addition to their curative power, they resolve problems, predict the future . . . their effective use of power is usually believed to rest on being chosen by divinity."[33] That is to say, the divine works in and through the shaman for the one who is in need; in this way, the authority given the shaman recognizes the power and bestowal of the divine. In his study of shamanism, Mircea Eliade writes that shamans are "of the 'elect,' and as such they have access to a region of the sacred inaccessible to other members of the community. Their ecstatic experiences have exercised, and still exercise, a powerful influence on the stratification of religious ideology, on mythology, on ritualism."[34]

In this way, holy persons, like the shaman, are exemplars. Ascetics and mystics are living evidence of the experiential dimension of a religious worldview. Indeed, the experience of these holy persons sets them apart; the fruit of their experience attests to a way of seeing, being, and knowing that validates and discloses the theological truth-claims of a given religious worldview.

CONCLUSION

The body a dazzling lamp, the pillar a lampstand: this is what one Christian onlooker saw when he gazed on the elderly ascetic Symeon, standing with arms outstretched atop a high pillar. Within the context of a religious tradition, ascetics and mystics illumine a particular means of encountering and of knowing the Other. They provide an example of the experiential dimension of a religious worldview and so also provide access to a way of seeing and of being human.

Additional Resources

Carmody, Denise Lardner, and John Tully Carmody. 1996. *Mysticism: Holiness East and West*. New York: Oxford University Press.

Freiberger, Oliver. 2006. *Asceticism and Its Critics: Historical Accounts and Comparative Perspectives*. American Academy of Religion Cultural Criticism Series. Oxford: Oxford University Press.

Harmless, William. 2008. *Mystics*. New York: Oxford University Press.

Kaelber, Walter O. 1987. "Asceticism." In *Encyclopedia of Religion*. Edited by Mircea Eliade. New York: Collier Macmillan.

Marcoulesco, Ileana. 1987. "Mystical Union." In *Encyclopedia of Religion*. Edited by Mircea Eliade. New York: Collier Macmillan.

Sharma, Arvind, ed. 1993. *Our Religions*. San Francisco: HarperSanFrancisco.

Smith, Margaret. 1977. *An Introduction to Mysticism*. New York: Oxford University Press.

32. These are described and discussed in chapters 2 and 5 of Lawrence Cunningham, *The Catholic Heritage: Martyrs, Ascetics, Pilgrims, Warriors, Mystics, Theologians, Artists, Humanists, Activists, Outsiders, and Saints* (New York: Crossroad, 1983).

33. Roger Schmidt, *Exploring Religion*, 2nd ed. (Belmont, CA: Wadsworth Publishing, 1988), 357.

34. Mircea Eliade, *Shamanism: Archaic Techniques of Ecstasy*, trans. Willard R. Trask, (Princeton, NJ: Princeton University Press, 1972), 7.

TECHNOLOGY AND RELIGION

Dr. A. K. M. Adam
University of Gasgow

Preface

A century ago, a person could expect no more than a few technological changes to contend with over a lifetime. Today, a host of technological changes and innovations occur daily. Each change—however small—has the capacity to either expand the conversation about religion or reduce it to trivial details. Each technological advance holds promise for bettering human life or diminishing it. Some technologies offer a panacea to life's toughest questions and can thrust people into dilemmas of religion and faith. What if molecular encoding becomes commonplace? What impact will this have on the religious imagination or religion itself? What if ubiquitous computing provides keystroke access to every known vice and virtue? What response do religions offer to the tidal wave of technology sweeping the world? How do religions engage technology? Why do some religions vehemently reject technological advances while others openly embrace them? In this chapter, A. K. M. Adam explores the landscapes of cyberspace, technology-saturated religion, and the human spirit.

Chapter Goals

- To critically reflect on religion in relation to technology
- To explore how technology intersects human experience and identity
- To consider what connotes spiritual experience and electronic spirituality
- To investigate the notion of what is "real" in relation to religion and human experience

INTRODUCTION

To grasp the relationship of technology to religion, let's begin by imagining religion *apart from* technology. Let's imagine a worshipper apart from walls and buildings, encountering the divine without mediation from any human products. To complete the worshipper's isolation from technology, we remove not only portable electronics, eyeglasses, watches, and jewelry but also any manufactured clothing. We will still not have attained pure isolation—our hypothetical worshipper has been immersed in technological devices throughout life and so must spend a long time naked in the wilderness to lose the habits of living in a technologically defined culture. After subsisting apart from all constructed devices for several weeks, shedding as much as possible the influences of technology, our worshipper might come optimally close to a technology-free confrontation with God.

The alternative extreme—saturating the worshipper with technology—may come more readily to mind. Technology-saturated religion might involve, for instance, participating in an online worship service in an interactive digital world. Even bodily encounters in face-to-face physical environments are technologically predetermined: different buildings afford different environments for worship; electrically amplified instruments enhance worship; our personal accoutrements, even our clothing, surround us with elements made possible through technology.

The relation of religion to technology, then, embraces a great deal more than the question of whether "toons" can pray. If modern worshippers worry over whether digital electronics threaten to corrupt religious experience, their grandparents worried about the intrusion of electrical light into sacred spaces, and their great-grandparents debated permitting the playing of musical instruments during worship. Some ancient *haruspices*[1] probably fretted over the distinction between bronze and iron implements for disemboweling a sacrificial sheep. The tension between technological support for religious purposes and technological impediments to religious practice is as old as humanity. The challenges that the current technological environment pose to religious thought involve issues that have provoked believers for millennia.

RELIGIOUS AND ETHICAL PROBLEMS WITH TECHNOLOGY

Some ancient roots of technological conflict derive from religions' divisions over the goodness of the material world. One person might describe technology as the optimization of human creativity and the materials of production. Advocates of this perspective might regard technology as intrinsically neutral, capable of being used for good or evil, or even as intrinsically good, an admirable exercise of ingenuity. To such a perspective, the evils we might associate with technology come from outside influences, not from the technology itself. On the other hand, some religions tend to regard the material world as mortal and transient at best, or worse as delusive, a trap for the spirit (*soma sema*, "the body is a tomb," as the Orphics and their successors proclaimed). To such an outlook, technology's benefits intensify the evilness of all material things by creating the false impression that material existence isn't so bad. One preliminary axis for assessing the relation of religion to technology, then, will be to draw a division between the pure spiritual realm and the corrupted material world. Adherents of such a perspective will either commit themselves to an ascetic renunciation of technology, or will try to determine a dividing line between tolerable manifestations of technology (such as clothing, shelter, and food preparation) and its impermissible uses (for entertainment, comfort, self-indulgence). The relation of technology to religion, in these cases, depends on beliefs about the nature of human, mortal products.

This preliminary division of religions into "pro-material" and "anti-material" camps

---

1. A *haruspex* foretold the future by inspecting the internal organs of sacrificed animals.

provides one quick-and-dirty way of sorting questions concerning technology. At the same time, it excludes intermediate options (a world-denying religion might argue that technology helps remove us from bodily limitations); and even extreme examples of world-renouncing religions can make allowance for *some* manufactured goods. A clock that enables a worshipper to observe the *adhans* (the muezzin's call that alerts Muslims to observe one of the five occasions of daily prayer) at the correct intervals, for instance, might be reckoned an acceptable technological advance, since it would help promote religiosity. Cell phones build up community, so they may be acceptable (as long as they're powered by batteries rather than the municipal power grid). But many modern congregations firmly reject the use of projection screens or electrically amplified instruments in worship. Religious communities discern the positive or negative value of particular technologies by articulating criteria that assess the device in comparison to the religious community's sense of identity (its charter texts, defining practices, goals, and perhaps even its entrenched habits).

Religious communities will judge particular technologies differently depending on the characteristics of the community and the technology in question. While few observers would regard an automobile as spiritually suspect, some religious communities eschew any device that endangers the bonds of proximity and neighborliness. That which the car makes possible (an *affordance*, to use the philosophical term) is mobility, but the community may put a higher priority on insularity. The car that *affords* a last-minute trip to the grocery store also *affords* a vacation among strangers in a remote, exotic location. The affordance of convenience may jeopardize the close-knit community that protects its beliefs from alien influence.

Not only are technological affordances accompanied by possibly unwelcome side effects, they also tend to conceal many of the effects that they foreclose. To remain with the automotive example, the car that makes it possible to rush out for pizza also makes it possible to ignore the numerous other food vendors along the way. The car also isolates the driver from the neighbors whose houses she might have walked past had she been on foot. And had she walked past the house of a neighbor who had just baked a pie, that neighbor might have invited her in, obviating the urgency of getting a pizza and building ties of friendship and sharing. The affordance of rapid transportation, then, conceals the effect of cutting riders off from their immediate environment. Furthermore, the easy availability of pizza tends to bring "convenience" to the foreground as a desirable quality. Though the drive burns costly fossil fuels, pollutes the air, and contributes to global warming, the technology relegates these effects to the background; a quick drive satisfies the perceived need for pizza now, but it invests our hunger in the oil drilling and refining industries and in an automobile that pollutes, degrades the environment, and contributes to global warming. Still further, the technology of pizza transportation conceals the labor of automotive workers, agricultural field hands, freight shippers, and on and on. The process of preparing a pizza from homegrown tomatoes and a home-baked crust involves a radically different set of practices and effects than the process of buying commercially prepared pizza. Add in the greater likelihood of someone being injured in a traffic accident, and those differences clearly pertain to religious identity and practice.

Somebody who adheres scrupulously to religious teaching that the whole living earth is sacred might reject automotive transportation across the board. A believer whose faith locates humanity as the crown and pinnacle of the universe might argue to the contrary, however, that the costs of mining, fabrication, manufacturing, and powering automobiles matter much less than the well-being that automobiles create for human beings. Religions whose tenets derive from what are seen as divinely ordained doctrines would assess automobiles differently depending on the extent to which the car reflects their deity's will. The same technology can bear many different religious significances, then, depending on the religion in question and the extent to which believers are willing to examine their technological investment on the basis of their professed faith.

Technology intersects with religion in at least one more way. As humans grow accustomed to the affordances and drawbacks of particular technologies, they tend to associate that technology with their own identity. A musician may sense her viola as an extension of herself; drivers frequently report problems they feel in their cars, as though the car were a prosthesis for transportation; and increasingly, computer users vest their hard drives with custodianship of their knowledge and memory. In these and countless other ways, the religious self involves not simply the bio-spiritual person (whose constituents have been parsed variously into body and mind; body, soul, and spirit; *rupa*, *vedana*, *samjna*, *samskara*, and *vijnana*; and innumerable other categorizations, depending on the religion in question). Technology constitutes some portion of the religious believer's identity—and if one judges by people's behavior, the technological component can take on tremendous importance.

If this seems an artificial inflation of technology into human identity, consider the case of a patient whose heart functions only with the assistance of an implanted pacemaker. Is that vital technology truly a part of the person's identity? A person with a motor neuron disease who relies on mechanical devices for mobility and electronic devices to communicate might reasonably sense her *self* to include the technological prostheses that enable her to function as effectively as she does. Such circumstances, where technology has become inseparable from the capacities that

express one's personhood, complicate any distinction between an organic and a technological aspect of a person's identity. Common examples of such technologies include eyeglasses, canes and walkers and wheelchairs, and prescription medications (which are frequently claimed to have the effect of "making me *myself* again"). If one acknowledges that technological appliances constitute a part of the "self" of a person who needs them to live and to function in the world, at what point does one disallow them for people who might manage without them, but who rely on them to support and enhance their organic selves' functioning?

DO CYBORGS PRAY TO ELECTRIC GODS?

The challenging area where humanity and technology converge provides a ripe topic for popular media. Science fiction abounds with robots who show greater "humanity" than nominally "human" characters; Philip K. Dick's novels *We Can Build You* and *Do Androids Dream of Electric Sheep?* (made into the cult classic film *Blade Runner*) meditate on the difficulty of distinguishing humanlike technology from mechanical, disaffected humanity. Film and television characters from the Bionic Woman and Six Million Dollar Man to Inspector Gadget, from the Jetsons' maid Rosie to Arnold Schwarzenegger's Terminator, all play on their audience's sense that technological constructs may display the traits that ordinarily suggest personhood (and that some who appear to be ordinary, organic people more closely resemble machines).

By the same token—only from the opposite direction—Alan Turing proposed a simple test to determine when a computer will have attained what we can plausibly call intelligence: if a human being cannot tell the difference between a human conversation partner and a computer partner, the computer can be characterized as intelligent. Though at this writing no computer has passed a rigorous Turing test, advocates of computer intelligence suggest that in a few years computers will be able to approximate human conversation and thinking.

The Turing test may adequately define a computer as intelligent (or it may not—not all theorists accept this premise), but that does not resolve the pertinent religious questions. A computer might be able to store data and interpret and formulate responses to verbal stimuli, but still not share qualities that invest human interaction with spiritual reality; without having souls or the capacity to recognize the illusory status of the phenomenal world, anthropoid robots might nonetheless convincingly simulate human behavior.

Moreover, religious observers will extend their moral evaluation of artificial intelligence to its entanglement with corporations, military agencies, espionage, and other sponsoring agencies. The technology of artificial intelligence does not develop isolated from political and commercial interests; rather, artificial intelligence exemplifies the way that technologies entail complexities and consequences that reach far beyond their apparent applications.

On the other hand, as scientists offer more and more neurological explanations of what hitherto had been experienced as the encounter of the human mind with transcendent reality, the very idea of a reality that transcends human capacities may evaporate. An apparently intelligent computer that reproduces electrical impulses identical to those produced by a human experiencing a mystical trance might represent an example of *electronic spirituality*. Since it's not clear how one could adjudicate a spiritual Turing test, the question of whether a "spiritual machine" would falsify religious claims of spiritual reality will remain open, possibly indefinitely.

DESERTS AND OASES OF REAL RELATIONSHIPS

These deliberations take us to the dizzying precipice from which all sorts of claims about reality come into question. The chance that technology can produce the *effect* of a profound spiritual experience by electrochemical intervention, for instance, raises the disconcerting implication that religion might be nothing more than the misinterpreted by-product of physiological, technological forces. Or—to return to cultural representations of technology—perhaps all the reality we perceive might turn out to be a technological construct, as in *The Matrix*. The worshipper who strips away all traces of manufactured human products in order to attain purity in the wilderness might, in theory, be plugged into a comprehensive virtual environment (right down to the digital bacteria).

Far-fetched as such a possibility might seem, it raises on a global scale some of the questions that concern many critics of technology. Technology's products, especially the products of digital technology, strike many observers as unreal. Digital technology may make it possible for a writer who lives in New Jersey to spontaneously chat with a friend in Japan, but skeptical colleagues may ask, "Are you real friends or 'virtual friends'?" Though my Japanese friend and I may have conversed more regularly and more deeply than my next-door neighbor and I, the brute fact of physical proximity renders my relationship with a neighbor more real to many observers. The question of what makes an event, item, person, or relationship "real" bears weighty consequences for religious reflection.

When religious observers call the reality of technology's effects into question, they frequently elide several senses of the word *reality*. A technologically mediated relationship may not be "real" in the same way that a relationship between two physically proximate people is "real," but some sort of relationship has actually been established, even if continents separate the two agents. My correspondent and I are not strangers to one another, even if we have not shared physical space. An object in a digital environment (let's say, a hammer) is real, even if it will not help us pound a physical nail. In this setting, the term *unreal* serves as a shorthand expression for "not fully real," or "lacking some essential property of the real." While some critics use the terms *real* and *unreal* to discuss features that technological constructs possess or lack, others use them to beg the question. They argue that the digital hammer is not real because it lacks a property essential to hammers, without making the case that such-and-such a property should be definitive of real hammers. If one stipulates that something must have weight, density, and physical extension in order to be a real hammer, one has simply excluded the possibility of a digital hammer from the outset—one hasn't shown that a digital hammer lacks reality, or explained why participants in the online environment have no trouble recognizing and naming the object as a hammer and manipulating it (within the limitations of the digital medium) as a hammer. One does not solve the problem of technological reality by defining it away.

My relationship with my friend in Japan differs from relationships based on physical proximity, but it is nonetheless real; the digitally represented hammer differs from the hammer in my toolbox, but it is nonetheless real. The technologically mediated instances of "relationship" and "hammer" entail particular affordances and constraints that distinguish them from those relationships and hammers to which I have access without computers and electricity (which have affordances and constraints of their own). I can communicate freely with my friend in Japan via digital technology; we can watch each other's expressions, hear our voices, interrupt, and gesture. We can even record our conversation and play it back later. None of this would be possible for us, separated by thousands of miles, apart from technological mediation. On the other hand, I cannot touch him, and my seeing and hearing have been limited by the quality of the cameras, microphones, transmission codes, and bandwidth on which our communication depends. I would almost always prefer to conduct my friendships over hot coffee and within handshaking range; since we cannot all fit around one table at the same time, however, and since we have jobs and families that constrain our possible locations, the affordance of technologically mediated community provides certain positive alternatives to physical presence.

IMAGINING WORSHIP IN A DIGITAL ENVIRONMENT

That being the case, the pertinent question for religious reflection shifts from "Are these things real?" to "How does the difference of technological mediation affect the religious significance of these relationships and objects?" This question allows us to evaluate the affordances to which technology gives ready access, while encouraging us to identify constraints in technology that inhibit growth in spiritual wisdom. Moreover, this question opens retrospectively to the deliberations with which religious thinkers have endorsed or rejected technologies over the millennia. As a consequence, we will be better equipped to arrive at well-reasoned responses to challenges that religious practice encounters in a technologically shaped environment.

The technological balance of affordances and constraints has long affected religious discourse. Whatever the purposes of such monumental structures as the ancient pyramids and temples, Stonehenge, stupas, or the moai of Rapa Nui, they required tremendous labor and technical ingenuity, and they provide evidence of construction technology and of the dedication of such technology for religious purposes. Paul of Tarsus is remembered for his use of ancient technologies of transcription and transportation in his communications. He was also aware that his letters involved constraints that his physical communication did not (and vice versa), as his letters preserved in the New Testament make explicit (see 2 Cor 10:11, 2 Cor 13:2, and Gal 4:20, and compare 2 Jn 12). What then makes for religiously appropriate and inappropriate uses of technology? Let's consider a few of the salient characteristics of technology in relation to religious practice and reflection.

Imagine, for example, a digital environment in which several "toons" (animated digital representations of active users, often known as "avatars"—itself a term with a strong religious heredity) gather to pray for an hour. While one might prefer that they meet in a single geographic location, the premise of an online prayer meeting sounds pretty good.

On the other hand, everyone involved might have spent that time in prayer off-line, saving electricity and obviating the need for computers to mediate their devotions. They might have prayed in solitude, or gathered with others who lived within walking distance. Few, if any, religious teachings require (or even recommend) that far-flung worshippers join their expressions of faith by means of telecommunications.

Sticking with the premise of an online prayer group, does it matter how the toons are depicted? Some users design toons to look roughly like themselves; others deliberately do the opposite. Some prefer toons that resemble animals; others prefer abstract, almost geometric representations. On one hand, it would seem as though it made little difference whether each participant's toon looked like a human being or a jumbled pile of hatboxes. On the other hand, some participants might express concern if a male member of the group selected a feminine toon. Many religious observers would hesitate to approve a prayer meeting in which humanoid toons participated without clothing—although such attire might represent a prerequisite for other traditions. The appearances of digital representations, then, and their congruence with the users who control them, constitute one set of criteria that might apply to online interaction.

Further, the prayer meeting might be praised or denounced based on the behavior of the toons. It might be reasonable to propose that their posture and gestures correspond to the posture and gestures used when they all gather physically in one place for prayer. The behavior of worshippers gathered in a physical space, however, has been determined on grounds that depend on human anatomy and the effects that one's actions have on others. If a squirrel, a pile of hatboxes, three humans, and an evanescent fog gather online for worship, it might seem fitting for the humans to remain still, perhaps kneeling; but hatboxes and fog banks are ill-equipped to kneel, and it might be difficult to determine which of a squirrel's positions constitutes the equivalent of a kneel.

Perhaps such speculations seem absurd, but the online environment appeals to many users for affording the opportunity to adopt a body image radically different from one's own physical appearance—whether that means trying out a different gender, different abilities, or a nonhuman body. On the Internet, anybody can be a dog, a cat, a dinosaur, or a pet rock.

If we more restrictively suppose that the online gathering has a serious religious purpose that excludes participation by atmospheric conditions and millinery containers, the next question might involve what counts as prayer in such an environment. A human typically prays in one of three ways: by speaking, by silently thinking the words that one might otherwise speak, or by adopting a wordlessly reverent frame of mind. (One could catalog numerous other legitimate modes of prayer, but these stand out as particularly common.) Some digital environments permit audio communication; these would make a congenial setting for spoken prayers. Many online environments, however, restrict aural communication. Such settings afford full opportunity for silent prayer, but if a participant were the group's leader, and hence required to communicate with others, she or he would have to type into a chat window.

Typed chat messages differ in many ways from audible verbal communication; online chat permits a much narrower range of typographic volume and intonation, for instance. Granted that a prayer spoken by a worship leader differs from a prayer typed into a chat window, one might offer varying religious evaluations of the extent to which the typed prayer fulfills the qualities of authentic, acceptable prayer.

DENSITY AND DEPTH IN DIGITAL SPIRITUALITY

All these considerations serve as the path that ascends gradually to a controversial precipice. Thus far, the discussion has concerned a relatively nonspecific "prayer meeting." Many religious gatherings, however, involve the purpose of effecting particular spiritual conditions. One paradigmatic religious ceremony is the sacrifice, in which something of particular value or meaning is offered to appease divine displeasure. Other common religious ceremonies include rites of initiation, of marriage, of communion—all may involve investment in the existential consequences of the ritual action.

For example, we might imagine an online purification ceremony. Such a ritual's explicit claim to change the status of the participant brings urgent focus to the interaction of religion and technology. The simplest analysis of the online purification ceremony would relegate it to the status of playacting, of no more religious importance than a movie wedding has for the actors in the film. If one compares a movie wedding, however, with the edited video recording of an actual wedding, one would have a hard time identifying the elements that distinguish them from one another. One can then separate the actors from the bride and groom by raising the question of intent; neither the marital actors nor the actor playing the role of the religious authority intend actually to bind themselves to the words they speak, whereas in the religiously binding marriage, all three and the congregation commit themselves to the premise that the ceremony changes the nature of the couple's relationship. The criterion of intent, however, might apply every bit as much to the online ritual as to an ancient *taurobolium*.[2] If the online officiant *intends* to purify the devotee, and if the devotee *intends* to seek purification, the online ceremony would fulfill at least one criterion of legitimacy.

Very well, then, assume for the purposes of argument that the religious officiant has been duly commissioned for the purification rite (and that assumption itself would bear further interrogation, since one might fret about the necessity of making sure that both the online character and its off-line operator be commissioned—must a toon be commissioned with religious authority if its operator has been?), and that the officiant types or speaks the words formally requisite for conducting a purification. The weightiest remaining objection to the validity of the online ritual is that the ceremony lacks the *matter* of a valid ritual action. To conduct a valid *taurobolium*, the devotee should stand under a grate over which a bull is sacrificed, such that the bull's blood gushes over the devotee. An online *taurobolium*

---

2. The *taurobolium* was a ritual from ancient Mediterranean cultures in which a devotee bathed in the blood of a freshly slaughtered bull.

might depict such events, but the extent to which a living creature has been slaughtered and blood applied to a religious believer remains in question. Although no physical animal has died nor has any physical believer been drenched in blood, the electronic manifestations of officiant, devotee, and sacrificial victim all played their roles according to established formulas. The validity of the online purification hangs, to a great extent, on whether a series of digital gestures can satisfy the religious expectation of a physical, material interaction.

The question of concrete materiality thus constitutes one decisive point of orientation for a religious understanding of technology. If legitimate religious ritual requires a direct physical interaction among participants and the sacred furnishings, then online religious rituals have been ruled out from the beginning. Some traditions will insist on material agency in religious action, on such grounds as the Christian teaching that the Incarnation of Jesus entails a divine affirmation of materiality, or the God of Israel's characterization of all creation as very good. Thus, the Roman Catholic Church has ruled that "the incarnational reality of the sacraments" prevents any mode of sacramental action online.[3] Protestant Christian traditions that define liturgical actions and effects differently might not see the grounds for rejecting the possibility of an online observance of the Lord's Supper. Still other traditions may allow that nonphysical interaction satisfies all the decisive characteristics of valid religious practice, whether because the material world stands opposed to everything spiritual or perhaps because physical and digital existence are equally illusory.

The Internet affords interaction among digital bodies, but those bodies lack important qualities of physical bodies: density, palpable texture, and especially depth. Users have become accustomed to construing digital media as three-dimensional;

the conventional expression "cyberspace" itself implies a spatiality to digital interaction. The habit of interpreting online communication as spatial, however, masks the two-dimensionality of the computer interface. While sophisticated graphic techniques can generate simulated textures, lighting, and gravitational models, the screen remains a smooth, flat field of representation. Screen-based communication—no matter how advanced—affords its conveniences at the expense of the dimension of depth that incalculably enriches human encounters with the physical environment.

Some critics pursue this line of criticism further, claiming that the literal flatness of the online environment entails a concomitant superficiality in online communication. Such observations gain credibility from the ratio of triviality to profundity in online discourse. Since it has become so very easy for anyone to publish any whim, opinion, prejudice, or general nonsense online, the whimsical, opinionated, prejudiced, and nonsensical pages tend to prevail over the carefully considered and profound (though the extent to which this differentiates the Web from a bookstore might be debated). Further, the pattern of affordance and constraint amplifies this tendency. The online environment affords instant access to broadcast publication and to innumerable sources of information, but that "instant" conceals all the resources that go into developing and sustaining the Internet itself, the physical computer, the operating system and protocols and browsing software, the costs for disposing of the waste these processes generate, and the uneven distribution of access. When one compares the benefit of enabling a superficial ignoramus to post inconsequential maunderings to all the costs that make such a publication possible, the Internet's lack of depth seems undeniable.

---

3. Pontifical Council for Social Communications, "The Church and the Internet," promulgated February 28, 2002.

The prospects for digital technology aren't quite so bleak, though. The two-dimensional space of online interaction has features unlike any flat thing that most users have dealt with before. For one thing, the two dimensions of screen space are infinite. The screens themselves show only small amounts of online information at any given time, but the information that one might display has been rising precipitously. Moreover, even if we regard online interaction as flat rather than spatial, the operation of hyperlinks shifts our screen from one page to another without passing through intervening space or pages. These hyperlinks make the flat environment of the Internet a mode of flatness unlike any other. Moreover, online technology is not flatly two-dimensional; the Internet interacts with *time* in distinctive ways. Ordinary discourse takes place in the transient flux of passing time, but digitally mediated interaction can be recorded and replayed. The Internet doesn't remember absolutely everything that's ever happened online, but it remembers a great deal more than one can readily imagine (as anyone can testify who has been tripped up by embarrassing details retrieved from Web archives). The moment of an online session passes, but the data stream endures. One might plausibly argue that the infinite hyperlinked flatness of online interaction and the availability of past interactions compensate to a great degree for the absence of depth. What the digital environment lacks in the traditional "third dimension" of depth, it supplies by abounding in other dimensions.

These different dimensions in digital technology seem mysterious and unnatural at first, less because of their intrinsic characteristics than because they are not yet familiar. Unfamiliar technologies partake of the arcane, the dangerous, and the magical—for the very good reason that they are indeed accessible only to an initiated few, and they can be risky (even after they've become commonplace, as automobile wrecks show). Technologies whose workings surpass their users' understanding are, in effect, magical. People who rely on magic share some unsettling similarities with those who rely on technology that they don't understand, and, as Arthur C. Clarke once said, "Any sufficiently advanced technology is indistinguishable from magic." As long as the boundary between magic and religion defies clear definition, participants in a culture shaped by "sufficiently advanced technology" may find themselves involved in magical/religious behavior and thought—whether they participate willingly or not.

WELCOMING DIGITAL NATIVES (AND STRANGERS)

In summary, the advancing edge of technology in the twenty-first century brings on a new generation of problems in the relation of technology to religion, but each technological transition—from fire and wheels onward—has generated religious challenges of its own. The complexities of pinning down digital technologies for evaluation appropriately reflect the complex of problems at the intersection of accelerating technological change and religious practice. Religious leaders and students of religion do not have access to a simple test for the legitimacy of particular technologies; whatever ethos they adopt will inevitably entail complications and frustrations.

Thus, the soundest approaches to the interaction of technology and religion will avoid aye-or-nay assessments that paper over complexities. A congregation whose ethos embraces technological modernity owes an account of what that implies about the ecological impact of consumer electronics and dependence on fossil fuels. Such a faith community will have to decide whether they are willing to alienate potential adherents who can't afford the latest hardware and software, or who can't figure out how to use it, or who object to the spiritual ramifications of investing so heavily in technological fashions.

By the same token, communities that forgo participation owe an account of what makes some technologies acceptable and others not. Why draw the line so as to include electric light and audio amplification, but exclude projecting hymn texts and illustrations on overhead screens? If they opt for preferential solidarity with people outside the charmed circle of advanced technology, they will want to work out the basis of their relation, if any, to the increasingly numerous denizens of the digital environment.

In cases where religious traditions have not formulated authoritative rulings regarding appropriate uses of technology (or where those rulings have come under critical reconsideration), one may look to the relation of affordances and constraints that a technology produces as a criterion. A Roman Catholic can approve of the construction of a physical space that affords anonymous confession of sins and absolution by an unseen priest who has been physically separated from the penitent; a Buddhist can approve the construction of prayer wheels that multiply a believer's repetitions of sacred expressions. One can submit e-mailed prayers to be inserted in the Western Wall of Jerusalem's temple mount, or arrange via the Web for *pujas* to be offered to Meenakshi by temple priests. Musical instruments enhance a listener's sense of harmony and help guide and reinforce congregational singing. The beneficial spiritual result of such technologies sanctifies their role in religious practice, although one might identify constraints that militate against their acceptance. The organ was unwelcome in churches well into the second millennium, and some Christian bodies still forbid any instrumental music in worship; some musical instruments were associated with licentious occasions, and untuned instruments or inept musicians disrupt congregational music

more than they enhance it. The confessional booth affords the freedom to anonymously confess sins, but it precludes visual observation of the penitent for signs of sincerity. Religious traditions rely on some technologies and repudiate others; they have always done so, and presumably always will.

The question of technology and religion, then, should be refined to address several more specific questions. First, by what terms does the ethos of a particular religion evaluate the products of human ingenuity? Are material products a snare and delusion? Or are they a reflection of a distinctive human capacity for constructive innovation? Do they in fact reflect the creative power of the divine?

The primary attitude toward technology then confronts particular technologies in relation to particular tenets of religion. Does the importance of a penitent's anonymity warrant authorizing online sacramental confession and absolution? Does the importance of a devotee's making a pilgrimage warrant allowing pilgrimage by proxy? Circumstance intersects praxis in ways that sometimes persuade religious leaders to allow unexpected intrusions of technology, and sometimes provokes them to exclude disruptive technologies. In each such case, general guidelines for envisioning technology encounter the religious community's specific needs, theoretical consistency encounters practical necessity, and believers reach some accommodation. When examined closely, there is no single question of "technology and religion," but a myriad of related questions, each inflected by different traditions and different applications of technology. While each religious group will arrive at its own determination, none is exempt from the necessity of articulating its ongoing interaction with technology.

Finally, both general and particular evaluations of technology should be compared to the power of a broader culture's influence on the religious tradition. Religious authority sometimes simply accepts developments from its surrounding culture, and sometimes pushes back against unwelcome encroachment. Technological change sometimes affects religion in ways that seem at first entirely benign, but that entail more ambiguous effects. The use of electronic amplification, to take one example, has profoundly altered the practice of liturgical communication. When a religious tradition confronts a particular technological development, the authorities are acceding to (or rejecting) both that technology and the cultural currents that pushed the technology to prominence. The meanings of culture, technology, and religion interweave so pervasively that they defy tidy segregation, but the rhetoric of religious evaluation sometimes reveals a stronger reliance on "what everyone knows" or "what we all use" than on distinctly religious reasoning.

CONCLUSION

The hypothetical devotee of the opening paragraph will try in vain to eradicate the traces that technology has left on her or his life, and the enthusiastic cyborg will not escape the persistent demands and impulses of organic, psychological, spiritual existence. While we stand to learn from pioneers who seek revelatory wisdom at the extreme limits of technological self-denial as well as from bleeding-edge early adopters who plumb the soul of digital avatars, we may learn more by observing closely the ways that religious teachers and practitioners negotiate the complications that lie between these extremes. In reasoning through the affordances and constraints, the benefits and drawbacks of particular technologies, believers bring to bear their sense of what is most important and most decisive in their faith.

Questions for Reflection and Discussion

- What are some obvious and subtle ways that technology impinges on the practice of religion?

- Select a technological artifact from your daily life. What does it afford? What effects does it obscure?

- How does the claim that the perceived world is a technologically sustained illusion compare to claims about existence and reality from various religious perspectives?

- In what ways do technologically mediated relationships fall short of relationships based on physical proximity? In what ways do they afford positive relationships that physical proximity does not?

- How do the varieties of technological mediation—handwritten notes, telephone calls, e-mails, instant messages, chat rooms, voice/video live chats, interactive avatars—affect the religious dimension of relationships and communication?

- Do the relationships between religion and technology trouble you? Why or why not?

- The text of this chapter was written online, with collaborative comments from readers around the world; what difference does this make relative to its claims?

Additional Resources

Borgmann, Albert. 2003. *Power Failure: Christianity in the Culture of Technology*. Grand Rapids, MI: Brazos Press.

Clarke, Arthur C. 1973. "Hazards of Prophecy: The Failure of Imagination." *In Profiles of the Future: An Inquiry into the Limits of the Possible*. Rev. ed. New York: Harper and Row.

Clarke, Arthur C. 1967. "The Nine Billion Names of God." In *The Nine Billion Names of God: The Best Short Stories of Arthur C. Clarke*. New York: Harcourt, Brace and World.

Dick, Philip K. 1972. *We Can Build You*. New York: Daw Books.

Dick, Philip K. 1969. *Do Androids Dream of Electric Sheep?* New York: New American Library.

Ellul, Jacques. 1967. *The Technological Society*. New York: Vintage Books.

Haraway, Donna Jeanne. 1997. *Modest_Witness@Second_Millennium. FemaleMan©_ Meets OncoMouse™: Feminism and Technoscience*. New York: Routledge.

Heidegger, Martin. 1982. "The Question Concerning Technology." In *The Question Concerning Technology, and Other Essays*. Translated by William Lovitt. New York: Harper Collins.

Kurzweil, Ray. 2000. *The Age of Spiritual Machines: When Computers Exceed Human Intelligence*. New York: Penguin Books.

McLuhan, Marshall. 1964. *Understanding Media: The Extensions of Man*. New York: New American Library.

Schultze, Quentin J. 2004. *Habits of the High-Tech Heart: Living Virtuously in the Information Age*. Grand Rapids, MI: Baker Academic.

STUDYING SCIENCE AND RELIGION

S. Brian Stratton
Alma College

Preface

Over the last five hundred years, science and religion have bumped up against each other at a number of key moments. The advent of Copernican and Galilean ideas, the emergence of the Enlightenment, modernism, the development of scientific method, and a host of other catalysts have thrust new questions on the world stage and invited religions to respond. Today, carefully constructed faith systems face questions about time, the nature of the universe, atomic principles, genetic research, and other topics that challenge tightly held positions about what connotes life and truth. Some fear the power of science to undo faith. Others are concerned that religious traditions simply cannot answer the questions raised by science. Students are acutely aware of the conundrums and paradoxes posed by scientific theories and inquiry in relation to religion and religious beliefs. In this chapter, S. Brian Stratton invites readers to explore and discuss the relationship between scientific and religious claims. Contemporary issues and controversies related to the intersection between science and religion are explored through noetic structures, worldviews, and correlations between the two.

Chapter Goals

- To reflect on the relationship between worldviews and noetic structures
- To provide a basic understanding of the worldviews of epistemology, metaphysics, axiology, anthropology, and theology
- To explore how science and religion might be related to each other—irrelevance, quasi-direct relevance, direct relevance, indirect relevance, and heuristic relevance
- To discuss specific ways that science may be important for religion
- To show how history, physics, physical cosmology, and evolution relate to the study of religion

INTRODUCTION

In the preface to his classic work *The Origins of Modern Science,* historian Herbert Butterfield claims the rise of science is the most important development in the history of Western culture since the rise of Christianity.[1] Like religion, science has deeply affected every aspect of human life—how we think and feel about the world and our place in it, how we morally and politically govern ourselves, and how we go about even the most mundane of daily tasks. It is perhaps surprising that scientists and theologians paid little attention to the relationship between these two great cultural forces for so long, but that is no longer the case. The relationship between science and religion is now one of the fastest-growing areas of interest in the study of religion, as evidenced by the endowed positions devoted to the topic springing up at universities and the attention-grabbing headlines in newspapers and magazines.[2] Unfortunately, too often the discussion in popular culture generates far more heat than light, as agenda-driven adversaries go for the throat or apologetic appeasers attempt facile, premature reconciliation. Both of these approaches show little real understanding of either science or religion and often distort each.

The issues involved in relating science and religion are many and complex, and it would be impossible for this chapter to solve them. Fortunately, our goal is more modest, namely, to help the reader begin to think intelligently, systematically, and critically about the relationship between science and religion. We will do this by addressing some basic questions about how to link the two and by introducing a few select topics that figure prominently in current discussions.

Before examining science and religion, however, we need to begin with a little philosophy, the third and often unacknowledged partner in any such conversation. In fact, the philosophical commitments introduced into science create many unnecessary controversies in contemporary discussions of science and religion.

NOETIC STRUCTURES, WORLDVIEWS, AND COHERENCE

The Greek roots of *philosophy* translate into "the love of wisdom." Historically, philosophy has used rational means to examine almost every conceivable question about life and the world. For the purposes of this chapter, *philosophy* will mean critical and constructive reflection on worldviews.[3]

A worldview is a small but important subset of a noetic structure (NS). Everyone has a noetic structure, understood here as the entire content of the propositions that a person believes and the relationships among those propositions. Noetic structures include four features: First, they include all beliefs a person holds regardless of whether they are true or false. (Normally, if a person discovers a belief is false, the person will remove it from the noetic structure.) Second, NSs include all beliefs a person holds regardless of the degree of certainty with which the person holds them. For example, most people will assert

---

1. Butterfield, *The Origins of Modern Science, 1300–1800* (New York: Free Press, 1965).

2. Examples include the recently endowed Starbridge Lecturer in Natural Science and Theology at Cambridge University and *Time* magazine's November 13, 2006, cover story, "God vs. Science."

3. For a full discussion of the following points, including the genesis of these ideas, see S. Brian Stratton, *Coherence, Consonance, and Conversation: The Quest of Theology, Philosophy, and Natural Science for a Unified World-View* (Lanham, MD: University Press of America, 2000).

with much more confidence that 2 + 2 = 4 than they will the exact number of people in a crowd at a public event. Third, NSs include all beliefs whether those beliefs are closely related or not. My belief that the Cincinnati Reds will not contend for the pennant this year is closely related to my belief that their pitching staff is very weak, but my belief that the Lone Ranger had the most magnificent horse of any cowboy has nothing to do with my belief that the chemical compound silver is written as Ag. Fourth, NSs include beliefs of varying importance that exert varying levels of control over the rest of the beliefs in the structure. If a deeply religious person were to give up his or her belief in God, it would affect practically every aspect of the person's life; if he or she gave up the belief that all swans are white, it would not.

A worldview constitutes the most important beliefs within a noetic structure, for it is *a conceptual scheme by which a person interprets and judges reality*. A worldview gives us a general picture of the world and helps us to make meaning out of what we encounter. Every person has a worldview whether he or she is aware of it or not, though many worldviews may not be the result of any serious thought or effort. Philosophers help people to understand their worldviews better, to improve them by eliminating inconsistencies or logical errors, and to provide new information that can challenge or strengthen these worldviews. Philosophers are in a solid position to help, for worldviews consist of at least five components corresponding to traditional philosophical concerns.

First, every worldview has an epistemology—a theory of the nature of knowledge, a method for finding knowledge, and a way to validate knowledge. Empiricists believe that knowledge comes primarily from experience; an empiricist claim from the everyday world of common sense

is "I'll believe it when I see it." Rationalists distrust the five senses as unreliable and instead put their trust in reason, believing the principles of mathematics or logic to be a surer path. Science has a strong empirical component and relies heavily on the use of mathematics; some have argued faith is present in scientific activity as well.[4] Christianity traditionally has believed that faith is a path to knowledge. Though the issues in epistemology are highly controversial, one can see that decisions about how knowledge is obtained and validated will play an important role in the study of the relationship between science and religion.

Second, every worldview includes metaphysics. Metaphysics is an even more controversial topic within philosophy than epistemology, but the traditional understanding of metaphysics as *the general principles or nature of ultimate reality* is sufficient at this level. Metaphysics is concerned about what is "most really real." Materialists hold that matter (or matter and energy) is the fundamental reality of the universe. Idealists, such as Plato, argue that the intelligible or mental are most real and are fundamental to the material. Monotheistic religious believers hold that God is the ultimate reality. Worldview commitments to metaphysical principles are indisputably relevant to discussions of science and religion. Time, for example, can be examined as an empirical component of rival scientific theories; something that as it "really is in itself" is beyond any particular partial scientific understanding, or as something that is in relation to a divine Creator of the world. Of course, differing worldviews will have differing opinions on the value or necessity of these matters, but being able to detect the metaphysical commitments of a given writer can greatly improve one's understanding of a particular issue when pondering science and religion, especially

---

4. See the work of scientist Michael Polanyi, *Personal Knowledge: Towards a Post-Critical Philosophy* (Chicago: University of Chicago Press, 1962).

when the philosophical intrudes on the scientific. Take this statement made in a popular presentation of the discoveries of modern astronomy: "The Cosmos is all that is or ever was or all that will be."[5] This may or may not be the case, but it is undoubtedly a philosophical claim rather than a fact about the universe discovered by contemporary science, since no contemporary cosmological theory entails this proposition. Careful and critical scrutiny of claims made in the discussion of science and religion is essential if any real progress is to be made in formulating a coherent worldview.

Third, every worldview has an axiology, a *way of making judgments about values*. Axiology includes ethics, which involves making judgments about moral values, and aesthetics, which involves making judgments about art or the experience of beauty. It is obvious the practice of science raises a broad range of ethical questions that society needs to address—questions in the areas of genetic modification of foods and animals, the use of nuclear energy, care for the environment, to name a few. Less obvious is the question of what role values (simplicity, for example) ought or do play in the epistemic judgment used in the acceptance of scientific theory, but this is an issue under much consideration by contemporary philosophers of science.[6] Perhaps what will be even more surprising to the reader is the question of what role aesthetics ought or do play in science. Consider these remarks of Nobel Prize-winning physicist Paul Dirac:

> It is more important to have beauty in one's equations than to have them fit experiment. . . . It

seems that if one is working from the point of view of getting beauty in one's equations, and if one has really a sound insight, one is on a sure line of progress.[7]

> Theoretical physicists accept the need for mathematical beauty as an act of faith. . . . For example, the main reason why the theory of relativity is so universally accepted is its mathematical beauty.[8]

These intriguing remarks support the importance of examining worldviews and suggest axiology is a topic that deserves more attention in the discussion of science and religion.

Fourth, every worldview addresses the question of anthropology or *an understanding of what it means to be human*. Making distinctions is an important part of developing critical intelligence, and distinguishing the human and the nonhuman is one of the most important classifications we make, with profound implications for discussions of science and religion, especially in terms of our ethical behavior. The debate about abortion, one of the most contested moral issues of our time, may help illustrate this point. Many pro-lifers believe that human life begins at conception and therefore oppose abortion as the unwarranted taking of a human life; many pro-choicers believe human life does not begin until much later and therefore that a decision to terminate a pregnancy can be acceptable. (Either position can be much more nuanced than this; the example here is to illustrate the powerful implications of distinguishing the human and the nonhuman in discussions of science and religion, with particular application to ethical behavior.)

---

5. Carl Sagan, *Cosmos* (New York: Random House, 1980), 4.

6. For a lucid discussion, see Ernan McMullin, "Values in Science," in *A Companion to the Philosophy of Science*, ed. W. H. Newton-Smith (Oxford, UK: Blackwell Publishers, 2000), 550–560.

7. Paul Dirac, "The Evolution of the Physicist's Picture of Nature," *Scientific American* 208 (May 1963): 47.

8. Paul Dirac, "Methods in Theoretical Physics," in *From a Life of Physics: Evening Lectures at the International Centre for Theoretical Physics, Trieste, Italy.* A Special Supplement of the IAEA Bulletin (1968): 22.

And fifth, every worldview contains a theology, or *critical reflection about the existence and nature of God*. One may believe or disbelieve in the existence of God (perhaps *atheology* would be a better word for this latter position), but the question of God's existence and what God might be like if God does exist is an important feature of a worldview. Theology is directly relevant to the question of the relationship between science and religion, for it usually serves as the worldview component that considers the relation between the two. For this reason, the terms *theology* and *religion* will be used somewhat interchangeably in this chapter.

A person desiring to develop into a mature critical thinker will want to have the clearest worldview possible. This means one will think rigorously about the conceptual scheme one uses to interpret the world, sift the evidence one examines, detect shams when they arise in one's noetic structure, and revise one's worldview components as necessary. One also needs to look out for logical contradictions and inconsistencies among beliefs. A mature thinker will seek coherence among the beliefs making up his or her worldview through a careful analysis of the components of one's noetic structure and find some way to integrate science and religion harmoniously within an understanding of the world. For this to happen, one needs to develop an understanding of how science and religion might be related.

Questions for Reflection and Discussion

- If every worldview has an epistemology—a theory of the nature of knowledge, a method for finding knowledge, and a way to validate knowledge—what is your epistemology and how does it relate to your understanding of religion?

- What is your understanding of what constitutes ultimate reality?

- How do you make judgments about values, what it means to be human, and the existence and nature of God?

- Do you agree that a person desiring to develop into a mature, critical thinker will want to have the clearest worldview possible? Explain.

THE RELATIONSHIP BETWEEN SCIENCE AND RELIGION

Scholars who study science and religion use a number of different typologies to describe the relationship between the two.[9] These categories are not particularly useful and are often distorting, however, for in attempting to categorize a thinker's general stance regarding the relationship between religion and science, they oversimplify and lose the subtlety and nuance of a given person's thought. To allow more precision in exploring links between science and religion, specific propositions or claims, not typologies, will be the focus. Scientific and religious propositions or claims may relate to each other in one of four ways: (1) irrelevance, (2) quasi-direct relevance, (3) direct relevance, or (4) indirect relevance.

A relationship of irrelevance holds when a scientific statement and a religious statement have

---

9. For examples, see Ian Barbour, *Religion and Science: Historical and Contemporary Issues* (San Francisco: HarperSanFrancisco, 1997); John Haught, *Science and Religion: From Conflict to Conversation* (Mahwah, NJ: Paulist Press, 1995); and Ted Peters, *Science and Theology: The New Consonance* (Oxford, UK: Westview Press, 1998).

nothing to do with each other. It is easy and even trivial to see how this can be the case; the two statements "The chemical composition of water is H_2O" and "Moses was God's agent to deliver Israel from bondage" could exist in a noetic structure without connection. A more serious claim is made by those who argue science and religion are irrelevant to each other because the two are totally independent and autonomous realms; they are noninteracting and noncompeting approaches to reality, each having its separate domain and methods with no bearing on the other. A good example of this type of approach is Stephen Jay Gould's NOMA or "nonoverlapping magisterial"[10] argument. Gould, a prominent paleontologist, evolutionary biologist, and science historian, wrote many delightful popular essays on science and its implications. According to Gould, science is about statements of fact, of how the world is, and religion is about moral values and spiritual meaning, with no intersection or mutuality between the two. Even if this is normally the case, however, it is still hard to see how science and religion could always remain closed off from one another. Knowledge about the natural world can be quite relevant to ethical considerations that fall in the realm of religion; theistic religious believers usually have some theology of nature in which they try to understand the natural world as God's creation; and, as noted above, axiological considerations do play a role in science. It is best to analyze questions of relevance between science and religion on a case-by-case basis rather than rely on a global principle that facilely dismisses any meaningful interaction between the two.[11]

When science and religion offer competing alternative explanations of the same data, there is quasi-direct relevance. An example is the rival explanations offered by mainstream geologic science and creation scientists for the existence and dispersion of marine fossils. Creation scientists use the Bible to argue these fossils exist due to their rapid creation and placement by the catastrophic flood associated with Noah and his ark; contemporary geology explains fossils by massive amounts of time and the slow action of forces like we observe today (plate tectonics, sedimentation, erosion, permineralization, and others). If one is concerned about intellectual coherence, quasi-direct relevance must be seen at best as a temporary state of affairs, for rival explanations are inconsistent with a fully integrated worldview. Statements of quasi-direct relevance are problems that need to be solved or obstacles that need to be overcome on the intellectual journey to a coherent view of the world. One (or perhaps both) of the rival explanations must contain errors or perhaps combinations of errors that are philosophical, theological, or scientific and will ultimately need revision in one's worldview.[12]

Direct relevance posits the closest relationship between science and religion and comes in two forms: (1) affirmative direct relevance, and (2) negative direct relevance. Affirmative direct relevance (ADR) occurs when

> a set S of scientific statements bears directly on theological doctrine D
>
> if D can be inferred from S.[13]

---

10. S. J. Gould, *Rocks of Ages: Science and Religion in the Fullness of Life* (New York: Norton, 1999).

11. For a full treatment of many types of irrelevance arguments see Stratton, *Coherence, Consonance, and Conversation,* chapter 2; this also includes a discussion of W. H. Austin's neglected but important book *The Relevance of Natural Science to Theology* (London: Macmillan, 1976).

12. An excellent point-by-point refutation of the errors made by scientific creationism in interpreting fossils can be found in Howard J. Van Till, Davis A. Young, and Clarence Menninga's *Science Held Hostage: What's Wrong with Creation Science and Evolutionism* (Downers Grove, IL: InterVarsity Press, 1988).

13. Of course, this principle could be formulated with a reverse relationship as well: a set of theological doctrines D bears directly on scientific statement S if S can be inferred from D; however, claims to support science with theology are rare and therefore the focus will be on the bearing science has on religion.

An example of ADR is the claim that big bang cosmology supports the Christian doctrine of creation.[14] Negative direct relevance (NDR) occurs when

> a set S of scientific statements bears directly on theological doctrine D
>
> if ~D (D is false) can be inferred from S.

An example of NDR is the claim that evolution refutes or at least strongly suggests the non-existence of God.[15] The question of claiming direct relevance for statements relating science and religion is a complex one, and caution is appropriate before adopting this stance. One must be careful not to draw support for a statement based on a mere superficial resemblance between a theological and a scientific claim, nor should the theologian tie his or her theology too closely to a scientific theory likely to be overturned. One should also be careful not to connect a scientific statement and a religious claim when there is no real logical entailment or clear relation between the two. For example, some scientists have tried to dismiss religion by claiming to have found that the reason humans have religious experiences is because evolution has in some way "hard wired" us to have them.[16] Even if this is the case, an explanation of why humans have a capacity for an experience or belief does not enable us to reject a belief. We have evolved the capacity to develop scientific

theories, of which evolution is one, but we do not discredit the theory because we can explain the path that enabled it, nor do we say that because we can explain the workings of an eye that what vision perceives does not exist. The religious believer could even argue, "Of course we are hard wired for religious experiences and belief for that is what God would want so God could communicate with us." One may defend the idea that religious beliefs and experiences do not come about as the result of an encounter with God, but the case for this claim will need supplementation by a number of other arguments and logical steps.

Indirect relevance, which comes in three forms, represents the most fruitful way to understand the relationship between science and religion, and the vast majority of those working on the study of science and religion are exploring this type of relationship. The indirect ways science might bear on religion are (1) methodological, (2) metaphysical, and (3) heuristic.

Methodological indirect relevance involves issues usually raised in epistemological considerations. A method is a way of going about something, and in this case refers to how science works to understand the natural world or how theology tries to understand God. Science can be methodologically relevant to theology in two ways. First, theologians often adopt a specific methodology to systematize their work or to impose a formal

---

14. See, for example, Robert Jastrow, *God and the Astronomers* (New York: Norton, 1978), 116. There are good scientific but even better theological reasons for not making this identification. See Ernan McMullin, "How Should Cosmology Relate to Theology?" in *The Sciences and Theology in the Twentieth Century*, ed. Arthur Peacocke (Notre Dame, IN: University of Notre Dame Press, 1981), 17–57.

15. See Richard Dawkins, *The Blind Watchmaker: Why the Evidence of Evolution Reveals a Universe without Design* (New York: Norton, 1986); *River Out of Eden: A Darwinian View of Life* (London: Phoenix, 1995); and *Climbing Mount Improbable* (London: Viking, 1996). A theistic answer to Dawkins's claims can be found in Alister McGrath, *Dawkins' God: Genes, Memes, and the Meaning of Life* (Oxford, UK: Blackwell Publishers, 2004).

16. See Steven Pinker, *How the Mind Works* (New York: Norton, 1997) and E. O. Wilson, *On Human Nature* (Cambridge, MA: Harvard University Press, 1978).

structure on beliefs held about God, and if the theologian conceives of his or her methodology as analogous with the methods of natural science or if he or she organizes beliefs about God within a formal structure like a science, then science may be said to be indirectly methodologically relevant to theology. A number of theologians have taken this approach. Theologian and philosopher Nancey Murphy, for example, has applied the "research program" understanding of scientific methodology developed by Imre Lakatos to Christian theology.[17] A second area of methodological concern is the traditional theological problem of sorting out the relationship between faith and reason. With the exception of radical postmodernism,[18] science is seen to be a rational enterprise, and it may offer clues that could be instructive to theologians dealing with questions of rational method, faith, and reason.

Metaphysical indirect relevance poses an even more complicated set of problems for the understanding of science and religion than epistemology. There is little agreement among those who call themselves metaphysicians about what it is they are attempting to accomplish,[19] so the discussion here will not attempt to be comprehensive but will restrict itself to specific examples.

PROCESS THEOLOGY

Process theology, developed from the work of Alfred North Whitehead, emphasizes the progressive or evolutionary nature of the world and holds that God is in process of development through interaction with a constantly changing world. The basic general category for understanding all of reality is the process of becoming with an emphasis on events rather than objects.

One of the most common approaches in discussions of science and religion views metaphysics as a conceptual scheme through which the results of particular disciplines can be systematized and interpreted. Process theology, based on the philosophy of Alfred North Whitehead, is one example of this approach and commands a wide following in religion and science discussions.[20]

Other thinkers are more cautious about the use of metaphysics in general and process metaphysics in particular. Problems with metaphysics include: (1) satisfactorily defining metaphysics (the leading definitions of metaphysics all are lacking);[21] (2) successfully justifying the adoption of metaphysics as *the* way to relate science and religion (no particular metaphysical system has yet been able to command wide enough support);

17. Nancey Murphy, *Theology in the Age of Scientific Reasoning* (Ithaca, NY: Cornell University Press, 1990). Many other theologians adopt particular scientific methodologies for their work; Ian Barbour's *Religion and Science*, quoted above, gives an excellent survey.

18. Postmodernism is a movement of several types of philosophical schools that resist definition but share a rejection of the leading themes of the Enlightenment, including the following: (1) optimism about the future and the inevitable progress of Western culture, (2) reason alone can establish a basis for morality and society, (3) reason, including scientific reasoning, can establish the truth about the world, and (4) reason transcends culture and can give a coherent and accurate picture of ultimate reality. Radical postmodernism offers the most extreme rejection of these principles. For a good treatment, see J. F. Lyotard, *The Postmodern Condition: A Report on Knowledge*, trans. G. Bennington and B. Massumi (Minneapolis: University of Minnesota Press, 1979).

19. See W. H. Walsh's summary article "Nature of Metaphysics," in vol. 5, *Encyclopedia of Philosophy*, ed. Paul Edwards (New York: Macmillan, 1967), 300–307.

20. Ian Barbour is arguably the best representative of integrating science and religion through process thought.

21. George Schlesinger discusses these points thoroughly in *Metaphysics: Methods and Problems* (Oxford, UK: Basil Blackwell, 1983).

and (3) the shift in discussions of metaphysics in the philosophy of science from conceptual system building, now largely seen as fruitless, to arguments about the metaphysical status of scientific theories (whether and in what sense one can speak of theories as true).[22] Building a metaphysical system to relate science and religion faces numerous problems, but it may be a challenge the reader wishes to take. The majority will probably find focusing on specific metaphysical problems, such as the nature of time, to be a more productive way forward.

Heuristic relevance is the belief that science and religion may suggest fruitful analogies for one another in method or even content. Science and religion can make useful suggestions for each other in ways that are exploratory, discovery-oriented, or that stimulate further investigation. Analogies of heuristic relevance are not so much purely formal correspondences as they are creative and instructive explorations of similarities and differences that encourage imaginative leaps or intuitions that produce new insights. One theologian exploring this area is Thomas Torrance, who has shown how James Clerk Maxwell's theological views helped spur his creativity in working on the electromagnetic field and how the scientific understanding of light can generate useful insights for theology.[23]

Of the three forms of indirect relevance, heuristic relevance is perhaps the most exciting and in need of further development due to its concern with creativity and new insights. Methodological and metaphysical relevance are important but are second-order reflections on science and religion, whereas the exploration of heuristic relevance has the potential to be genuinely useful to both science and theology within the disciplines themselves.

Questions for Reflection and Discussion

- How do you understand the relationship between science and religion — irrelevance, quasi-direct relevance, direct relevance, indirect relevance, or something else? Explain.

- What do you think about heuristic relevance? Does it suggest a way forward for new insights about correlations between science and religion? Explain.

PARTICULAR TOPICS IN SCIENCE AND RELIGION

This section will focus on particular issues currently under debate in the discussion of science and religion. It will begin with the question of whether science is important to religion and close with an examination of major contemporary topics in the study of science and religion, including issues raised for religion by particular sciences.

Is Science Important for Religion?

There are four major reasons theologians, particularly those explicitly working out of a religious tradition, should see the natural sciences as

---

22. See Stratton, *Coherence, Consonance, and Conversation*, 82–86.

23. Thomas Torrance, *Transformation and Convergence in the Frame of Knowledge* (Grand Rapids, MI: Eerdmans, 1984), and *The Christian Frame of Mind: Reason, Order, and Openness in Theology and Natural Science* (Colorado Springs, CO: Helmers & Howard, 1989).

important for religion. First, theologians need to develop a theology of nature; that is, an understanding of the natural world as God's creation and as witness to the glory of God (Ps 19:1–4). Nature, understood in this way, traditionally has been described as one of the "Two Books" that reveal God—the Book of Scripture and the Book of Nature. Science would definitely have bearing on reading the Book of Nature. Second, there are important ethical reasons to see science as relevant to theology. The Judeo-Christian tradition teaches that human beings are to be good stewards of God's creation, heal the sick, feed the hungry, and help the poor; and the natural sciences can help people understand how to protect ecosystems, how to prevent diseases by understanding their causes, how to grow better crops, and how to address countless other issues associated with human flourishing. Third, there are certain points of interaction between theology and science, including those where conflict might be possible. For example, if a religious believer accepts that God acts in the natural world, including ways that are out of the ordinary or miraculous, he or she needs to answer the question of how God's activity relates to a world that explains events in terms of regular and identifiable natural causes. Do physical processes allow room for a Creator to act? Does God act only through regular natural processes or can God act in unique ways to bring about results that do not fit the normal expectations of nature? And, if God does act in unique ways, how does this take place and can it be identified explicitly? And fourth, the theologian may see science as relevant to theology in the apologetics for his or her tradition. Apologetics is the rational defense of religious belief and includes both turning back objections to the faith and

stating positive reasons why one should adopt a particular religion. Understanding the natural sciences is essential for this activity, for there are those who claim science renders religious belief untenable and any religion that expects to be taken seriously from an intellectual point of view is going to have to come to terms with modern science.

One question plaguing the beginner thinking about science and religion is "There is so much to think about—where do I start?" One obvious answer would be to begin with what is of interest, but scientific theories will vary in importance according to people's concerns. Perhaps a useful way to begin is to use the categories for scientific theories developed by Roger Penrose.[24] The categories are: (1) Superb, (2) Useful, and (3) Tentative.

Superb theories exhibit phenomenal range, accuracy, and mathematical elegance, and only a handful of theories fall into this category, such as quantum theory and Einstein's general and special theories of relativity. Superb theories are the most important and demand the most attention. Useful theories have some scientific experimental support but have not yet achieved nor may ever achieve the observational accuracy and predictive power of Superb theories. Useful theories mentioned by Penrose include the quark model of subatomic physics and the big bang theory of the origin of the universe.[25] Tentative theories make up the largest number of scientific theories and lack any significant scientific experimental support; they may contain good ideas or simply be misguided (string theory, for example). Useful and Tentative theories can be raised to a higher category over time if successful and subsumed under other theories that become Superb, or they can fade away. It is clear Useful and Tentative

24. Roger Penrose, *The Emperor's New Mind: Concerning Computers, Minds, and the Laws of Physics* (Oxford, UK: Oxford University Press, 1989), 152–155.

25. The latter's stock definitely has been on the rise since the publication of Penrose's book.

theories will need to be treated case by case, with successful theories requiring more attention as they rise in status over time and others meriting little, if any, attention. If Penrose's classification of theories is correct, heuristic comparison poses the most relevance for religion, and direct relevance probably will be rare.

History

One of the most exciting and fruitful areas in studying science and religion is that of the history of the understanding of the relationship between the two. Earlier historical accounts heavily emphasized the conflict between the two. Two highly influential studies, J. W. Draper's *History of the Conflict between Religion and Science* and Andrew Dickson White's *A History of the Warfare of Science and Theology in Christendom*, portray a battle to the death between conservative irrational religious dogmatism and progressive rational science.[26] The conflict between Galileo and the Roman Catholic Church figures prominently in both accounts, and numerous examples illustrate the warfare between science and religion. The warfare model has left a seemingly indelible mark on the popular understanding of the relationship between religion and science, as evidenced by its treatment in contemporary media.

In recent decades, historians have criticized this warfare perspective as highly selective and oversimplified. Science and religion are not monolithic blocks or even unified forces in battle against one another. Historical study actually shows a complex relationship between the two, with layers of thinking and nuance even within the same person and groups.[27] The Galileo affair, so often used as the exemplar of conflict, actually

was a highly complex event involving many more issues than just the scientific evidence for a heliocentric view of the universe versus biblical literalism or church dogma. The historical study of the relationship between science and religion is relatively new, and the future holds many opportunities for the scholar seeking deep understanding of this rich and subtle topic.

Physics

Physics is a science that deals with basic structures, processes of change, and interactions of matter and energy. Three areas of study within physics that have implications for religion are relativity, quantum theory, and chaos and complexity.

Einstein's special and general theories of relativity challenged the dominance of Sir Isaac Newton's work in physics and created a new way of looking at the universe. The special theory interrelated measurements of space, time, and mass for objects moving uniformly with respect to an observer, and implied a space-time continuum and the equivalence of mass and energy. The general theory related accelerated motion, gravitational force, and the curvature of space and led to conclusions that the universe is finite, curved, and may be unbounded rather than infinite, and that space is expanding. Both theories raise epistemological and metaphysical points of interest for theology.

First, relativity does not mean relativism, for relativity, while insisting on the importance of reference frames in observing the universe, does hold to observer-independent standards for knowledge (the speed of light and the form of physical laws). Second, relativity shows we cannot always rely on common sense to understand the universe (as in

26. John W. Draper, *History of the Conflict between Religion and Science* (New York: D. Appleton, 1874), and Andrew Dickson White, *A History of the Warfare of Science with Theology*, 2 vols. (New York: D. Appleton, 1896).

27. Two fine studies illustrating this point are John Hedley Brooke, *Science and Religion: Some Historical Perspectives* (Cambridge, MA: Cambridge University Press, 1991), and the essays collected in *God and Nature: Historical Essays on the Encounter between Christianity and Science,* David Lindberg and Ronald Numbers, eds. (Berkeley, CA: University of California Press, 1986).

our notions of space and time); human experience is limited, and epistemic humility is important. Third, space and time are part of a single continuum and are empirical features of the universe, not ultimate or infinite, as some philosophers have thought. Past, present, and future are relative to the observer, which has implications for how one might understand God's knowledge of and action within the world. And fourth, relativity describes an interconnected universe that is a multileveled whole: space and time are inseparable and mass is a form of energy, to name two examples of interconnection. The total interconnection of the physical world breaks down many traditional dualisms embraced by Western thought and has deep implications for any theology of nature or attempt to form a coherent worldview.[28]

Quantum theory challenged the old orbital model of the atom. Formulated in the 1920s, quantum theory treats the properties of atoms and subatomic particles as wave functions that are represented by mathematical operators that allow predictions of probability but not exact values for observable events.[29] Most of the philosophical interest in quantum mechanics centers on three issues: (1) the observer-observed relationship, (2) indeterminacy, and (3) nonlocality. The interpretation of each of these is highly controversial and problematic at best, but at least a sketch of the issues involved is possible.

The observer-observed relationship or the "measurement problem" concerns how great a role the observer plays in determining the outcome of an event. To observe is to interfere, thus we do not yet have a certain answer to the question: "What is the state of an electron before (or if no) humans try to measure it?" The measurement problem has led to wide speculation about quantum mechanics and the nature of reality.[30] One thing is clear—understanding is a participatory and relational process with implications for both epistemology and metaphysics. The more bizarre issues raised by the measurement problem are probably not going to be solved anytime in the near future but are highly interesting for those seeking to create a coherent worldview.

Indeterminacy is related to the Heisenberg Uncertainty Principle and states that the more accurately we determine the position of an electron, the less accurately we can determine its momentum, and vice versa. What is the basis of this uncertainty? Different answers include the following: (1) human ignorance, (2) an inherent limitation imposed on us by experiment or conceptualization, or (3) genuine indeterminacy in nature, for there are genuine alternative possibilities in the atomic world. Each of these positions has its defenders, and each has different implications for an attempt to create a coherent worldview. For example, if genuine alternative possibilities exist in the world, there is room for some kind or degree of freedom; if electrons are governed by deterministic hidden variables, making a claim for freedom is much more difficult.[31]

Nonlocality, as proposed by John Bell and confirmed by Alain Aspect, refers to the counterintuitive "togetherness in separation" by which

---

28. The theologian Thomas Torrance has reflected most on the implications of relativity for theology; readers are encouraged to look at his work, especially the books referenced above.

29. For an excellent short introduction to quantum theory, see John Polkinghorne, *The Quantum World* (London: Penguin Books, 1986).

30. For a treatment of differing interpretations, see John Wheeler and W. H. Zurek, eds., *Quantum Theory and Measurement* (Princeton, NJ: Princeton University Press, 1983), and Zvi Schreiber, "The Nine Lives of Schrödinger's Cat," master's thesis, University of London, 1994, *http://arxiv.org/PS_cache/quant-ph/pdf/9501/9501014v5.pdf.*

31. For a defense of genuine indeterminism in nature, see John Polkinghorne, *Belief in God in an Age of Science* (New Haven, CT: Yale University Press, 1998).

quantum entities that have once interacted with each other retain a power of instantaneous mutual influence no matter how far apart they separate. This principle leads to greater evidence of the interconnectedness of reality as well as suggests some potentially fruitful heuristic connections between science and religion.

Chaos theory and complexity are two relatively new sciences that have implications for religious belief.[32] Chaos theory states that chaotic systems are nonlinear, in that a very small initial change can result in a subsequent very large change. Unlike deterministic systems, infinitesimally small uncertainties in chaos systems can lead to enormous uncertainties in predicting behavior; for example, a butterfly fluttering its wings in the Amazon can theoretically alter weather in China. Complexity refers to the emergence of higher levels of order in the self-organization of systems with many components. Both of these new sciences are nonreductionistic; that is, they defy the claim that understanding something is the equivalent of reducing it to its lowest level of explanation; higher-level explanations are necessary. Theologians have looked to chaos theory and complexity to articulate fresh understandings of human freedom, the emergence of biological life, and how God may act in the world.[33] There are controversial aspects to each of these approaches, but it does appear these new sciences at least encourage creative explorations to a greater degree than previous deterministic systems.

Physical Cosmology

Physical cosmology is a branch of astronomy that is concerned with questions of the formation, structure, and evolution of the universe. Two primary topics in cosmology have been of most interest to those seeking to integrate science and religion: (1) the big bang and (2) the anthropic principle.

The big bang cosmological model asserts that the universe expanded to its current state from a singularity (t = 0), a primordial condition of infinite density and temperature and zero volume in which the laws of physics as we know them break down. The universe has a finite past of fifteen to twelve billion years. There is impressive and increasing evidence for the big bang and the theory has no serious challengers.[34] The big bang does give our universe a beginning, but the question of whether or not it is an absolute beginning is open. Opinions on the religious implications of the big bang have varied. It is certainly tempting to read theological import into the theory and some religious figures, like Pope Pius XII, have yielded, claiming the big bang supports the biblical idea of creation.[35] Others, like John Polkinghorne, view the big bang as irrelevant to the Christian understanding of creation.[36] Robert John Russell defends a type of indirect relevance between theology and theory.[37] Quentin Smith, on the other hand, argues the big bang makes atheism

32. Treatments can be found in James Gleick, *Chaos: The Making of a New Science* (New York: Viking, 1987), and M. Mitchell Waldrop, *Complexity: The Emerging Science at the Edge of Order and Chaos* (New York: Simon and Schuster, 1992).

33. A good overview of these issues is in Christopher Southgate et al., *God, Humanity, and the Cosmos: A Textbook in Science and Religion* (Harrisburg, PA: Trinity Press International, 1999).

34. A good list of evidence and an accessible introduction to cosmology, mixed with speculation about what it all means, is provided in the popular book by Joel Primack and Nancy Abrams, *The View from the Center of the Universe* (New York: Riverhead Books, 2006).

35. Pope Pius XII, "Modern Science and the Existence of God," *The Catholic Mind* (March 1952): 182–192.

36. John Polkinghorne, *The Faith of a Physicist: Reflections of a Bottom-Up Thinker* (Minneapolis: Fortress Press, 1994).

37. Robert John Russell, "Finite Creation without a Beginning: The Doctrine of Creation in Relation to Big Bang and Quantum Cosmologies," in *Quantum Cosmologies and the Laws of Nature*, eds. Robert J. Russell, Nancey Murphy, and Chris Isham (Vatican City State: Vatican Observatory Publication, 1993).

more likely.[38] Whatever the truth may be, reflection on the meaning of the big bang for religious belief is likely to take one on a substantive intellectual quest.

The *anthropic principle* is an umbrella term covering a variety of formulations stressing the precise physical constants and conditions needed in the universe to allow the emergence of intelligent carbon-based life.[39] According to this principle, if the constants and conditions were only slightly different, life would not have emerged. The most widely accepted version, the Weak Anthropic Principle (WAP), states that given the fact that observers of the universe exist all possible universes are not equally probable. If the fundamental physical constants of the universe such as the mass of an electron or the force that holds an atom together were different, there would be no life to observe the universe. The more controversial Strong Anthropic Principle (SAP) goes further and argues the universe must have properties that will allow life to develop. Variations on the SAP include: (1) the Design-Centered Anthropic Principle (DCAP), which holds the universe is biocentric because it was designed to be by a higher power; (2) the Participatory Anthropic Principle (PAP), which holds that the existence of sentient carbon-based observers is needed to create the universe; and (3) the Final Anthropic Principle (FAP), which holds that once sentient life comes into existence it must exist forever. Reactions to the anthropic principle and its variants have been widely mixed. Richard Swinburne has argued that the anthropic principle increases the epistemic probability there

is a God.[40] Even those who do not accept the anthropic principle as an argument for the existence of God, like scientist and agnostic Paul Davies, see the theistic implications:

> It is hard to resist the impression of something—some influence capable of transcending spacetime and the confinement of relativistic causality—possessing an overview of the entire cosmos at the instant of its creation, and manipulating all the causally disconnected parts to go bang with almost exactly the same vigour at the same time, and yet not so exactly co-ordinated as to preclude on the small scale, slight irregularities that eventually formed the galaxies, and us.[41]

Those who oppose the anthropic principle have taken two strategies: (1) to dismiss the constants as mere coincidences, and (2) to propose a "many worlds" alternative in which our universe is survivor of a possibly infinite number of failed worlds.[42] The first is certainly possible even though it strains credibility. The second has three problems: (1) there is no evidence for any other possible worlds nor can any be found since the other domains would be beyond our observational powers, (2) there are a significant number of unresolved questions and difficulties within each of the "many worlds" options offered, and (3) the use of an infinite number of worlds to explain this one world seems to be a clear violation of Ockham's Razor, or the value of simplicity in explanation. This has led some philosophers, like John Leslie, to argue that God is a superior hypothesis to explain the "fine tuning" of the universe for life.[43] It is clear however

38. William Craig and Quentin Smith, *Theism, Atheism, and Big Bang Cosmology* (New York: Oxford University Press, 1993).

39. The standard discussion is John Barrow and Frank Tipler, *The Anthropic Cosmological Principle* (Oxford, UK: Clarendon Press, 1986).

40. Richard Swinburne, *The Existence of God*, (Oxford, UK: Clarendon Press, 1991).

41. Paul Davies, *The Accidental Universe* (Cambridge, MA: Cambridge University Press, 1982), 95.

42. A helpful discussion of the variants of the "many worlds" view can be found in Ian Barbour, *Religion and Science: Historical and Contemporary Issues* (San Francisco: HarperSanFrancisco, 1997), 206–207.

43. John Leslie, *Universes* (London: Routledge, 1989).

that whether one decides to accept some version of the anthropic principle or reject it, the choice made will reveal much about and have a ripple effect on one's worldview.

Evolution

No other scientific theory generates as much passion in the science and religion discussion as does Charles Darwin's theory of evolution. Controversies about evolution continue to occur and to be a regular feature in American media. This is somewhat surprising given the tremendous scientific acceptance and evidence for evolution.[44] Complete rejection of Darwinian evolution on scientific grounds is rare to almost nonexistent among scientists, and the main opposition comes from those who see evolution as incompatible with their religious beliefs.

INTELLIGENT DESIGN

"The theory of intelligent design (ID) holds that certain features of the universe and of living things are best explained by an intelligent cause rather than an undirected process such as natural selection. ID is thus a scientific disagreement with the core claim of evolutionary theory that the apparent design of living systems is an illusion."[47]

"Scientific creationism," of both a young earth and old earth variety, defends Genesis 1–3 as an accurate depiction of the origins of the species (or *kinds* to use their preferred term).[45] The issue separating the two is obviously the age of the earth. Young earth creationists commonly set an age limit of about ten thousand years for the world's existence; old earth creationists are willing to take the days of Genesis as referring to much longer periods. To say the overwhelming majority of scientists repudiate scientific creationism is to put it mildly.

Other opposition to Darwinian evolution, which claims not to be based on religious belief, comes from intelligent design theory, which is well represented by Phillip Johnson, William Dembski, and Michael Behe.[46] Intelligent design theorists are not necessarily biblical literalists, but they view Darwinism as incompatible with theism and insufficient to explain the emergence of information-rich or irreducibly complex biological structures.

Intelligent design has fared little better than scientific creationism, but it certainly has generated a lively discussion.[48] There are atheists who agree with the creationists and intelligent design proponents that Darwinian evolution is incompatible with a belief in God, and they argue that since evolution is true, it is God,

---

44. For an accessible survey of the evidence for evolution, see Michael Ruse, *Can a Darwinian Be a Christian?* (Cambridge, MA: Cambridge University Press, 2001), chapter 1.

45. The former position is represented by Henry Morris, ed., *Scientific Creationism*, 2nd ed. (El Cajon, CA: Master Books, 1985), the latter by Hugh Ross, *Creation and Time: A Biblical and Scientific Perspective on the Creation-Date Controversy* (Colorado Springs, CO: NavPress, 1994).

46. Phillip Johnson, *Darwin on Trial* (Washington, DC: Regnery Gateway, 1991); William Dembski, *The Design Inference: Eliminating Chance through Small Probabilities* (New York: Cambridge University Press, 1998); Michael Behe, *Darwin's Black Box* (New York: The Free Press, 1996).

47. Definition taken from the Web page of the Intelligent Design Network, *http://www.intelligentdesignnetwork.org*.

48. For a collection of pro and con essays, see Robert Pennock, ed., *Intelligent Design Creationism and Its Critics* (Cambridge, MA: MIT Press, 2001).

not evolution, that must go.[49] The majority of religious believers seem to find evolution compatible with religious beliefs, as do the majority of scientists and philosophers, even if the latter are disinterested in religion.[50] Some theologians, like Arthur Peacocke, take a very positive view of Darwinian evolution and see it playing a constructive role within Christian theology, enriching the understanding of God as Creator.[51] As the diversity of views indicates, evolution, like other areas in the discussion of science and religion, provides stimulating possibilities for reflection and incorporation into one's worldview.

CONCLUSION

It is impossible to cover all the topics relevant to the discussion of science and religion; indeed the issues raised by the topics covered here are far from complete. Many fascinating areas such as neuroscience, cybernetics, the origin of human life, the possible future human creation of life, and the ethical issues raised by science and technology remain for your exploration.

I would be remiss not to mention one final area of tremendous importance in discussions of religion and science in today's multicultural world: the plurality of human worldviews. Men and women representing all the rich diversity found in our world are concerned about these issues, and it would be a shame for differing communities not to share their wisdom and insights with one another. If the reader is interested in further pursuing issues related to science and religion, he or she is encouraged to join with others similarly interested in developing their worldviews. Discussion groups, many of them funded by the John Templeton Foundation, are available in cities around the world and are affiliated with the Metanexus Institute. The Metanexus Institute is a valuable resource, for it is a community committed to fostering interdisciplinary, intercultural, and inter-religious collaboration in pursuit of new insights and a better future.[52] Representatives of many different worldviews attend sponsored conferences to share ideas, engage in serious debate, and seek common ground. Come join the conversation.

Questions for Reflection and Discussion

- What are some of the possible advantages to approaching the relationship between science and religion by studying history?

- How does the measurement problem in physics relate to the study of religion?

- In what ways might the study of cosmology aid or hinder the study of religion?

- What additional questions might be raised about the relationship between religion and science?

---

49. See the earlier works cited by Richard Dawkins and Daniel Dennett, *Darwin's Dangerous Idea* (New York: Touchstone, 1995).

50. For discussion of this point, see Michael Ruse, *Can a Darwinian Be a Christian?*

51. Arthur Peacocke, *Theology for a Scientific Age*, (Minneapolis: Fortress Press, 1993).

52. The Web site for Metanexus is *http://www.metanexus.net/institute/*.

Additional Resources

Barbour, Ian. 1997. *Religion and Science: Historical and Contemporary Issues*. San Francisco: HarperSanFrancisco.

Barrow, John, and Frank Tipler. 1986. *The Anthropic Cosmological Principle*. Oxford, UK: Clarendon Press.

Butterfield, Herbert. 1965. *The Origins of Modern Science, 1300–1800*. New York: The Free Press.

Craig, William, and Quentin Smith. 1993. *Theism, Atheism, and Big Bang Cosmology*. New York: Oxford University Press.

Davies, Paul. 1982. *The Accidental Universe*. Cambridge, MA: Cambridge University Press.

Dawkins, Richard. 1996. *Climbing Mount Improbable*. London: Viking.

Dawkins, Richard. 1995. *River Out of Eden: A Darwinian View of Life*. London: Phoenix.

Dawkins, Richard. 1986. *The Blind Watchmaker: Why the Evidence of Evolution Reveals a Universe without Design*. New York: Norton.

Dennett, Daniel. 1995. *Darwin's Dangerous Idea*. New York: Touchstone.

Dirac, Paul. 1968. "Methods in Theoretical Physics." In *From a Life of Physics: Evening Lectures at the International Centre for Theoretical Physics, Trieste, Italy*. A Special Supplement of the IAEA Bulletin.

Dirac, Paul. 1963. "The Evolution of the Physicist's Picture of Nature." *Scientific American* 208 (May).

Draper, John W. 1874. *History of the Conflict between Religion and Science*. New York: D. Appleton.

Gleick, James. 1987. *Chaos: The Making of a New Science*. New York: Viking.

Gould, S J 1999. *Rocks of Ages: Science and Religion in the Fullness of Life*. New York: Norton.

Haught, John. 1995. *Science and Religion: From Conflict to Conversation*. Mahwah, NJ: Paulist Press.

Jastrow, Robert. 1978. *God and the Astronomers*. New York: Norton.

Leslie, John. 1989. *Universes*. London: Routledge.

McGrath, Alister. 2004. *Dawkins' God: Genes, Memes, and the Meaning of Life*. Oxford, UK: Blackwell Publishers.

McMullin, Ernan. 2000. "Values in Science." In *A Companion to the Philosophy of Science*. Edited by W. H. Newton-Smith. Oxford, UK: Blackwell Publishers.

McMullin, Ernan. 1981. "How Should Cosmology Relate to Theology?" In *The Sciences and Theology in the Twentieth Century*. Edited by Arthur Peacocke. Notre Dame, IN: University of Notre Dame Press.

Metanexus. *http://www.metanexus.net/institute/*.

Murphy, Nancey. 1990. *Theology in the Age of Scientific Reasoning*. Ithaca, NY: Cornell University Press.

Peacocke, Arthur. 1993. *Theology for a Scientific Age*. Minneapolis: Fortress Press.

Pennock, Robert, ed. 2001. *Intelligent Design Creationism and Its Critics*. Cambridge, MA: MIT Press.

Penrose, Roger. 1989. *The Emperor's New Mind: Concerning Computers, Minds, and the Laws of Physics*. Oxford, UK: Oxford University Press.

Peters, Ted. 1998. *Science and Theology: The New Consonance*. Oxford, UK: Westview Press.

Pinker, Steven. 1997. *How the Mind Works*. New York: Norton.

Polanyi, Michael. 1962. *Personal Knowledge: Towards a Post-Critical Philosophy*. Chicago: University of Chicago Press.

Polkinghorne, John. 1998. *Belief in God in an Age of Science*. New Haven, CT: Yale University Press.

Polkinghorne, John. 1994. *The Faith of a Physicist: Reflections of a Bottom-Up Thinker*. Minneapolis: Fortress Press.

Polkinghorne, John. 1986. *The Quantum World*. London: Penguin Books.

Pope Pius XII. 1952. "Modern Science and the Existence of God." *The Catholic Mind* (March).

Primack, Joel, and Nancy Abrams. 2006. *The View from the Center of the Universe*. New York: Riverhead Books.

Ruse, Michael. 2001. *Can a Darwinian Be a Christian?* Cambridge, MA: Cambridge University Press.

Continued . . .

Additional Resources

Continued . . .

Russell, Robert John. 1993. "Finite Creation without a Beginning: The Doctrine of Creation in Relation to Big Bang and Quantum Cosmologies." In *Quantum Cosmologies and the Laws of Nature: Scientific Perspectives on Divine Action*. A Series on Divine action in scientific perspective, v. 1. Robert J. Russell, Nancey Murphy, and Chris Isham, eds. Vatican City State: Vatican Observatory.

Sagan, Carl. 1980. *Cosmos*. New York: Random House.

Schlesinger, George. 1983. *Metaphysics: Methods and Problems*. Oxford, UK: Basil Blackwell.

Schreiber, Zvi. 1994. "The Nine Lives of Schrödinger's Cat." Master's thesis, University of London. *http://arxiv.org/PS_cache/quant-ph/pdf/9501/9501014v5.pdf*.

Southgate, Christopher, et al. 1999. *God, Humanity, and the Cosmos: A Textbook in Science and Religion*. Harrisburg, PA: Trinity Press International.

Stratton, S. Brian. 2000. *Coherence, Consonance, and Conversation: The Quest of Theology, Philosophy, and Natural Science for a Unified Word-View*. Lanham, MD: University Press of America.

Swinburne, Richard. 1991. *The Existence of God*. Oxford, UK: Clarendon Press.

Torrance, Thomas. 1989. *The Christian Frame of Mind: Reason, Order, and Openness in Theology and Natural Science*. Colorado Springs, CO: Helmers & Howard.

Torrance, Thomas. 1984. *Transformation and Convergence in the Frame of Knowledge*. Grand Rapids, MI: Eerdmans.

Van Till, Howard J., Davis A. Young, and Clarence Menninga. 1988. *Science Held Hostage: What's Wrong with Creation Science and Evolutionism*. Downers Grove, IL: InterVarsity Press.

Waldrop, M. Mitchell. 1992. *Complexity: The Emerging Science at the Edge of Order and Chaos*. New York: Simon and Schuster.

Wheeler, John, and W. H. Zurek, eds. 1983. *Quantum Theory and Measurement*. Princeton, NJ: Princeton University Press.

White, Andrew Dickson. 1896. *A History of the Warfare of Science with Theology*. New York: D. Appleton.

Wilson, E. O. 1978. *On Human Nature*. Cambridge, MA: Harvard University Press.

CHAPTER 14

RITUAL STUDIES

Dr. Kendra G. Hotz
Rhodes College

Preface

Religions specify what is of ultimate importance—what is to be valued above all, what grants meaning to life and all of reality, what is worth ordering one's life around. Religions offer their adherents ways of organizing reality and determining priorities. Ritual acts serve as markers of that vision. They indicate how a religious community sees the relationship between human life and the broader cosmos.

To illumine the ways in which religions construct and sustain meaning through ritual practices, this chapter examines eight central concepts in ritual studies. Kendra G. Hotz examines the ways in which rituals encode a community's values. What constitutes a life well lived? How are individuals incorporated into a religious community? How do belief and practice interact in a life of faith? Hotz proposes that the study of ritual provides a way into the subdermal layers of religion and religious ideas that are not readily accessible at other junctures of human experience.

Chapter Goals

- To introduce readers to ritual markers in religious practice
- To introduce readers to ways of understanding religious rituals and practices
- To invite critical reflection on the place of ritual markers in human experience

INTRODUCTION

This chapter explores central concepts from the field of ritual studies that shed light on religious practice. But before we can explore how scholars of ritual studies interpret religious practice, we first need a sense of what ritual practices look like in lived religious traditions. We begin, then, with a brief description of ritual practices in three religious traditions.

Judaism. "From the moment he awakens until the time he retires, an observant Jew fills his day with words of gratitude to God," observes Howard Greenstein. "He recites a blessing for washing his hands and face, for setting foot on the floor, for attending to his bodily needs, and for dressing in his customary garments."[1] Codes of ritual purity determine what may or may not be eaten or touched, what is to be sought out and what avoided. These same ritual enactments mark and interpret the ordinary cycles of human life and include prayers as the day begins and ends; a ritual bath, the *mikveh*, at the ebbing of a menstrual cycle; and the washing of utensils used to prepare meals. Every moment of life, for an observant Jew, is to be lived in awareness of God's goodness. Every act may be interpreted in light of God's desire for human flourishing and God's commands for human community. Ritual blessings reinforce intentional daily living and impart sacredness to the ordinary moments of life.

Rituals not only reinforce the sacredness of the ordinary but also mark and interpret moments of extraordinary transition. Judaism ritually marks a child's entry into the covenant community with a naming ritual that includes circumcision for male children. In this ritual, parents bring their children before the community to be marked verbally and physically as participants in the ancient covenant with God. Again at adolescence, these same children celebrate the bar mitzvah (for boys) or bat mitzvah (for girls) and are acknowledged as full members of the adult community of faith as they begin to take responsibility for their own participation in that community and signal their acceptance of its norms and values. Just as birth and the transition to adulthood are marked and interpreted ritually, so also marriage and death find their place in a Jewish religious sense of the world through ritual acts.

Roman Catholic Christianity. In 1439, the Council of Florence of the Roman Catholic Church issued a decree that enumerated seven sacraments that ritually carry a person from birth to death, physically marking and verbally interpreting important moments of transition in human life.[2] Even today these sacraments are understood as outward and visible signs of an inward and spiritual grace and have the effect of connecting the individual to a larger community of faith.

The decree explains how these sacraments function in the course of a human life:

The first five sacraments are intended to secure the spiritual perfection of every man individually; the two last are ordained for the governance and increase of the Church. For through baptism we are born again of the spirit; through confirmation we grow in grace and are strengthened in the faith; and when we have been born again and strengthened we are fed by the divine food of the mass; but if, through sin, we bring sickness upon our souls, we are made spiritually whole by penance; and by extreme unction we are healed, both spiritually and corporeally, according as our souls have need; by ordination the Church is governed and multiplied spiritually; by matrimony it is materially increased.[3]

Baptism, typically celebrated shortly after birth, marks one's entry into Christian life. Confirmation, typically celebrated in early adolescence, marks one's entry into mature faith. Matrimony and ordination mark entry into two different life paths. The Mass and penance provide regular support and correction in Christian

1. Greenstein et al., *What Do Our Neighbors Believe? Questions and Answers from Judaism, Christianity, and Islam* (Louisville, KY: Westminster John Knox Press, 2007), 89.

2. Council of Florence, 1439, "Decree for the Armenians," Medieval Sourcebook, *http://www.fordham.edu/halsall/source/1438sacraments.html#amen*; site maintained by Paul Halsall. Original Source: James Harvey Robinson, ed. *Readings in European History*, Vol. 1 (Boston: Ginn and Company, 1904).

3. Ibid.

living. Extreme unction offers comfort to "the sick who are in fear of death."[4]

The Roman Catholic sacramental system constructs a world thick with signs and symbols and ritual words and actions, through which the profoundest questions about human existence can be encountered and illuminated: a child is marked with water while the name of God is invoked, a dying person is anointed with oil while forgiveness is pronounced. Every milestone of life between birth and death is ritually marked and thus brought under the interpretive canopy of the Catholic Christian faith.

Islam. The Five Pillars of Islam, the acts that constitute the very heart of Muslim faith, likewise are thick with ritual. To be a Muslim one must confess that there is one God and that Muhammad is his prophet, pray five times daily, give alms, fast during the month of Ramadan, and, if able, make a pilgrimage to the holy city of Mecca. The confession of faith becomes woven into the ritual life of a Muslim because it is heard five times each day during the call to prayer. This call to prayer ritually marks the passage of the day from dawn to noon, from midday to dusk and to evening. The prayers themselves involve not only ritual words but also bodily movements. Muslims at prayer face Mecca, bow, kneel, and prostrate themselves before God, while reciting prayers and verses from the Qur'an. Muslims mark their time and their food ritually by fasting in daylight hours during Ramadan. And the highlight of Muslim ritual life is the pilgrimage to Mecca, or the hajj. The hajj itself involves four days filled with ritual acts such as circling and kissing the Kaaba, the central shrine of Islam, and participating in a ritual stoning of Satan. The rites of confession, prayer, fasting, almsgiving, and making pilgrimage are each so well woven into Muslim life that they constitute the

very meaning of being Muslim, being one who submits to the will of God. These ritual acts highlight and answer the most basic questions about what it means to be human and to be obedient to God.

Every culture, every religion, to a greater or lesser extent makes use of such ritual markers. But what are these rituals? What do they mean? How do they function? Clearly, when new parents bring a child before the community of faith to have him named and circumcised or to have her marked with the waters of baptism, they do so in the context of certain beliefs about the practice and about the community. When mourners gather for a funeral, they do so with a sense of what makes for a good life. The ritual itself expresses, partially constructs, and reinforces a normative view of human life. Rituals offer answers, however provisional and fluid they may be, to the basic questions of human life: What constitutes a life well lived? What does this community value? How is the value of a human life judged? Ritual practices serve as markers of value, places where participants are confronted with their greatest hopes for life and with their most basic judgments about what they most value in life. Ritual practices are always interwoven with faith commitments and embedded in specific cultural contexts. Without all three elements—practices, beliefs, and contexts—we cannot understand what is happening in a particular ritual.

Rituals, then, open many questions for the student of religion. Can we examine particular rituals to discover what is valued in a community? What is regarded as meaningful? as sacred? Ritual studies is the discipline that attempts to answer these questions. This chapter will introduce eight of the central concepts used in this field of study.

---

4. Ibid.

Questions for Reflection and Discussion

- What are the principal ritual markers in the religion with which you are most familiar?
- In what ways are ritual markers important or unimportant for human experience?

- What ritual markers have you found to be significant in your life and what made them so?

RITUAL: A PRELIMINARY DEFINITION

Before we can employ ritual studies to explore the religious significance of ritual acts, we need to say some things about what a ritual is. What kinds of actions count as rituals? What makes a ritual action different from other kinds of activities? Why are some actions, like a pilgrimage or baptism, regarded as rituals, while others, such as driving to work or brushing one's teeth, are not?

According to Stanley Tambiah, a ritual is "a culturally constructed system of symbolic communication. It is constituted of patterned and ordered sequences of words and acts."[5] Let's consider that definition one phrase at a time. First, a ritual is *culturally constructed*. Rituals, in other words, are not natural. They do not happen automatically the way breathing, eating, and seeking sexual intimacy do. A ritual may offer an elaboration on such natural events, but it is not itself natural. For example, traditions such as *hesychasm* in certain strands of Christian eastern orthodoxy and yoga in some Indian communities include meditative practices that involve controlling the breath. Nearly every religious community has developed rituals surrounding common meals and marriage. So, a ritual may be linked with a natural, universal feature of human life, such as breathing, eating, and mating, but it will be encoded with meanings derived from a particular culture. In the case of a ritual associated

with birth, such as Christian baptism, a basic hygiene behavior—washing—becomes a means of marking a child as a member of a particular faith community. The ritual washing has the effect of making a child who was naturally a member of a family, culturally a member of the church. Circumcision in Jewish communities works in a similar way. The ritual marks a child with the sign of the covenant so that he is no longer simply the child of his parents, but is now also a child of the covenant.

Second, a ritual involves a *system of symbolic communication*. Think, for instance, of the Muslim obligation to pray five times each day facing Mecca. A Muslim finds meaning in the acts only as they are embedded within a broader system of symbols. If the words of the prayer, the direction one faces, and the acts of prostration are to lend meaning to one's life, one must know the story of the prophet, understand the centrality of Mecca in that story, and share the value of submission to the will of God. A similar system of interacting symbols underlies a Christian rite associated with death. In extreme unction (last rites), a priest uses oil that has been blessed to make the sign of the cross over the dying person's eyes, ears, nostrils, mouth, hands, feet, and loins, while offering a prayer asking God to forgive the person for whatever sins have been committed by sight, or hearing, and so on. Each act—the prayer, the anointing, making the sign of the cross—points beyond itself to some deeper and socially constructed meaning. Understanding the

---

5. Tambiah, "A Performative Approach to Ritual," *Proceedings of the British Academy* 65 (1979): 119.

content of a particular symbol requires attention to a broader system of symbols. What, for instance, does the cross signify? The content of that symbol can only be properly conceived when one connects it with Christian accounts of the death and Resurrection of Christ. What is happening to the dying person's body is interpreted in light of what happened to Christ's body.

Third, rituals involve *patterned and ordered sequences*. Rituals can be identified in part because the same act and the same words are repeated in precisely the same way each time. If we observe someone standing near a wall, briefly bowing from the waist, then moving on as though nothing unusual has happened, we might safely assume that no ritual has taken place. Perhaps the person dropped something and was looking to see where it had fallen. But suppose we see the same person repeatedly bowing and notice that he is repeating a phrase over and over again. Perhaps we notice that he returns to this wall on a regular basis to repeat this activity. Especially if we happen to be standing near the Western Wall (sometimes called the Wailing Wall) of the Temple Mount in Jerusalem, we will recognize this activity as a Jewish prayer ritual. There is something about the repetition itself that indicates to us the ritual nature of this event.

Finally, the patterned repetitions of rituals involve both *words* and *acts*. Consider the committal of the body at a Christian funeral: mourners release a handful of dirt onto the casket, which has been lowered into the ground, while a minister intones "ashes to ashes, dust to dust." The action of covering the casket with dirt is coupled with the verbal reminder of the Judeo-Christian creation myth that the human body was formed from the dust of the earth, to which it returns at death. Likewise, in the Mass, the priest pronounces the words of institution, the story of how Christ shared his Last Supper with his disciples, while breaking bread and pouring wine into a cup.

With this working definition of a ritual, let's turn to some of the central concepts in the discipline of ritual studies to see how they can help us understand what is happening in religious rituals.

Questions for Reflection and Discussion

- Could fraternity and sorority rituals be understood as religious activities? Why or why not?

- If a ritual is not performed properly would the ritual lose significance for the one who performs it or for those who engage in it?

RITUAL TYPE: RITES OF PASSAGE

Many of the rituals considered in this chapter are associated with life's beginning, ending, and moments of significant transition. In the field of ritual studies these are known as *rites of passage* and can be distinguished from other types of rituals such as sacrifice. In *The Rites of Passage*, Arnold van Gennep explores how rituals facilitate the movement of an individual from one stage of life or social status to another, such as from childhood to adulthood, single to married life, or life to death. He argues that such transitions occasion a kind of crisis that the ritual helps to resolve by moving the individual through a process that begins with *separation* from the old state, a time of *transition* during which the person is suspended "betwixt and between" and is without a fixed status, and finally *incorporation* into a new state. Some rites of passage may focus more heavily on one part of the process or another. Van Gennep argues that funeral rites, for instance, focus primarily on separation, while marriage rites lean toward incorporation, and initiation rites focus on transition.[6] Yet all rites of passage, according to van Gennep, serve the function of resolving social crises related to the identity and status of group members—a crisis that is generated precisely by the transitions that inevitably occur across the course of a lifetime. As one moves from childhood to adulthood, from a single state into a married one, from adulthood into old age, and from life into death, the group must find ways to cope with the new and changing status of its members.

Some of the features of van Gennep's theory can be seen in the rituals surrounding birth practiced in traditional Chinese society. Anthropologists Martha Fried and Morton Fried describe these practices in their book *Transitions: Four Rituals in Eight Cultures*.[7] Giving birth is an important time of transition for a woman as she moves into the new social role of motherhood. When she is ready to give birth, the woman will separate herself from others by going into the birthing room in her home. Only a midwife and perhaps some older women from her family will be present. After giving birth, a woman is expected to observe a thirty-day period of complete rest known as *tso yueh*. During this time, she must not bathe, read, clean the birthing room, or eat certain foods. This is a period of transition, during which she is unlikely to have visitors other than her mother-in-law or mother. Even her husband is unlikely to have contact with her during this period. At the end of *tso yueh*, the family incorporates the child and new mother into the family with a special celebration.

In the sacrament of baptism, especially for infants, the process of separation, transition, and incorporation is greatly compressed. This rite of passage marks the transition through which the child's identity is no longer determined primarily by his or her family of origin, but by membership in the Christian church. As the ritual begins, parents hand their child over to sponsors. These sponsors may be designated as Godparents or may be leaders in the congregation. It is these sponsors who present the child for baptism. This simple act of handing the child over to sponsors marks a moment of separation from the old, family identity. During the time of transition, the sponsors are asked to renounce evil and affirm faith on behalf of the child. Finally, the infant is handed to the officiant, who pours water onto her head three times while saying, "I baptize you in the name of the Father, and of the Son, and of the Holy Spirit." The imagery used to describe what happens during this ritual washing is that of mortification and renewal. The infant is understood to participate in the death of Christ and to be resurrected to new life with Christ. Once this transition is complete, the child is welcomed into her new identity as a member of the Christian church. She has been incorporated—which literally means taken into the body—into the church, the body of Christ.[8]

6. Van Gennep, *The Rites of Passage*, trans. Monika B. Vizedom and Gabrielle L. Caffee (Chicago: University of Chicago Press, 1960), 11.

7. Martha Fried and Morton Fried, *Transitions: Four Rituals in Eight Cultures* (New York: Norton, 1980), 51–57.

8. The contrast between the birthing rituals in traditional Chinese society and the sacrament of baptism raises interesting questions about what specifically makes a ritual religious. Some Enlightenment assumptions discussed in the sections "Theory and Practice" and "Belief and Practice" may tempt observers of these practices to assume that cultural practices not specifically articulated within an institutional structure that resembles a Christian church are not, in fact, religious. But if we work with a broader definition of religion—one that acknowledges religion as a meaning system that connects human life with transcendent reality and thereby confers ultimate meaning—then the distinction between cultural and religious practices begins to break down.

FUNCTION: CONSERVING AND TRANSFORMING SOCIAL STRUCTURES

One of the central questions of ritual studies concerns the function of ritual. What purpose does it serve? Although many attempts have been made to answer this question, here we will look at two efforts to identify how ritual functions with respect to social organization.

In *The Elementary Forms of the Religious Life*, a seminal work first published in 1915, Émile Durkheim proposes that religious rituals reinforce the existing structures within a given society. If, for example, a social group holds that men are superior to women, then its ritual life will reinforce hierarchical gender roles. Rituals, and religious rituals in particular, function as a kind of social glue that holds society together by ensuring that members of the society accept their socially constructed roles as natural and God-given. According to Durkheim, religion is simply the phenomenon of sacralizing the social order, of assuming that the social order is the will of God. Ritual plays an important role in cementing social bonds because it generates powerful emotions that help individual members of a society feel connected to something that transcends their individual lives. But since the transcendent reality to which they feel connected is simply a projection of the sacralized social order, the effect of eliciting such powerful emotions is to strengthen the individual's commitment to the group. Durkheim calls this emotional effect of ritual "collective effervescence."[9]

To understand what Durkheim means by collective effervescence and its ability to generate and reinforce social cohesion, think about a sporting event, a nonreligious event that is not obviously a ritual. Even a casual observer can see how the crowd shares powerful feelings of elation or disappointment as the home team triumphs over or loses out to the opposing team. As individuals within the crowd shout chants together and experience similar emotions, their identities as fans of this team (or citizens of that nation, as in the Olympics) are reinforced.

How might a religious ritual do the same? Think back to the example of infant baptism from the previous section. In this case, the community in question is the Christian church. This can be understood either as the community of all believers everywhere or simply as the concrete community of a particular congregation. Powerful social bonds hold together members of the Christian church, and baptism reinforces those bonds in multiple ways. Members of the congregation are expected to be active in ensuring that the child is raised in the Christian faith. They are to set an example of Christian living, provide opportunities for education in the tradition, and support the family. The rite of baptism provides a concentrated moment when members of the congregation make explicit their intention to act in these ways. Their vows, or at the very least the vows of the sponsors, are an integral part of the rite. They give voice to the community's role in shaping the identity of the child.

If religious rituals can function to reinforce social structures, can they also play a role in transforming those structures? The influential ritual theorist Victor Turner argues that they can. In his book *The Ritual Process: Structure and Anti-Structure*, Turner argues that ritual is as much related to process and transformation as it is to structure and stability.[10] Turner explores the

---

9. Durkheim, *The Elementary Forms of the Religious Life*, trans. J. W. Swain. (New York: The Free Press. 1965), 258.

10. Caroline Bynum has offered a systematic critique of Turner's theory regarding ritual's transformative aspect. She suggests that his theory may account for the perspective of the privileged within a society, those who may temporarily move into a liminal space. But it does not account for the experiences of those, such as women, who are already marginalized within a society by their lower status. See Bynum, in *Readings in Ritual Studies*, Ronald Grimes, ed. (Upper Saddle River, NJ: Prentice-Hall, 1996), 71–86.

nature of the transitional phase in van Gennep's description of rites of passage. He notes that this transitional phase is like passing over a threshold when one moves from one room to another. The Latin term for a threshold is *limen*, and so Turner refers to this state of transition as one of liminality. In the liminal state, the individual lacks identity because he or she is no longer the old self (a child, for instance) but has not yet become the new one (an adult).

Turner especially explored rites of initiation among the Ndembu of central Africa.[11] The Ndembu initiate boys into the responsibilities of adult life through a ritual called *mukanda*, which involves an extended period of isolation during which the boys are circumcised and instructed by the older men in the customs of their society. This ritual does ultimately reinforce social structures,

by initiating the boys into the roles that they will play as men, but Turner points out that to effect this transformation, the liminal stage creates a new, albeit temporary, society—what Turner terms a *communitas*[12]—that does not conform to the norms of ordinary Ndembu society. For instance, regardless of social status, all boys are treated as equal in the *communitas*, and they form lifelong friendships that will prove crucial to their ability to thrive later. Because the boys-becoming-men reside in this alternative *communitas* during the transition, they are exposed to other possible ways of ordering society that open creative possibilities for them as they enter their new roles as Ndembu men. Turner suggests that a similar kind of *communitas* may be formed in North America in military academies and fraternities and sororities.[13]

Questions for Reflection and Discussion

- How might human experience give rise to religious rituals?
- Can you think of examples of ritual that reinforce the status quo?
- In what ways might rituals enable people to enter new ways of

understanding themselves and the world around them?

- To what extent do you think the practices of the Ndembu describe specifically religious ritual? Where would you draw the line between religious and cultural practices?

PERSPECTIVE: THEORY AND PRACTICE

If rituals that mark life's beginning, ending, and important transitions have the effect of solidifying or transforming social structures, does this function exhaust the meaning of the ritual? Does the scholar of religion explain everything about

the Ndembu rite of initiation by describing its function in forging friendships that facilitate adult social life? Does baptism mean anything beyond the function it serves in cementing group loyalty?

These questions concern the role of perspective in religious studies. The adherent of a religion participates in its ritual life with quite a different

---

11. Turner, *The Forest of Symbols: Aspects of Ndembu Ritual* (Ithaca, NY: Cornell University Press, 1967).

12. Turner, *The Ritual Process: Structure and Anti-Structure* (Ithaca, NY: Cornell University Press, 1969), 96.

13. Turner, *The Forest of Symbols*, 101.

perspective from the scholar of religion who observes the ritual. These differing perspectives illumine certain features of an experience and obscure others. The question is whether the gap between the practice of a ritual and a theory about it can be bridged.

Consider the ritual of committing the body to the ground in Christian burial rites: the scholar, with an external perspective, may draw attention to ways that rituals of mourning provide a needed disruption to the ordinary ordering of daily life so that mourners may express their grief in ways that ultimately will not disrupt everyday social life. The function of the funeral is, in part, to provide a socially acceptable space for otherwise disruptive behaviors, and this space allows for continuity of social life. But if you ask a participant in the ritual, someone with an internal perspective, you are unlikely to hear this explanation of the purpose and meaning of the funeral. The meaning of the funeral for the believer is quite different from any social function it might serve, and the believer is unlikely even to be cognizant of that function in the midst of participating in the ritual. In Christian traditions, the funeral serves as witness to the resurrection and anticipates the renewal of the human body in God's redemptive work.

To some degree, then, the dynamics of ritual described by scholars are inaccessible to participants. Likewise, there are aspects of the ritual—indeed, perhaps the deepest structures of its meaning—that are inaccessible to an observer. Some scholars of ritual have attempted to bridge this gap by becoming participants in the rituals they observe. As Ronald Grimes explains of Victor Turner, he "not only observed, interpreted, and theorized about ritual; he also participated in it and created it. In fact, he was initiated by the Ndembu. Though he recognized the boundary between theory and practice, he regularly crossed it."[14] To what degree might such participation grant the scholar a share in the adherent's perspective? To what degree might it represent a kind of scholarly colonizing of religious terrain? These questions remain open for debate.

In her careful analysis of the history of ritual studies, Catherine Bell presents a dramatic proposal about the gap between theory and practice. She argues that traditionally scholars of ritual "assume that there is a substantive phenomenon at stake, not simply an abstract or analytical category."[15] In other words, those who advance a *theory* about ritual do so with the assumption that a given *practice* is really, essentially, a ritual. This means that ritual is something real in the world, that it has some objective reality, and that rituals can therefore become objects of study. But Bell proposes that ritual is in fact simply a heuristic device that scholars use to classify and describe certain behaviors. Bell calls this assumption that ritual is an objective reality *ritual reification*.

We can take an example from the book *Transitions* to understand better what Bell means by ritual reification. The authors offer descriptions of four rituals from eight different cultures. In the chapter on birth, for instance, we find descriptions of the practices surrounding parturition among five groups: the !Kung, a nomadic tribe of the Kalahari Desert; the Hausa Muslims of Nigeria; the Tlingit tribe of southern Alaska; the Tikopia, a Polynesian culture recently converted to Christianity; and traditional Chinese families living in Taiwan. The authors describe how pregnant !Kung work alongside others until their contractions begin and then go outside of the village to deliver the child on their own, unless it is a first birth, in which case the mother

---

14. Grimes, "Ritual," in *Guide to the Study of Religion*, Willi Braun and Russell T. McCutcheon, eds. (New York: Cassell, 2000), 266.

15. Bell, *Ritual: Perspectives and Dimensions* (New York: Oxford University Press, 1997), 253.

may be assisted by other women. By contrast, a Hausa woman may be surrounded by many women from her family and a midwife when she delivers. The practices of women from a variety of cultures while pregnant and during parturition are described as rituals. But are they?

Bell proposes that Western scholars of religion are accustomed to thinking in dualistic categories, such as sacred and secular, belief and practice, that are foreign to the world-interpreting assumptions of most of the communities they investigate and describe. Labeling a practice "ritual" assists these scholars in "negotiating cultural differences."[16] But labeling a practice as ritual tempts scholars to imagine that they stand on scientifically objective ground, from which they can view the activities of those who are "other"

in an unbiased manner. This has the effect of privileging the perspective of the theorist over that of the practitioner. The assumption that one may discover a universal theory to account for the varieties of practices labeled "ritual" may also lead to inattentiveness to the particularities of the practices under observation. The scholar who observes behaviors surrounding birth in two different cultures and labels them as birthing rituals may begin to seek an explanation of the behavior that encompasses both events. Seeking this common explanation, however, may cause the scholar to overlook, suppress, or dismiss aspects of the events that are not common. Bell cautions scholars, therefore, not to confuse *ritual* as a useful category of analysis with the reification of ritual that posits it as an actual entity in the world.

Questions for Reflection and Discussion

- What is the difference between observing and participating in a ritual activity?
- How might observer participation in a ritual change its nature and the experience of others for whom it was intended?

- Some teachers encourage students to make religious site visits in order to help students better understand different practices of religion. Given what you have read so far in this book, do you find value in this practice? Explain.

BELIEF AND PRACTICE

The eighteenth-century Enlightenment philosopher Immanuel Kant expressed a hope that religion would one day be entirely rational—that it would exist solely within the limits of reason alone.[17] For Kant, this rational religion would be shorn of the accretions of tradition, childish superstitions, and superfluous ritual. Rational religion would be solely a matter of correct

belief that motivates enlightened individuals to live moral lives.

This Enlightenment view that belief constitutes the true essence of religion and that moral practices are its only natural expression has been enormously influential in Western thought. As a result, Western scholars of religion have often assumed that the correct way to study religious traditions is to discover and describe what the adherents of those traditions believe. Rituals, it

16. Ibid., 259.
17. Kant, *Religion within the Limits of Reason Alone* (New York: Harper Torchbooks, 1960).

has been assumed, simply express these beliefs, and the scholar can observe ritual practices to glean insight into the beliefs of the religion concerned. Van Gennep, for instance, draws a sharp distinction between religion and magic.[18] According to van Gennep, religion is rooted in theory—a cosmology, for instance—and its ritual practices are simply worshipful expressions of that theory. Magic, on the other hand, is rooted in technique and its ritual practices are designed to accomplish some particular end.

The Enlightenment view of religion entailed the assumption that the cognitive content of a religion takes precedence over its ritual practices, which simply express and reinforce beliefs. But this assumption runs contrary to the lived experience of religion in many contexts. In the Christian tradition, for instance, the relationship between worship practices and belief has long been summarized by the Latin phrase *lex orandi, lex credendi*, which means that the law that governs prayer is identical to the law of belief. The worshipful act of praying determines the shape and content of doctrine. Praying and believing are inseparable. Prayers do not merely reflect beliefs; they shape them. Christian sacramental theology reinforces the mutuality of belief and practice in its traditional affirmation that the sacraments function *ex opere operanto*—literally, they work because of the work that is done. That is, the sacraments are effective because the grace of God works objectively through the sacramental action. Baptism does not simply symbolize the community's faith and intentions to rear the baptized child in that faith; rather, baptism *confers* faith. Likewise, the priest's actions in extreme unction do not merely symbolize the hope of the faithful that God will forgive the dying person; rather, the sacramental action, which includes the words spoken, *effects* absolution.

The external perspective of the scholar who anticipates that the ritual simply expresses Christian beliefs, in other words, misses a crucial component of what the faithful themselves understand as the meaning of these rites. Such rites do point to a system of beliefs, to deeply held convictions about what constitutes a good life. But the rites do more than point to such beliefs; they also participate in and, at least in part, construct that good life. To live a good life, in other words, is to have one's birth, everyday life, and death marked by these rites. A good life, as understood in Jewish communities, is marked by the sign of the covenant in circumcision, sustained by prayers of gratitude over every aspect of waking life, and remembered by members of a community who rend their clothing in grief for the death of a loved one. A good life, as understood in much of the Christian tradition, is one immersed in the waters of baptism, sustained by the body and blood of Christ offered in communion, and absolved of sin through penance and anointing. A good life, as understood in Muslim communities, is lived by the confession that there is one God, sustained by daily prayers, and fulfilled in the giving of alms. These rites not only *express* beliefs about a good life, they also *make* a good life.

The Western, monotheistic traditions cited here are only a starting point. The faithful of many—indeed, most—other religious traditions likewise maintain that belief and practice are inseparable, that practices not only express but also partly constitute the values of the religious community. To discover the meaning of these religious rituals, then, requires more than extracting a ritual from its context and placing it beside other, supposedly similar rituals from other traditions for purposes of comparison. Understanding the rituals that make and express

---

18. Van Gennep, *The Rites of Passage*, trans. Monika B. Vizedom and Gabrielle L. Caffee (Chicago: University of Chicago Press, 1960), 14.

the fundamental values of a religious community requires becoming deeply immersed in the cultural contexts in which these rituals happen. It requires noting how those contexts, the beliefs of religious communities, and the particular practices of a particular rite are interwoven.

THE BODY

The Enlightenment perspective described above is not only likely to advance a false priority of belief over practice but also to be deeply inattentive to the importance of the body and embodiment in religious ritual. Clearly, if it is belief and not practice that marks the essence of religion, then it is the mind and not the body that serves as the primary site of religious activity. Yet even a casual observer of religious practices, especially worship practices, will note the central role that physical acts and objects play in them: upon entering the sanctuary, many Christians mark themselves with water and the sign of the cross; during morning prayers Jews bind phylacteries to their foreheads and arms; five times a day devout Muslims bow, kneel, and prostrate themselves in prayer; during the annual festival of Ganesa, Hindus dissolve the statue of this god of passageways in the river. Bodily movement into and within worship spaces and the use of material objects within that space are of central importance in religious rites.

Physical acts and objects within religious rituals are of such central importance because of the way that they relate to a religion's cosmology—its way of specifying the essential nature of reality. Religions specify what is of ultimate importance—what is to be valued above all, what grants meaning to human life and all of reality, what is worth ordering one's life around. Religions offer their adherents ways of organizing

reality and of determining what their priorities ought to be. Religions entail a comprehensive vision of how every aspect of reality is related to that which is of ultimate importance and to every other aspect of reality. Ritual acts serve as markers of that vision. They indicate how a religious community envisions the relationship between human life and the broader cosmos. The body, then, is a bearer and locus of meaning in ritual activity.

Catherine Bell explains that "the fundamental efficacy of ritual activity lies in its ability to have people embody assumptions about their place in a larger order of things."[19] When Muslims prostrate themselves in prayer, they indicate in physical form their submission to God, who governs all of reality and their individual lives. In this act of prayer, the Muslims embody their place within a cosmos ruled by the will of God. When Jews bind phylacteries to their foreheads and arms, they physically bind themselves to the law of God and to the covenant community that received that law and bound itself to God through the covenant with Abraham. In this ritual act, Jews embody their place within a world where God acts in history, making and renewing the covenant with Abraham, Moses, David, and all of their ancestors. When Christians mark themselves with water and the sign of the cross, they remind themselves that Christ suffered bodily for them and that they have been incorporated into the redemptive work of Christ's death and Resurrection through the waters of baptism. In this ritual act, Christians embody their place within a world where God has become human—has lived, died, and risen as a human person—and thereby enabled humanity to be redeemed and restored.

The ritual act reminds the participants of their place in the cosmos, but it is also far more than a memory prompt. The ritual act also

---

19. Bell, *Ritual: Perspectives and Dimensions* (New York: Oxford University Press, 1997), xi.

constructs for the participant the very cosmology it enacts. The ritual also communicates the values of the community and its sense of ultimate importance to the faithful. Rituals, in other words, actively form persons for a particular kind of religious life, for a particular way of framing reality and of responding to others within and beyond the boundaries of the community. The body, in other words, not only bears ritual meaning but also generates that meaning. By participating in the ritual life of a community by embodying its values, individuals are formed as members of that community, as persons who perceive the world as Jews or Muslims or Christians.

THE BODY AND COMMUNITY BOUNDARIES

Anthropologist Mary Douglas has observed that the role the body plays in religious ritual indicates strongly how a community establishes and maintains boundaries. In her classic study of food laws in ancient Israel, for instance, Douglas notes that the people refused to consume certain kinds of animals, such as pigs and shellfish, and that the choice of which foods were permitted and prohibited was not arbitrary.[20] On the contrary, the ancient Israelites viewed the world in which they lived as one in which God had overcome primordial chaos with order. By their food choices, the Israelites aligned themselves with God's ordering power over against the forces of chaos. They noted that animals with a cloven hoof chew cud. Pigs violate this orderly arrangement because they have cloven hoofs, but do not chew cud. Likewise, animals that live in the water have gills and scales. Shellfish violate this order because they live in the water but do not have scales. Ancient Israel, as a community aligned with the order of God, prohibited the consumption of the chaotic foods, and keeping these food laws was a central marker of their identity. The food laws, in other words, marked the boundaries of the community and helped to maintain those boundaries. Assimilating to the surrounding cultures meant giving up the observance of such food laws. Since sharing meals is such a foundational activity of human communities, the Israelites' choice to set limits on which animals could be consumed and how those that were consumed should be slaughtered was a powerful way to establish and maintain social boundaries.

Douglas claims that the function of ritual in establishing and maintaining boundaries in ancient Israel not only applied to determining who was and was not a member of the group but also to social roles within a group. For instance, she studied their ritual purity laws as they related to sexuality, such as the prohibition against homosexuality. Here too, she notes an attempt to regulate boundaries (in this case, the boundaries of the human body) and suppress ambiguity (in this case, the clarity of two gender roles: women who are attracted to men and men who are attracted to women). She uses the term *group* to specify the strength with which the boundaries between insiders and outsiders are set and *grid* to specify the strength of regulations regarding social roles for individual members of the group.

A society with a strong sense of group will be relatively closed to outsiders, whereas one with a weak sense of group will have much more permeable boundaries. A society with a strong grid will be relatively hierarchical, with clear social roles that individuals must assume based on characteristics such as age and sex. A society with weak grid will allow for more social mobility. Because ritual activity reinforces boundaries, Douglas hypothesizes that societies

---

20. Douglas, *Purity and Danger: An Analysis of the Concepts of Pollution and Taboo* (London: Ark Paperbacks, 1984).

with strong group and grid are likely to engage in a greater degree of ritual activity. Likewise, ritual activity would be less prevalent in societies without clearly fixed boundaries and with open social roles.

Consider the *mukanda* initiation rite of the Ndembu. The rite ensures that young boys assume their place as men who are able to meet their responsibilities within Ndembu society. The rite solidifies the boys' identification with the social role expected of them. It reinforces the grid. Following Douglas, we might expect that as the Ndembu come into greater contact with outsiders or as their understanding of social roles

changes, the rite might decline in significance. In the United States, we can observe a similar pattern. In the nineteenth century, among the upper classes at least, gender roles were much more scripted than today. Women and men had distinct spheres of activity and influence. At the same time, fraternal organizations such as the Masons and their corollary organizations for boys, women, and girls flourished; these organizations employed highly ritualized initiation ceremonies and a hierarchical structure. But as gender roles have become more fluid in the United States, membership in such organizations has declined.

Questions for Reflection and Discussion

- What religious activities could be identified as places where belief and practice are separable?

- How might a ritual act construct for a participant the cosmology it enacts?

- In what ways have you been formed for religious life?

- What aspects of your formation would you want to question and why?

- Are there specific religious rituals that could be harmful for physical and psychological reasons? If so, what are they and why would they be harmful?

- In what ways might your presence at a ritual change the experience for all involved?

SPEECH ACTS

As much as rituals concern the body—its movement, boundaries, and engagement with physical objects—they also involve words. And just as bodily actions bear meaning and also generate it, so too do words. We are often tempted to think of words simply as signs that point to reality. We say "dog" in order to point a listener to a furry canine. This is one way that words function, and certainly this function is crucial in basic communication. It is also important in ritual communication. But words in general, and ritual words in particular, have an important function beyond

"pointing" to objects; they also communicate ideas and values to the participants.

But words perform other functions as well. In his work *How to Do Things with Words*, philosopher J. L. Austin points out that we use words not only to point to reality but also to do things; his theory, therefore, is known as speech-act theory. Think, for instance, about taking a vow. At a wedding, bride and groom exchange vows; these vows do not describe the reality of matrimony, they generate it. It is precisely the act of saying "I take you to be my wife" or "I take you to be my husband" that accomplishes the action of marrying. Austin refers to these events as *performative utterances* because in them the words pronounced are the activity undertaken. In the utterance, the speaker performs the act.

Austin's speech-act theory has important implications for ritual studies. When a priest pours water over a child's head and says, "I baptize you in the name of the Father, the Son, and the Holy Spirit," the priest is not describing the action taken. Instead, the utterance is an intrinsic part of the sacrament being performed. Saying "I baptize you" is as necessary to the efficacy of the rite as is pouring the water. Likewise, the pronouncement of absolution in the sacrament of extreme unction does not so much communicate information about forgiveness to the dying person as it participates in the reality of that forgiveness.

As religious communities ritually mark important transitions in life, they use words to communicate value and to generate meanings that carry the traditions of the community forward from one generation to the next.

CONCLUSION

Throughout this chapter we have explored central concepts in ritual studies to discover how that field may shed light on the ritual practices of faith communities. Stanley Tambiah's definition of a *ritual* as "a culturally constructed system of symbolic communication, [which] is constituted of patterned and ordered sequences of words and acts," provides a useful starting point for noting some of the most prominent features of ritual acts.[21] We've explored theories about the structure of ritual rites of passage and noted how such rituals might serve either to conserve or transform social structures. We have noted the importance of perspective in analyzing rituals. Some aspects of the ritual life of a faith community may be obscured for its adherents, but other aspects may be inaccessible to the disinterested scholar. We've noted how belief and practice intersect, how the body bears and generates ritual meaning, how rituals can mark the boundaries of the community, and how speech-acts mirror the communicative and generative aspects of the body in ritual.

As you consider instances of rituals that are familiar to you, make use of these categories. Do they help you see features of those rituals that were not obvious to you before? Do they miss anything vital to the ritual? As you deploy these categories in the analysis of ritual, remember that they do not function as discrete concepts. Each of these concepts will overlap with others in ways that lend subtlety and nuance to your analysis. For instance, speech-act theory and the analysis of rites of passage intersect where performatory utterances are central to rituals such as weddings and rites of initiation. Likewise, the relationship between belief and practice may best be illumined when the student of religious ritual attends to the role of body and of speech-acts and to how body and speech-acts may serve either to conserve or transform social structures. The individual concepts explored here, in other words, are complex and interrelated. This complexity is only natural because religions are vital, multifaceted ways of organizing the world. They offer rich, multifaceted views of what is of ultimate value, of what makes life worth living. Perhaps nowhere else but in their ritual lives do students of religion have such a ready opportunity to explore and analyze that richness.

---

21. Tambiah, "A Performative Approach to Ritual," *Proceedings of the British Academy* 65 (1979): 119.

Questions for Reflection and Discussion

- How are vows and promises potentially religious acts?
- In what ways do words change your perceptions about yourself and others?
- What is the significance of your name? Is there any religious significance associated with it?

- Are there any ritual activities in which you would decline to participate? Why or why not?
- If all ritualized activities were to cease tomorrow, would various forms of religion disappear? Why or why not?

Additional Resources

Austin, J. L. 1975. *How to Do Things with Words*. 2nd ed. Cambridge, MA: Harvard University Press.

Bell, Catherine. 1997. *Ritual: Perspectives and Dimensions*. New York: Oxford University Press.

Bynum, Caroline Walker. 1996. "Women's Stories, Women's Symbols: A Critique of Victor Turner's Theory of Liminality." In *Readings in Ritual Studies*. Ronald Grimes, ed. Upper Saddle River, NJ: Prentice-Hall, 71–86.

Council of Florence. 1439. "Decree for the Armenians." Medieval Sourcebook. *http://www.fordham.edu/halsall/source/1438sacraments.html#amen*. Site maintained by Paul Halsall. Original source: James Harvey Robinson, ed. 1904. *Readings in European History*. Vol. 1. Boston: Ginn and Company.

Douglas, Mary. 1984. *Purity and Danger: An Analysis of the Concepts of Pollution and Taboo*. London: Ark Paperbacks.

Durkheim, Émile. 1965. *The Elementary Forms of the Religious Life*. Translated by J. W. Swain. New York: The Free Press.

Fried, Martha Nemes, and Morton H. Fried. 1980. *Transitions: Four Rituals in Eight Cultures*. New York: Norton.

Greenstein, Howard R., Kendra G. Hotz, and John Kaltner. 2007. *What Do Our Neighbors Believe? Questions and Answers from Judaism, Christianity, and Islam*. Louisville, KY: Westminster John Knox Press.

Grimes, Ronald L. 2000. "Ritual." In *Guide to the Study of Religion*. Willi Braun and Russell T. McCutcheon, eds. New York: Cassell, 259–270.

Kant, Immanuel. 1960. *Religion within the Limits of Reason Alone*. New York: Harper Torchbooks.

Rothkrug, Lionel. 2006. *Death, Trust, and Society: Mapping Religion and Culture*. Berkeley, CA: North Atlantic Books.

Smart, Ninian. 1995. *Worldviews: Crosscultural Explorations of Human Beliefs*. Englewood Cliffs, NJ: Prentice-Hall.

Tambiah, Stanley. (1979) "A Performative Approach to Ritual." *Proceedings of the British Academy* 65: 119.

Turner, Victor. 1967. *The Forest of Symbols: Aspects of Ndembu Ritual*. Ithaca, NY: Cornell University Press.

Turner, Victor. 1969. *The Ritual Process: Structure and Anti-Structure*. Ithaca, NY: Cornell University Press.

Van Gennep, Arnold. 1960. *The Rites of Passage*. Translated by Monika B. Vizedom and Gabrielle L. Caffee. Chicago: University of Chicago Press.

Yust, Karen Marie, Aostre N. Johnson, Sandy Eisenberg Sasso, and Eugene C. Roehlkepartain, eds. 2006. *Nurturing Child and Adolescent Spirituality: Perspectives from the World's Religious Traditions*. London: Rowman and Littlefield.

About the Authors

Paul O. Myhre

Paul O. Myhre is associate director of the Wabash Center for Teaching and Learning in Theology and Religion, in Crawfordsville, Indiana. His current research and teaching involves Native American religions, art and religion, and undergraduate research. Recent essays include "Painting as Sacrament: A Search for Dali's Sacramental Imagination," "Edvard Munch's Embrace of Loss and Grief through Painting and Printmaking: 1885–1900," and "Encountering Navajo Cosmology through Sand Paintings."

Debra Majeed

Debra Majeed is associate professor and chair of philosophy and religious studies at Beloit College, in Beloit, Wisconsin. Her research and writing reflect her concern with issues of social, political, racial, and religious injustice, particularly in regard to women. She has contributed to *CrossCurrents*, *Journal of Feminist Studies in Religion*, *Teaching Theology and Religion*, and *Deeper Shades of Purple*, among other publications. Her current project, *Encounters of Intimate Sisterhood: Polygyny in the World of African American Muslims*, is forthcoming from University Press of Florida. Majeed also has served as a resource on the study of religion for several media groups, including the *Washington Post*, and has appeared on National Public Radio's "News & Notes."

David C. Ratke

David C. Ratke is associate professor of religion at Lenoir-Rhyne University, in Hickory, North Carolina. He is the book review editor for *Dialog: A Journal of Theology* and has published widely in Christian theology and history. His published books include volumes on ecclesiology, the nature and authority of scripture, and bioethics. He is currently preparing an edited volume on the relationship of religion and higher education. He teaches a wide variety of courses: introduction to Christianity, ethics, religion and culture, history of Christianity, religion and science, world religions, and general humanities. He is a former pastor and current pew occupant.

Dianne L. Oliver

Dianne L. Oliver is chair of the department of philosophy and religion and associate professor of religion at the University of Evansville, in Evansville, Indiana. She teaches courses in world religions, Christian theology, and ethics, especially in the area of peace and justice. Several of her publications focus on the work of Dorothee Soelle, twentieth-century theologian, mystic, and activist, including *Dorothee Soelle: Essential Writings*, and an essay in *The Theology of Dorothee Soelle*. She has done work on the purpose of higher education and the role of religion in undergraduate education, published in such journals as *Perspectives in Religious Studies* and *Teaching Theology and Religion*.

Karl N. Jacobson

Karl N. Jacobson is assistant professor of religion at Augsburg College, in Minneapolis, Minnesota, and an ordained pastor of the Evangelical Lutheran Church in America. His teaching includes general introductions to religious studies, comparative scriptures, biblical studies, and biblical languages. He is a coauthor of *Crazy Talk: A Not-So-Stuffy Dictionary of Theological Terms* and *Crazy Book: A Not-So-Stuffy Dictionary of Biblical Terms*. His articles have appeared in *Word & World* and *Lutheran Forum*, online in the

SBL-Forum, and in the *Encyclopedia of the Bible and Its Reception.*

Rolf A. Jacobson

Rolf A. Jacobson is associate professor of Old Testament at Luther Seminary, in St. Paul, Minnesota, and an ordained pastor of the Evangelical Lutheran Church in America. His teaching, writing, speaking, and research reflect his commitment to the mission of the church in service of God's word. He is the author of *Many Are Saying: The Rhetorical Function of Direct Discourse in the Hebrew Psalter* and a coauthor of *Crazy Talk: A Not-So-Stuffy Dictionary of Theological Terms* and *Crazy Book: A Not-So-Stuffy Dictionary of Biblical Terms.* His articles have appeared in various publications, including *Theology Today, Word & World, Interpretation, Teaching Theology & Religion, The Lutheran Journal of Ethics,* and in various collections of essays.

S. Brent Plate

S. Brent Plate is currently visiting associate professor of religion at Hamilton College, in Clinton, New York, and has taught previously at Texas Christian University, the University of Vermont, and the University of Glasgow. He is author/editor of several books, including most recently *Religion and Film: Cinema and the Re-Creation of the World.* Earlier books include *Blasphemy: Art That Offends; Walter Benjamin, Religion, and Aesthetics; Representing Religion in World Cinema;* and *The Religion and Film Reader.* He is cofounder and managing editor of *Material Religion: The Journal of Objects, Art, and Belief.*

Jack A. Hill

Jack A. Hill is associate professor of religion (social ethics) at Texas Christian University, in Fort Worth, Texas, where he lectures on ethics, ecology, and world religions. In addition to teaching and writing, Hill has coordinated peace and justice programs and served as an ethics consultant for churches, universities, and grassroots organizations in the United States, Fiji, and South Africa. He is a trained mediator, teaching mentor, and former pastor. His books include *Ethics in the Global Village: Moral Insights for the Post 9-11 USA, Seeds of Transformation: Discerning the Values of the Next Generation,* and *I-Sight: The World of Rastafari.*

Darlene Fozard Weaver

Darlene Fozard Weaver is associate professor of theology and director of the Theology Institute at Villanova University, in Villanova, Pennsylvania. An ecumenically trained moral theologian, Weaver specializes in moral anthropology and ethical theory. Weaver teaches undergraduate and graduate courses in theology and ethics; her classes regularly cover issues in fundamental moral theology, ethical theory, ethics and the family, sexual and reproductive ethics, and health care ethics. She is the author of *Self Love and Christian Ethics* and the forthcoming *Involvements with God and Goods: Persons and Actions in Christian Ethics.* She is coeditor of and contributor to *The Ethics of Embryo Adoption and the Catholic Tradition.* Weaver has contributed essays to scholarly journals, including the *Journal of Religious Ethics,* as well as to a number of edited volumes.

Swasti Bhattacharyya

Swasti Bhattacharyya is associate professor of religion at Buena Vista University, Storm Lake, Iowa. As an applied ethicist, her work examines ethical issues such as cloning, stem cell research (and other bioethical issues), environmental ethics, and peace and justice from different religious perspectives (Christian, Buddhist, Hindu, Jain, Jewish, Muslim). She has published in *International Journal of Gynecology and Obstetrics* and the *Journal of Bioethical Inquiry,* contributed chapters to several books, and is the author of *Magical Progeny, Modern Technology: A Hindu Bioethics of Assisted Reproductive Technology.* Her current project focuses on the living legacy of Vinoba Bhave.

Daniel G. Deffenbaugh

Daniel G. Deffenbaugh is associate professor of religion at Hastings College, in Hastings, Nebraska, and author of *Learning the Language of the Fields: Tilling and Keeping as Christian Vocation.* His articles and reviews have appeared in such publications as the *Journal of the American Academy of Religion, Soundings, Teaching Theology & Religion,* and *Sojourners.* He has a variety of scholarly interests that extend beyond the study of theology and ecology, including religion and the arts, the role of sacred space in world religious traditions, and environmental history. When he is not teaching, he spends as much time as possible gardening organically and keeping bees.

Bernadette McNary-Zak

Bernadette McNary-Zak is associate professor of religious studies at Rhodes College, in Memphis, Tennessee, where she teaches courses in the interdisciplinary humanities program and in early Christian literature and history. Her primary research interest is in Christian monastic life and thought. She has published several articles in this area and is the author of *Letters and Asceticism in Fourth-Century Egypt*.

A. K. M. Adam

A. K. M. Adam began hacking computers in 1977 and worked in computer graphics for several years before entering ministry in the Episcopal Church. He teaches New Testament at the University of Glasgow, after terms as professor of New Testament at Duke Divinity School, Princeton Theological Seminary, and several other schools, and he has ministered to congregations in Florida, New Jersey, and Illinois. His research and writing focus on hermeneutics: how do we make ourselves understood, and how do we figure out what others want us to understand? He is frequently invited to preach in congregations around the country and to speak at academic and technological conferences. He has written and edited numerous books, including *Faithful Interpretation, Reading Scripture* *Church* (with S. Fowl, K. Vanhoozer, and F *Handbook of Postmodern Biblical Interpretat Is Postmodern Biblical Criticism?*, and *Making New Testament Theology*.

S. Brian Stratton

S. Brian Stratton is associate professor of phi phy and religious studies at Alma College, in A Michigan. He is the author of *Coherence, Consona and Conversation: The Quest of Philosophy, Theolo and Natural Science for a Unified World-View, t* forthcoming *Creation and Fall in an Age of Science*, an numerous articles on philosophy and the relationship between science and religion. He has received college and state awards for teaching.

Kendra G. Hotz

Kendra G. Hotz is assistant professor of religious studies at Rhodes College, in Memphis, Tennessee, where she teaches courses in theology, church history, and the Bible. She has coauthored three books exploring the theological dimensions of religious practices: *Shaping the Christian Life: Worship and the Religious Affections, Transforming Care: A Christian Vision of Nursing Practice*, and *What Do Our Neighbors Believe? Questions and Answers from Judaism, Christianity, and Islam*.

Index

Tables are referenced with "t" and sidebars with "s" after the page number.

215

Weber, Max, 23, 92
Wee-sa-kay-jac (Cree spirit),
 37–38
When Religion Becomes Evil
 (Kimball), 103
whirling dervishes, 159
White, Andrew Dickson, 186
White, Lynn, Jr., 138, 147
Whitehead, Alfred North, 183
Williams, Delores, 24
womanism, 24–25, 85–86
women
 ashrams for, 130–31
 gender roles, 13, 207
 religious ethics and, 85–86
 religious study methodologies
  centering on, 23–25

Woolgar, C. M., 76
World Community of Al-Islam,
 121s
world-renunciation practices, 157
worldview
 Buddhism, 143–44
 Christian, as cause of environmental crisis, 137, 138
 components of, 178–80
 defined, 82, 178
 as ethical analysis component,
  81
 Native American, 140–41, 143
 as noetic structure subset, 178
 Taoist, 145
 Vedantic Hindu, 142–43
wu-wei, 145

Y

Yahweh, 39
Yerushalmi, Yosef Hayim, 72–73
yin and *yang*, 145
yoga, 155
Yom Kippur, 155
Yoruba, 73–74

Z

zakat, 87, 88, 92, 126s, 133
Zen Buddhism, 74, 143–44, 155